ROBERT VAUGHN'S NEW BOOK,
"THEN AND NOW, OR THIRTY-SIX YEARS IN THE ROCKIES"
IS WELCOME WHEREVER IT GOES.

THE FOLLOWING ARE EXTRACTS FROM LETTERS TO THE AUTHOR.

I have read the book with much interest and have realized more than ever the debt we owe to the brave pioneers. It is one of the best sources for the future historian. I like especially the perfect simplicity of your narrative and have been much moved, in many places your book by your rich and profound feeling. Any glimpse into another life is precious, and when you give us not simple narrative, but so often the key to your own heart.

From Rev. Leslie Willis Sprague,
New Jersey.

Robert Vaughn, Esq.
Dear Sir—We saw your book, "Then and Now, or Thirty-six Years in the Rockies," at Governor J.K. Toole's house last evening. The directors of the State Historical society requested me to ask you to send a copy to the library.

Respectfully,
Laura E. Howey,
Secretary and Librarian of State
Historical Society, Helena, Montana.

Reliability is its strongest recommendation, being founded upon the personal experiences and observations of the author. The whole is embellished by the finest half tones from photographs in portraiture and scenic art, and notable by the presentation of several of the celebrated paintings of C.M. Russell, "the cowboy artist." In statistical value the work stands without peer.

E.K. Abbott.

"I have just returned from the east and find here your book. I greatly appreciate your remembrance of me, and I am glad to have the story of your life on the frontier."

James J. Hill,
President Great Northern Ry.,
St. Paul, Minn.

"I am in receipt of a copy of your excellent book. I consider it well worth the price demanded and beg to enclose check for $2.50. I cannot refrain from congratulating you on the excellence of the work.

J.M. Kennedy,
State Senator, Anaconda, Mont.

In Robert Vaughn's book, "Then and Now," many remarkable adventures and incidents of the early days in the northwest are truthfully and graphically related that would otherwise have been lost, as man of the actors therein have already passed away, and soon all cognizant of these stirring events will be gone. It is a valuable book which I have greatly enjoyed reading.

From Hon. Granville Stuart.

Headquarters Department of Dakota, Inspector General's Office, St. Paul. My Dear Pioneer: Your book, "Then and Now, or Thirty-six Years in the Rockies," is before me. As my nomadic army life has measurable qualified me to pass judgement upon this production of your reminiscent pen, I gladly bear testimony to its accuracy in which you have described the many events belonging to the period when no transcontinental line or wire disturbed the aboriginals or whites in their contest for supremacy.

Yours truly,
Philip Reade.

It covers the most interesting period and I am having great pleasure in reading it.

From Gen. Nelson A. Miles,
Washington, D.C.

I say to you without flattery or desire to flatter you as its author, that it should be in the hands of every resident of this state.

From Judge John W. Tattan.

"Then and Now" being a book replete with the pioneer days of Montana, should have a place not only among the books of every family in this state, but it should be found in all public libraries of the country. That Mr. Vaughn has been able to compile a work so interesting and valuable, is due to his past familiarity with Montana's early history, and to his ability to present his sketches in a most pleasing manner.

Paris Gibson,
U.S. Senator from Montana.

I have read your book; it is very interesting from beginning to finish and will prove a valuable aid in preserving the early history of Montana, for it is from such works that the true history of the Northwest will in time be written. It is a duty we old settlers owe to the future generation to put into shape our early recollections and experiences in the West and leave them for the future historians. Your work is well gotten up.

From Judge Frank H. Woody.

I [am] very much pleased with the mechanical appearance of the book, but its historical and literary value far exceeds the appearance.

John G. Evans, Butte, Montana.

As a history of the early settlement of the West it is the most accurate and comprehensive insight into frontier life that I have ever had the pleasure of reading. From a literary point of view I regard it as one of the highest order.

James Donovan,
Attorney General of the
State of Montana.

Mr. Robert Vaughn:

Dear Sir—I have before me a copy of your book entitled "Then and Now, or Thirty-six Years in the Rockies." It is attractive and valuable, containing a record of events of times the history of which must be of great future interest.

Marion P. Maus,
Lieutenant Colonel and Inspector General
of the Pacific Coast.

I am impressed with the fact that there is a sincerity in the narrative which should render it of great interest. It will not be many years before there will be precious few of you left to write on the striking events which occurred in the upbuilding of that state, and 20 or 30 years from now when people wish to know of the early days of the west they will be required to obtain their information from just such sources as your book.

O.D. Wheeler,
St. Paul, Minn.

"It is of rare literary merit."

From General Warren

I consider it a book that is wanted by the pioneers and particularly by the late comers, as it fills in a space of which we have no history at all. Send me six copies.

A.M. Holter.

It is written in a simple and graphic style and portrays in a vivid manner the dangers, trials and triumphs of the men whose heroic efforts made it possible for modern civilization to transform this part of the northwest from a wilderness into a flourishing state.

From Judge R.W. Berry.

I consider the book a valuable one. The simple directness of its style carries conviction the truthfulness of its statements. While the tenderness of that touching picture of the boy's farewell to his parents reveals a poet's soul, I am richer than I was yesterday, not in money, but in something worth more to me.

From Rev. William N. Moore.

This kind of work cannot and should not be done second-handed, for no matter how truthfully and painstaking the writer may be, there will always be found lacking that delicacy of touch and candor of expression that is possible only to one who has lived through and experienced all that is narrated. You have done the work well.

S.M. Emery, Ex-Superintendent State
Agricultural College, Bozeman, Montana.

frontispiece of first edition

ROBERT VAUGHN.
Courtesy Montana Historical Society, Helena

THEN *and* NOW

OR,

THIRTY-SIX YEARS IN THE ROCKIES

Personal Reminiscences of Some of the First Pioneers
of the State of Montana.

INDIANS AND INDIAN WARS.

The Past and Present of the Rocky Mountain Country.
1864–1900.

by
Robert Vaughn

FARCOUNTRY
PRESS

First edition published by the author, 1900.

ISBN 1-56037-198-6

Dedication

Arvonia Elizabeth Vaughn, Great Falls, Montana.

My Dear Little Daughter:

The following series of letters, which include a short history of Montana's early days, together with a brief sketch of your father's life and a copy of my letter to you, giving an obituary of your dear mother, I dedicate to you, knowing that they will be appreciated, and hoping that you will have the pleasure of reading them after I am gone.

Your affectionate father,

ROBERT VAUGHN.

GREAT FALLS, MONTANA, MAY 15TH, 1900

Author's Preface

It may not be out of place to explain how this book came to find its way into print. It was written for my little daughter, in the form of letters at various times, and not intended for publication, but many friends after reading them insisted that they should be published. One said: "You must not wait until you are dead before these letters are given to the world."

As my desire is, by the grace of God, to live many years yet, I now present these letters to the reader, supplemented by others from old time friends who braved the perils and dangers of pioneer life; and as they are intended to be a part of the history of this great state, care has been taken to keep strictly to the truth.

It is hoped that a line here and there will be appreciated by those who ride in palace cars as well as the old pioneers who came west in prairie schooners.

ROBERT VAUGHN.

Contents

Introduction

"Who were the pioneers of Montana? They were the brave men and noble women who came here first;... They were the heroes who rescued this beautiful mountain land from the hands of the savages and laid the foundation and molded the destiny of this great state."

ROBERT VAUGHN, 1899

Robert Vaughn is the quintessential Montana pioneer. By his own definition, he had arrived in Montana Territory in the 1860s, worked hard, took risks, involved himself in civic affairs, and prospered. Most important, he had remained on the Montana scene—long enough for his story of "the early days" to hold credence. Vaughn was born in Montgomeryshire, Wales, on June 5, 1836, the third of six children. He spent his youth working on the family farm and received only a minimal formal education. At the age of nineteen he moved to London and engaged in flower gardening and in learning the English language.

Robert then sailed for America and arrived in New York City in 1858. When filing his citizenship papers, the clerk of court misspelled his name—which was "Vaughan," not "Vaughn." Because of legal difficulties, Robert agreed to the revision—although the change annoyed him for the rest of his life.

Between 1858 and 1864, the young Vaughn stopped to work

in Rome, New York, Palmyra (which he recalled as being in Ohio) and Youngstown, Ohio, and McLean County, Illinois. He reached a booming Alder Gulch on July 13, 1864. His overland route followed the Oregon Trail to Fort Laramie and then, as a member of Joe McKnight's train, the Bridger Cut-off to Virginia City.

There Vaughn tried his hand at placer mining and followed the rush to Last Chance Gulch late in 1864. He mined near Helena and opened a meat market at Nelson Gulch. In 1869 he located in the Sun River Valley, where he became the area's first private stockman and received the first homestead patent in Chouteau County.

The energetic Robert built a solid ranching operation near the present-day town of Vaughn, his namesake, west of Great Falls. He specialized in blooded stock and raised some of the best horses in the Territory. During the 1870s and 1880s, the ranch sat relatively close to the Blackfeet Reservation, and Vaughn experienced repeated encounters with local Indians and with other bands moving through the area.

In 1886 Robert Vaughn married Elizabeth Donahue of Toronto, Canada. She was thirty-one years old and he was fifty. To them was born a daughter, Arvonia Elizabeth, on January 1, 1888. The mother died as a result, however, and Robert assumed the responsibility of raising their child. It is to the young Arvonia that Vaughn writes the series of 1898-1900 letters that comprise the bulk of *Then and Now*.

Two years after the death of his wife, Robert sold his ranch on the Sun River to Captain Thomas Couch and removed downstream to the fledgling settlement of Great Falls. A fast friend of the community's founder Paris Gibson, Vaughn speculated in real estate, invested in the building of commercial blocks, and bankrolled local mining operations.

As Great Falls grew, so did the wealth and influence of Robert Vaughn. In 1893 he married again, this time to Ella De

Vee of Indiana. This relationship failed, however, and Robert returned to raising his daughter Arvonia in their Vaughn Block apartments. He became both an Elk and a Mason and involved himself in the Society of Montana Pioneers. Membership in that organization required an applicant's arrival in Montana prior to December 31, 1868.

By the turn of the last century, Robert Vaughn's personal kindness and honest public dealings had gained him widespread respect in Montana. Great Falls residents called him "Uncle Bob" to recognize his optimism, his boosterism, and his lack of pretension. In his later years, severe rheumatism caused Robert much pain and forced him to use a cane and/or a crutch. Yet he never complained. At a gathering to honor his eightieth birthday in 1916, Paris Gibson remarked (*Great Falls Tribune*, June 16, 1916):

"I first met Robert Vaughn in Fort Benton when he was 43 years old, my own age being 49. I was at once impressed with the personality of this man. He was erect and strong, and there was something in his bearing and his words that gave evidence of his courage and his honesty...Love of God and man is his religion, and what broader foundation can there be for man's life work?"

Robert Vaughn died in the Great Falls home he shared with his daughter Arvonia and son-in-law H. M. "Max" Sprague on March 23, 1918. His longtime Methodist friend, the Reverend W. W. Van Orsdel, eulogized Vaughn to throngs of mourners at the funeral. "Brother Van" remarked (*Great Falls Tribune*, March 27, 1918):

"'Uncle Bob' Vaughn was a pioneer of pioneers...This class of brave men and women are passing on rapidly, and their brave acts and heroic deeds made progress possible. They should be ever in our minds and thoughts as we note the growth of this great commonwealth.

"Robert Vaughn will be missed in his home and in places where he held council with his friends. Throughout all his eventful life, he did things worthwhile in his home life, in his Christian life, in the lodges, and in the community. We are all bereft."

* * * * * * *

For a man who saw himself first and foremost as a Montana pioneer, Vaughn's greatest legacy is this volume, initially published in 1900. The complete title of the work is instructive: *Then and Now; or, Thirty-Six Years in the Rockies. Personal Reminiscences of Some of the First Pioneers of the State of Montana. Indians and Indian Wars. The Past and Present of the Rocky Mountain Country, 1864-1900.* Interestingly, Robert copyrighted the work in Arvonia's name.

Vaughn stumbled on a neat convention with his series of "letters to my daughter." The first, heartfelt piece was penned in 1888, just a month after the death of his wife and Arvonia's mother. But he did not begin the rest of the writings until ten years later, in 1898.

In this 43-letter set (written between January 14, 1898, and May 30, 1900), he addresses his personal history, life in territorial Montana, Indian War issues, and aspects of "modern" (i.e., 1900) Montana. One of the real strengths of this work is Vaughn's inclusion of complementary sources. These materials range from obscure newspaper pieces, to official government documents, to letters from principals involved in specific events.

The richest sources are the solicited reminiscences of Vaughn's pioneer friends. Many of these one-of-a-kind pieces appear only in this volume. Vaughn was a good friend of Charlie Russell, the "cowboy artist," since both were long-time Great Falls residents. Russell authorized the use of eight pieces of his artwork in the original publication. Interestingly, both Vaughn and Russell used the "then and now" convention to advantage in their creative work.

Vaughn liberally invoked his "then and now" theme to illustrate the "progress" that white civilization has brought to Montana's Indian wilderness in the short span of thirty-six years. In many ways, this volume is one lengthy advertisement for Manifest Destiny, Christianity, and the Euro-American way of life. But who would expect less, given the time period in which it was written and given the experiences of the author?

Vaughn's heritage and perspective propelled him to justify—even to champion—the eradication of Indian cultures by white society. Yet this was not an easy task for him. He could handle it better on the broad, impersonal, cultural level (page 270): "They are naturally treacherous, savage, and cruel to those they are not at peace with—be it the whites or their own race, it makes no difference."

Yet on the personal level, Vaughn's innate humanity gets in the way of haughtily conquering another individual—however necessary. Following an account of Piegans stealing his horses and then returning them (pp. 91-93), Vaughn remarks, "That was the only time the Indians ever stole anything from me." Thus a topic like inter-tribal horse theft allows the author to speak admiringly of the personal characteristics of tribal participants. Vaughn's accounts of early days in the Sun River Valley especially reveal this perplexing dichotomy between dealing with the Indian culture and dealing with the Indian individual. "Then and now"—in terms of Indians—ultimately creates a tough moral dilemma for "Uncle Bob." His cultural guilt is never fully assuaged. It underlies much of his writing on Indians—even when he assumes, as in the old saw, "the only good Indian is a dead Indian."

In other realms, the convention of "then and now" to mark time and progress works with fewer moral or ethical glitches. The transportation comparison (p. 42) between "then" taking mules from Virginia City to Helena in 1864 and "now" arriving at the Capital City on a sleek, black, steam-belching locomotive in 1900 is a graphic image. Similarly, the change (p. 255) in communities from mining-era boom camps "propagating crimes and greed, and filling the air with blasphemy" to respectable towns with "well selected libraries" and "the best class of educational and beneficent institutions" puts "then" in stark contrast with "now."

Most impressively, the wilderness of "then" has become the boom economy of "now" (p. 254):

"…And the sturdy stroke of the miner, followed by that of the mechanic, farmer, stockman, and manufacturer has brought out her hidden treasures, until today Montana is the wealthiest state in the Union in proportion to its population."

What must not be forgotten, however, is that all this genuflection at the altar of "progress" is done at the expense of the indigenous peoples who inhabited Montana "then." Robert Vaughn knew it in 1900, just as well as the modern reader knows it today.

* * * * * * *

At some point during the process of writing his series of letters, Vaughn's initial purpose of documenting his life for his daughter changed. As friends sampled his efforts, they encouraged him to seek a wider readership for his work.

So, rather than write solely for a daughter whom he feared he might not see grow to adulthood, "Uncle Bob" began to write for an audience of contemporary Montanans. Chapters on "The Sioux War," "The Nez Perces War," "the Indian Messiah and the

Ghost Dance," "Yellowstone National Park," and Butte's "Greatest Mining Camp on Earth" are the results. Today's reader benefits from these particular letters by gaining an insightful 1900 perspective on these key historical events and places.

* * * * * * *

In 1987 Clyde Milner II wrote an intriguing piece addressing the phenomenon of "Montana pioneerism" entitled "The Shared Memory of Montana's Pioneers" (*Montana, the Magazine of Western History*, XXXVII, 1 [Winter, 1987], 2-13). Here Milner notes the propensity of early white Montana settlers not only to make history but also to preserve and promote that history.

In the course of characterizing these Montana pioneers, Milner identifies several topics common to their reminiscences: the overland journey; Indian threats; life in the early gold camps, particularly vigilante actions; harsh weather; encounters with wild animals; starting enterprises from scratch. Sample cases from Granville Stuart to Wilbur Fisk Sanders and Conrad Kohrs illustrate this commonality of focus.

To Milner, the shared memory of these Montanans produced a shared identity for the pioneers—it defined a pioneer. For an early settler to address these topics was to validate his pioneer status.

Again, Robert Vaughn proved the quintessential pioneer. Vaughn eagerly displays all of the contents of the pioneer's kitbag in *Then and Now*. He survived the requisite overland journey to Virginia City, experienced multiple Indian encounters in Montana, prospected in both Alder Gulch and in Last Chance Gulch, observed the Vigilantes at work, encountered harsh weather as well as wild animals, and started several business enterprises from scratch. In fact, Vaughn's hard work and ingenuity made his Sun River ranch one of the premier livestock operations in the Territory.

Thus *Then and Now* becomes a testimony to "Uncle Bob's" pioneer status. His use of the reminiscences of other pioneers aids in producing a "collectively remembered past." Historian Milner would have certified Vaughn as a legitimate Montana pioneer. To cinch the designation, Robert conspicuously became a member of the Society of Montana Pioneers and served as its Cascade County vice-president in 1890.

* * * * * * *

Pioneers not only plant the flag, they also raise the level of society and they stay around to develop the economy. Vaughn quotes an 1869 citizens' comment to this effect (p. 276):

"Ours is a contest between civilization and barbarism, and we must risk our lives and sacrifice our hard-earned property to defend them, unless the general government gives us the means of defense. To this we are entitled, as we have left homes of comfort in the East to plant civilization in the wilderness..."

The citizens' assertions are Vaughn's opinions also (p. 87):

"Some people, after reading this letter, may say that it was wrong for those daring men and brave women to go into such a country, occupied only by savages. Well, that may be so, but the unexplored West never would have been developed were it not for the immigrants, miners, and prospectors who had the ambition, courage, and pluck to commence to conquer. They are the 'John the Baptists' of civilization. They are the founders of states that are represented by stars in our banner and of those yet to come.

"I came to Montana when a young man. Now I am old,...but there is nothing that can rob me of the pride and glory of being a 'hero of Montana'—one of those who stood by its cradle."

Indeed, Robert Vaughn is a legitimate Montana pioneer.

Then and Now is his testament. To curious readers more than a century after its initial publication, it affords a rare glimpse into the early white settlement of Montana. This volume—a remarkable contribution to "the Montana story"—has been too long out-of-print. Welcome back!

* * * * * * *

To Montana Pioneers*
By Robert Vaughn

Montana pioneers were they,
Who opened the Wilderness Gate,
That civilization might come,
And transform it into a state.

They were the brave pioneers who,
Away, away westward went
O'er countless miles of trackless plains
When stirring were the events.

Most popular way to go west then
Was in a prairie schooner,
Though there were other outfits
Would get them there much sooner.

What a long and perilous journey
Was the trip across the plain,
Out in cold and stormy weather,
Tugging through mud and rain!

Many fights they had with Indians,
Who were watching night and day,

For a chance to steal and plunder
And to run their stock away.

Those came first went to the mountains
In small bands to hunt for gold.
They had bloody fights with Indians,
Endured hunger, fear and cold.

One was killed near the camp fire
While drinking his cup of tea,
Another arrow rent the air
And came near killing me.

Later others came and settled
In the valleys and the plains.
They, too, fought some desperate battles,
In which many a one was slain.

In those battles with the savages
Many a pioneer then did fall,
And as many of the enemy
Answered to the rifle's call.

Blessed be those noble women
Who then crossed the trackless plain.
They were the "Red Cross" in those battles
To the wounded and the slain.
It cost twelve hundred lives or more
To win the glorious victory,
That now the people of this state
May live in peace and plenty.

Honor the memory of those who've
Passed over the Great Divide
To rest in Camp Eternity
On the plain on the other side.

After all we greatly enjoyed
Life on the wild frontier,
As long as we had a grub-stake mine
And the Indians not too near.

As a general thing our health was good
(When Indians were not near),
And as a rule we had plenty to eat,
Antelope meat and deer.

And when the holidays would come
We had a Christmas dinner,
A partridge, venison and plum-duff,
We cared for nothing better.

Little we thought that we were then
Paving the way for a state,
Paving the way for Montana,
MONTANA, The Treasure State.

* * * * * * *

DAVE WALTER
HELENA, MONTANA — JULY 2001

*Helen Fitzgerald Sanders, *A History of Montana*, Vol. 2
(Chicago: Lewis Publishing Company, 1913), 958.

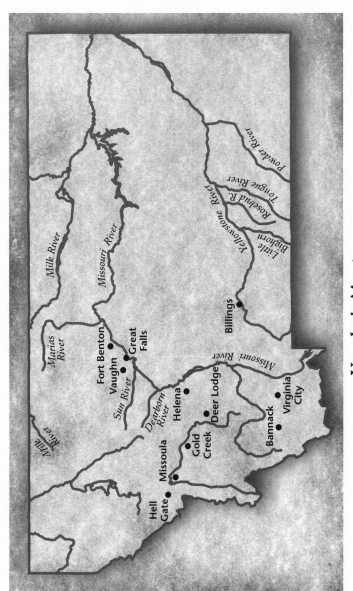

Vaughn's Montana

THEN *and* NOW

OR,

THIRTY-SIX YEARS IN THE ROCKIES

From Home to the State of Illinois.

I was born in Wales June 5, 1836, and was reared on a farm until I was nineteen years old. My parents' names were Edward and Elizabeth Vaughan. There were six children—Jane, Hugh, Robert, Edward, John and Mary. Edward lives in the old home at the present time. His address is: "Dugoed Bach, Dinas Mowddwy, Mereoneth Sheir, G.B."

My parents were of good family; by that I mean they and their ancestors were good Christian people, father and mother were members of the Episcopal Church. Father was a warden as long as I can remember. Mother was my only teacher. She taught me to obey, to tell the truth, to be kind, to respect others and above all to fear God.

I left home when I was between nineteen and twenty. At this time I could speak but the Welsh language. I had a great desire to learn to acquire English; therefore I went to Liverpool, where sister Jane lived. I secured employment from the Hon. Benjamin Haywood Jones to work in a flower garden at his beautiful home on the West Derby Road. He was a rich banker in the city. I remained there over a year. Brother Hugh had gone to America a year before I left home, locating near Rome, N.Y. In the fall of 1858, instead of going home as I intended, I concluded that it would be a good idea for me to go to America and see my brother; then return in four or five months. So, without the knowledge of my parents, I took passage on board a steamship named the "Vigo" bound for New York. I was on the ocean twelve days and a half. As soon as I landed I wrote home and stated what I had done, and that I would be back home in four or five months, and at that time it was my honest intention to do so. From New York City I went to my brother's, and stayed with him about three months; then I went to Palmyra, Ohio, to see Aunt Ann, my father's sister. I was right at home now, and my father was satisfied since I was in the care of his sister. I was there over a year, going thence to Youngstown, Ohio, where I worked for Joshua Davies on a farm, and in the coal mines. From here I proceeded to McLean county, Illinois, where my brother had been for two years. I farmed with him one summer, then I went to Fairbury, Livingston county, and mined coal until 1864. During all this time I wrote home regularly and received letters in return. Instead of going home I was continually getting further from it. Somehow I could not resist the desire of venturing into the unsettled regions of the West. I kept drifting further and further until I found myself in the heart of the Rocky mountains, six thousand miles from home.

In this way forty-one years elapsed since I left my childhood home, but the picture remains in my memory as though it were but yesterday; everything appears to me as it was the last time I saw it. The house still seems the same; the ivy creeping up its walls; the sycamore, alder, birch and spruce trees stand there like sentries guarding it. The rose bushes and the evergreens in front, the hollies where the sparrows huddled together at night, the orchard and the old stone barn; and I imagine—

"I see the quiet fields around,
I stroll about as one who dreams;

'Til each familiar place is found,
How strangely sweet to me it seems.

"The old and well known paths are there,
My youthful feet so often pressed;
Gone is the weight of manhood's care,
And in its place a sense of rest.

"The broad expanse before me lies,
Checked here and there with squares of green;
Where, freshly growing crops arise,
And browner places intervene."

I see the dancing rill flowing by the garden gate, and the great arch of white thorn overspanning the passage way that led to the main road. There my mother embraced and kissed me and bade me good-bye for the last time. Here my "only teacher" gave me her last instruction, it was this: "My dear son, be careful in selecting your companions to go out with in the evenings. God be with you, good-bye."

Oh, how sweetly her voice fell on my listening ear,
And now, I imagine those soft words I hear;
If I ever view her silent grave,
My tears will flow like tidal wave.

There she stood staring at her wandering boy leaving home. We watched one another until a curve in the road took me out of sight; that was the last time I saw my mother. Father came with me about a quarter of a mile. We spoke but very little; we were both very sad. Suddenly father turned to me and took me by the hand and said: "Well, my son, fare thee well, be a good boy." I was weeping bitterly and after I had gone a little way I looked back and saw father leaning against a gate which led to the meadow, with both hands on his face; this caused my tears to flow faster than ever. I shall always believe that father was praying for me then. And that was the last time I saw him. Father and mother are now sleeping in the silent tomb. But in my memory they appear like statues as I saw them last, and that was forty-one years ago. Mother standing at the gate with tears in her eyes waving the kind and tender hand that soothed and fondled me when I was a babe, and father leaning on that rude gate with his face buried in his hands offering a prayer in my behalf. Nothing can efface that vision from my memory. Mother more than once said in her letters to me that she always remembered me in her prayers. I often think that I might not have fared so well and perhaps be a worse man than I am, were it not for the prayers of my father and mother.

ROBERT VAUGHN.

GREAT FALLS, MONT., MARCH 20, 1898

Crossing the Plains.

I left Fairbury, Livingston county, Illinois, March 4, 1864, in company with James Gibb, John Jackson, James Martin, and Sam Dempster and wife, destined for the new gold fields in Idaho, for the Territory of Montana had not then been created.

Our mode of traveling was with a four-horse team and a farm wagon. A great portion of Illinois and Iowa was then but sparsely settled; we would travel for hours without seeing any signs of habitation. The roads were very bad through those states; and it took us twenty-five days to come to Council Bluffs, which was then but a small frontier settlement. An old man, one of the inhabitants of the place, called my attention to two small hills on the bluff above the village and said: "It was there General Fremont, with his men, held a council before crossing the river to traverse the plains to California, and from this incident the town derives its name." We crossed the Missouri on a ferry boat. Omaha had scarcely twelve hundred people. Here we made up a train of sixty-five wagons, some drawn by oxen. It was a mixed train as far as the destination was concerned. Some were going to California, Oregon, Washington, and Salt Lake, but mostly to the new gold diggings in Idaho. We were to travel together as far as Utah.

Our trail was on the north side of the North Platte river as far as Fort Laramie, following most of the way the surveying stakes on the line of the Union Pacific Railway. For several hundred miles, while we traveled in the Platte river valley, we passed over fine land for agriculture. Here we met a great many Indians of the Pawnee tribe, but all appeared to be friendly. I was approached by one of them, who came and asked me to give him some coffee; he was over six feet tall, and had a very large bow and arrows. I made a mark on a big cottonwood tree and stepped off fifty paces and told him if he put an arrow in that mark I would give him some coffee. At once he began sending his arrows, every one piercing the tree about two inches in depth, and the fourth one into the center of the mark. I gave him his coffee. On another occasion I put my hat on a bunch of sage brush for two Indian boys to shoot at for a piece of bread; the next thing I knew there was an arrow through my hat. Several days, when traveling in this valley, not a stick of timber of any kind could be had; the only fuel we could obtain was buffalo chips which were abundant.

The mail carrier told us that after passing a place called "Pawnee Swamp," which was about fifty miles west of Fort Kearney, we would be in the Cheyenne and Sioux country, and that those Indians were very hostile to the whites. It was two days after we crossed this line before we saw an Indian. The third morning at day break, when I was on guard, I discovered one from a distance who was coming towards our camp. I kept watching him; finally he came to me and spoke, at the same time making signs; of course I did not understand either. While going on with his gibberish and making those motions with his hands he stepped up and patted me on the breast and on my vest pocket. I told him in plain English that he was getting a little too familiar for a stranger, and to keep away from me. Then he picked up a stem of some dried weed about the size of a match and scratched it on a stone as a person would when lighting a match. This convinced me that he wanted some matches. I gave him half a dozen and he thanked me, or at least I thought he did, for he gave a kind of grunt with a faint smile and went back in the direction he came from.

In the afternoon of the same day we crossed a small creek; on its bank there was a newly made grave in which a young woman twenty-two years of age had been laid to rest. At the head of the grave, for a head-board, a round stick, which had been used at one time for a picket pin, was placed, and on this some unskilled hand had written with a pencil "In memory of_____," the name I could not decipher, but the words "dear daughter" were plainly written, which indicated that there was a parent present to kiss her marble brow before it was lowered into the silent tomb. This instance made a deep impression on me then when viewing that lonely grave in the heart of the wilderness and thinking of its occupant, who possibly was once the center star in some lovable family, but was left there alone in her earthen couch to sleep and rest forever; and when, on the coming of spring, no one would be there to even pluck wild flowers and lay them on the grave of the unfortunate young traveler. What more sorrowful sight could there be than witnessing those parents leaving that sacred spot before continuing their westward journey, and, when on that ridge, taking the last look at the little mound by the winding brook in the valley below? Here the curtain drops on this pitiful scene; the emigrant train is out of sight and all is over.

At Fort Laramie we met the noted frontiersman, John Bozeman, after whom the city of Bozeman, Montana, was named. He sought to organize a train to take a cut-off route east of the Big Horn mountains. There was also a man by the name of McKnight, who was a trader at this place. He had two wagons loaded with goods for Alder Gulch, each wagon being drawn by four fine mules, and he was getting up a train to go west of the Big Horn mountains and through the Wind River country. McKnight said to me that he wanted about one hundred wagons and about five hundred good, resolute, determined men and they would get through all right. I told him that there were five of us, and that we would accompany him. There were scores of wagons passing Laramie every day and most of them were bound for the new gold diggings.

The first day we got twenty wagons to join the McKnight

train, and we pulled out about a quarter of a mile in the direction we were to travel. This new camp was a kind of "refin-
ery;" here one and all might consider the perils, dangers and
privations likely to be encountered. The faint-hearted ones
took the safer route by way of the South Pass. However, in a
few days we had four hundred and fifty men and over one
hundred wagons. We were aware that we were going to travel through several hundred miles of an untrodden wilderness,
where Red Cloud and Sitting Bull reigned over twenty or thirty-five thousand savages, so it was very necessary for us to be
well armed and organized. Before starting we took a vote and
selected a captain and two lieutenants, and a committee of
three to examine every one and see if he was prepared with
guns, sufficient ammunition, and if his outfit was substantial
enough to make the trip. A paper was drawn in which was in-
serted a provision that we were to stand by and defend each
other at all hazards; to this we all signed our names. We realized that it was a perilous undertaking, but we pressed on-
ward. We depended a great deal on our guide. He was a tall,
well-built, straight, dark-complexioned, resolute and intelligent man; he was reared in Canada and had been in the
employ of the Hudson's Bay Company. He was a famous
scout and versed in the language of every Indian tribe from the
Platte to the Saskatchewan, and was both feared and respected by all. He was a brave and true man, whose tact and
courage, on more than one occasion, resulted in avoiding trouble with hostile redskins.

Roll was called every evening. Each man had to be on
guard in his turn for four consecutive hours during the night.
To form the camp the first wagon had to make a circle until it
faced the hindmost one, and each one followed forming thus
a stockade, the horses being driven past the inside hind wheel
of the wagon in front; after unhitching the tongue was thrown

EARLY DAY FREIGHTER—OX-TEAMS PULLING COVERED WAGONS.
Courtesy Montana Historical Society, Helena

over the wheel and rested on the axle. At night all the horses and tents were on the inside and those standing guard being on the outside. We invariably formed our camp in this way, and were always on our guard, for no man can tell when danger may be near in an Indian country. When there is not an Indian to be seen it is the time they are the most likely to make an attack. An incident I well remember. The writer and Gibb were ahead of the train and about half a mile on one side from the direction we were traveling. Crossing a small ravine we saw two Indians hiding under some willows. They pretended not to see us. It is probable that there were many more in that vicinity, although there was no indication of the kind.

One day we came through a Sioux village of eighty-five tepees; there were from two to three hundred Indians, chiefly women and children. On a slope of a hill near by were over eight hundred horses in charge of six Indians. Though we camped at noon but a short distance from them, only two approached us, and their actions were different from those of the other Indians whom we met. When the Sioux came to our camp they would go from one tent or wagon to another in a sullen manner with a contemptible look as if they were going to massacre every one of us, and likely the reason they did not was that we had taken them unawares and before they had time to prepare, besides we were as good as an equal number of soldiers if it had come to fighting. But by the year following they were better prepared, for they had obtained guns and ammunition from the traders. They killed many immigrants. And the year succeeding traveling through that part of the Sioux country was entirely discontinued, and Fort Phil Kearney was established. A few months later all the soldiers, eighty-one in number, were killed by the Indians—not one was left to tell the story. And, these savages kept up their murderous deeds until the Sioux war of 1876.

Many times I thought of the perils and dangers that we escaped on that eventful journey, of which I now give an account.

It was against the rules of our camp for any one to kindle a fire after dark. The object was to prevent the Indians from locating us at night. We were obliged to camp where an abundance of water could be obtained. A small spring would not meet our requirements, for we had nearly three hundred horses, sometimes we had to make long drives to the next stream or a place where there was plenty of water. Other times we had to stop, from early noon until next day, for we could not make the drive in one afternoon. For the balance of the day we frequently had considerable sport by playing several games, shooting at a mark, short and long distance jumping, wrestling and foot racing; but as the journey grew longer the contraction of the muscles put a stop to the latter three. On one of those long evenings we saw a torch light at the base of a mountain not far off. It was swung back and forth for several minutes. It was an Indian sign, and that put a stop to all games for that evening. We looked for trouble that night, but had none. We were all happy and had no sickness on that trip. There were six or seven men from the southern part of Illinois who had the ague at the time they joined the party, but as we came nearer to the mountains all traces of it disappeared and returned no more. It was hard for us to secure game of any kind, for the Indians kept driving it away as we went, and it was not prudent for us to venture far from the course we were pursuing to look for any. We saw many deer and buffaloes, but they were a long ways off; occasionally we would get some of the smaller game. We traversed much good grazing land where water was plenty; also many valleys with rich lands for farming and an abundance of good timber.

The atmosphere was very clear when we first saw the Rocky mountains. They were several hundred miles distant;

an old Californian pointed them out. They appeared to be of immense height and it was difficult to convince many of us that they were mountains, for they looked more like thunder clouds to us who came from the prairie states. Every day brought us nearer, and soon the perpetual snow was visible, then the green pines and the rocky cliffs above the timber line, where no vegetation exists, were plain to be seen, and, as I gazed at those high rocky peaks, reaching above the clouds, it was plain to why the Rocky mountains were called "The Rockies."

It did not take many days to skirt those lofty mountains and wind our way through their canyons, listening to the rebounding echo of our wagons rattling over the rocks and boulders as we went.

In one of those narrow valleys in the mountains we camped one June day for dinner. Trout was abundant in the creek. On both sides there was a dense growth of pine. Thinking that it was a good place to look for deer, I took my gun and climbed the mountain side until I reached where the land was almost level. After I had gone about a mile, I arrived at an opening in the woods; two or three hundred yards away I saw a large brown bear and elevating my gun I took aim at the big brute; just then a second thought came to me, and I said to myself: "If I kill it, all well and good; if I only wound it I'll get the worst of it." I paused for a minute, looking at the bear, and the longer I looked the larger it seemed; the bear stood and looked at me, and finally he walked away slowly, occasionally looking back. I was walking as the bear did, only in the opposite direction. Soon the bear stopped and faced towards me and I made a bee-line for the camp, for I was not looking for that kind of game that day.

We frequently passed trees in the branches of which a dead Indian was placed on a kind of scaffold eight or ten feet above the ground. This place of burial was constructed of poles and branches of trees tied together with strips of rawhide. The remains were carefully wrapped in beaded and painted robes, in Indian fashion, and secured with rawhide ropes to the scaffold. Thus the dead Indian rested, high and dry, on his sacred roost until his gorgeous couch was destroyed by the elements and his bones picked by birds of prey. We also passed several scaffolds built on four forked stakes, on which remains of Indians were placed, and wrapped in the same manner as those on the trees.

Very often some aged Indians would visit our camps and go from one tent to another and peep in as if they were counting to ascertain how many there were. We treated them kindly and gave them something to eat; they always asked for matches and were very fond of tobacco. Our guide warned us that they were spies and for us to have our guns in a conspicuous place so they could see our strength. We had many obstacles to contend with on our journey. One day we had to travel forty miles without water. It was very hot; many of the horses giving out, their tongues being swollen until they protruded from their mouths. At another time we had to let the wagons down the mountain with ropes, with the hind wheels locked; and we had to cross rivers on rafts and wagon boxes; again fording streams where there was great danger of being taken down by the surging waters. Four of our men came very near losing their lives in this way; but being good swimmers they avoided drowning. We crossed the Powder, Clark's Fork, Rosebud and Yellowstone rivers and many other streams. The first we came to were very high, for at that time the snows were melting off the mountains.

Upon reaching the Rosebud we pitched our tents and camped till the next morning. It was in the latter part of June; the trees and shrubs were in full foliage and the wild flowers perfumed the air. The Rosebud is one of the prettiest rivers I ever saw; like all mountain streams the current is swift and its water as clear as crystal. Its beds are inlaid with pebbles of all imaginable colors, with occasional large boulders, where the speckled trout hides as one approaches the water's edge. Along its bands are groves of ancient trees, with underbrush of many varieties and wild roses in great profusion. The bottom lands for miles are but nature's meadows, while the rolling hills, as far as the eye can see, are a vast pasture land dotted here and there with clumps of timber. Although away from civilization, the small birds flutter among the branches, singing their sweet songs with as tender cadence as if in somebody's front yard in the civilized East. The same can be said of nearly all of the streams and valleys that we crossed and came through on our journey. On first view of these beautiful landscapes a person would think that some prehistoric race had cultivated these fertile valleys and planted those ancient trees and groves that grew as uniform as if the ground had been laid out by some expert landscape gardener. On further observation, we could see high, tempest tortured towers of grand masonry work, which had withstood the elements for ages. All is but the handiwork of nature, directed by the Great Architect of the Universe.

When in the Yellowstone valley we saw from a distance a party of Indians all mounted and coming towards us. Our captain at once gave orders to form into a camp, and, before the Indians got near, we were formed into a stockade and ready for battle, if necessary. As the Indians approached our guide stepped forward about two hundred yards to meet them. They were eighty-five in number. Then they whipped their horses to greater speed and began yelling. When within about two hundred yards of him, he lifted his hand and the Indians stopped as if they were shot. The chief of the party and our

AN INDIAN SCAFFOLD BURIAL.
Courtesy Montana Historical Society, Helena

guide had a sign talk for a few minutes; the chief came forward and stated that they were "Crows" and he wished to know who we were. He was informed who we were and where we were going. They talked for about ten minutes, then the balance of the Indians came forward and were invited to come to our camp. They were mounted on good horses and had on their war paint and all were stripped to their waists. We gave them bread and coffee and took a smoke with them. Smoking with an Indian signifies that he is friendly. They all left very peaceably and never came back. They were the last Indians we saw until we got to Alder Creek.

Some distance after crossing the Yellowstone river the writer and two others were considerable ahead of the wagons and crossing our course was a ripple of clear water. The sun was hot and the effect of the heat made us thirsty. All three, nearly at the same time, got down to quench their thirst with the sparkling water. The first one cries at the top of his voice: "My God, it is hot;" the second remarked: "Well, boys, we must be near to the jumping-off place," while the third thought that we were getting near to the infernal regions. However, it was a great wonder to us, for this was the first hot spring that we had ever seen.

This spring is to-day the renowned Hunter Hot Springs, a place of resort for its mineral properties, where hundreds of people are treated every year for rheumatism and kindred diseases. It has fine hotel accommodations and all modern conveniences and improvements for the comfort of its patrons. What was "then" but a ripple of hot water is "now" a Western Saratoga.

After a journey of two thousand miles over plains and sandy deserts, up the hills and down the canyons, crossing rivers and through many beautiful valleys, fatigued by much suffering, hardships and dangers, we arrived in Alder Gulch

July 13, 1864. We found it to be a great camp, and were told how many dollars to the pan and how rich the mines were, and of the "road agents" robbing and killing people; of the organization of the vigilance committee and the good work they were doing by hanging the desperadoes, and suppressing lawlessness. Not until we arrived did we learn of the organization of the Territory of Montana, for it was completed May 26th, while we were in the wilderness. Truly, Montana "then" was but an infant in its cradle.

ROBERT VAUGHN.

FEB. 11, 1898.

On a Stampede to the Yellowstone.

In September, 1864, James Gibb, Jack Williams, Charles Howard, myself and a man named Wilson, left Alder Gulch on a "stampede" to the upper Yellowstone country. It was reported that a rich gold discovery had been made not far from the canyon at the Yellowstone river. Each of us procured a saddle pony, and a pack horse. We undertook to follow the base of the mountains; crossing the headwaters of the Madison, Jefferson, and Gallatin rivers. We were traveling by direction of a map and the use of a compass, but made the mistake of keeping too near the mountains, for we were delayed several times by the dense pines that grew so thick in some places that we had to chop our way through. In one small valley there was a great quantity of petrified wood. And in the bed of the creek nearly all the stones were petrifactions. I remember that we stopped on the banks of this creek for dinner. The mountains were very steep. On a cliff about one hundred yards off stood a Rocky mountain goat. At first we thought it a domestic sheep, for it was very white, bleated, and acted as if it was glad to see us. But then, as there were no settlers within several hundred miles, we could not imagine how a sheep could get to such a place. While we were discussing the matter, the animal leaped over cliffs and up the mountain as if it was on level ground, and this satisfied us all that it was a Rocky mountain goat. Not one of us had seen one previously. The next day we came to a small lake on top of a mountain, on approaching which we could see a big black bear rooting in the edge of the water, but it disappeared before we had a chance to shoot. After that we were on the watch for bear. Sometimes we would travel for several miles on a well-beaten trail made by wild animals. At one time Jack Williams was considerably in advance of the balance of the party, and on one of these game trails, at a point where the ground was a little marshy so an impression of any kind would show very plainly. Suddenly we could see Jack coming around the bend helter-skelter as fast as his pony could carry him, saying that he had seen the track of a grizzly bear coming straight towards him. I asked, "Do you mean to say that you saw a grizzly bear coming straight towards you?" "No," said Jack. "I saw its track coming this way." "And you went after the bear, did you?" Jack studied a minute and said: "I'll be hanged I never thought of that, but I'll tell you, boys, those tracks are fourteen inches long and eight inches wide; I don't care what direction they point to, the sight of them is enough to convince a man when he is alone that he has not lost any bears." On the seventh day we camped on the Yellowstone and stayed until the next morning. The river was not wide, but the current was very swift and the banks and the bed of the stream were very rocky. It was a fine place for trout fishing, and we caught some that weighed two pounds. We could not see any indications of travel up the river, but we went as far as the canyon. Wonderland was not known then. We concluded that the new Eldorado was not in that direction, so we turned back and went down the valley for many miles; we did some prospecting along the route. Finally we found about fifty men working in a place which had been named Emigrant Gulch. There were but few taking out gold in paying quantities; most of them were prospecting in the gulch and on the bars. We remained there several days but found nothing that we thought would pay, although a great deal of gold has been taken out of this gulch since. Consequently we decided to go home. This time we took the lowland until we reached the emigrant trail. On our way, on the divide between the Yellowstone and Gallatin valleys, we saw about one hundred and fifty elks all in one herd, on a slope of a hill, grazing. Grass was abundant and game was plentiful;

JOHN BOZEMAN.
Courtesy Montana Historical Society, Helena

wherever we traveled we had all the trout and deer meat that we could eat. At the crossing of the Gallatin we met Mr. John Bozeman, for whom the City of Bozeman, Montana, is named, as I have mentioned in a previous letter. The last time that I met him was on the North Platte. There were with him three or four Indian people. He was returning from Alder Gulch, having made a successful trip with a train of emigrant wagons, of which he was guide. He brought this train, which was about one hundred and twenty wagons, from the North Platte river and by his "New Bozeman route," east of the Big Horn mountains, to the Yellowstone valley and thence to the gold fields; now he was on his way back to organize another train for the same place and by the same route. Some time afterwards and but one day's travel from the place where I met him last he was murdered by the treacherous Indians, for whom he had done many kind acts. Thus the brave pioneer and frontiersman John Bozeman, came to the end of his route. We had been very lucky; we saw but few Indians; the weather had been delightful, and all enjoyed the trip. We saw grand scenery, groves of lofty pines, natural parks stocked with wild deer and elks, brooks of clear water where the speckled trout played among its pebbles and had all the harbor to themselves; beautiful springs bursting forth from the mountain side, still higher the majestic peaks stood in bold relief above the mountain pines, where lay the perpetual snow; and to render man's enjoyment complete, his lungs are filled with pure mountain air perfumed with scent of pines and herbs that grow everywhere. I know of no place like the mountains for one that loves nature in all its glory.

After twenty-nine days of "roughing it" we returned to Alder Gulch, not any richer, but wiser, men.

ROBERT VAUGHN.

FEB. 12, 1898.

The Discovery of Alder Creek, the Richest Gulch on the Globe.

On April 9, 1863, several courageous miners met at Bannock City, and formulated plans to organize an expedition to the country of the Yellowstone and Big Horn rivers for the purpose of prospecting for gold, and if successful, the idea was to lay out townsites, and so forth. James Stuart, a brother of Granville Stuart (now of Butte), and William Fairweather, were the prime movers in getting up the expedition. It was agreed that those who were going to join the expedition should meet at Rattlesnake creek the next day. There the form of organization was to be adopted; the original manuscript, which is now in the possession of the Historical Society of Montana, reads thus: "Having determined to explore a portion of the country drained by the 'Yellowstone' for the purpose of discovering gold mines and securing townsites, and believing this object could be better accomplished by forming ourselves into a regularly organized company, we hereby appoint James Stuart captain, agreeing upon our word of honor to obey all orders given or issued by him, or any subordinate officer appointed by him. In case of any member refusing to obey an order or orders from said captain he shall be forcibly expelled from our camp. It is further understood and agreed that we all do our equal portions of work, the captain being umpire in all cases, sharing equally the benefits of the said labor both as to the discovery of gold and securing townsites.

"(Signed.) James Stuart, Cyrus D. Watkins, John Vanderbilt, James N. York, Richard McCafferty, James Hauxhurst, Drewyer Underwood, Samuel T. Hauser, Henry A. Bell, William Roach, A. Sterne Blake, George H. Smith, Henry T. Greery, Ephraim Bostwick." George Ives overtook the party the next day; he had not yet signed the agreement, but he intended doing so.

William Fairweather, Lewis Simons, Bill Sweeney, Thomas Cover, Barney Hughes, Henry Edgar and Rogers intended to meet Stuart and his party at a given place, but on account of losing their horses they failed to make the connection, but arrived there three or four days after Stuart and his party had passed. They took their trail, making as good time as possible, with the expectation of overtaking them in two or three days. But, on the upper Yellowstone, they were met by a large party of Crow Indians who took them prisoners. And this is the reason why the "Bill Fairweather party" and "the James Stuart party" became separated. The consequence was that Fairweather and his men were forced to turn back, and, when returning from what they thought was an unfortunate trip, they discovered Alder Gulch, which proved afterwards to be the richest gulch in the world. And it appears to a man in the moon that the Crow chief had a hand in making this discovery, and likely if Bill Fairweather had thought of it he would have staked him a claim.

When the news reached Bannock that Fairweather's party had made a rich discovery everybody rushed for the new Eldorado, and in a few days Bannock was almost deserted. June 6, 1863, the Fairweather district was organized (in Alder Gulch), with Dr. Steele president and James Fergus recorder. And then and there the sills and rafters of the State of Montana were hewn.

Since then over $85,000,000 has been taken out of this remarkable gulch.

Recently a correspondent of the Anaconda Standard had an interview with the Henry Edgar referred to, which interview was published in the "Standard" Sept. 5, 1899, from which the following extracts are taken. Mr. Edgar said:

"In February, 1863, I sold my claim, which was No. 8 on Stapleton's bar at Bannock, and went to Deer Lodge to get an outfit for this expedition. We intended to join Stuart's party,

WILLIAM H. FAIRWEATHER.
Courtesy Montana Historical Society, Helena

which left Bannock about the same time we departed from Deer Lodge. That was the latter part of April or the first part of May. We were in reality bound for the Black Hills. Simmons accompanied us as our guide. There were six in the party. We had got two days' travel below the mouth of Clarke's Fork in the neighborhood of Pompey's Pillar, when we were captured by the Indians. There was no fighting. That would have been sure death, they so far outnumbered us. They took us into camp and made medicine over us for three days.

"It was jointly through Bill Fairweather and Lewis Simmons that we were saved. I do not understand why it was, but a rattlesnake would never bite Bill. When he saw one he would always take it up and carry it along with him. They never seemed to resent anything he would do with them and he never killed one. As we were going towards the Indian village he picked up a rattlesnake, and just at the outskirts of the village he picked up another. When the Indians saw him come in with a rattlesnake on each arm they were awed. He put the snakes in his shirt bosom and Simmons told the Indians that he was the great medicine man of the whites.

"They took us into the medicine lodge, where a large bush was placed in the center. They marched us around that several times and finally Bill said if they repeated it he would pull up the sacred medicine bush. They marched around us again and Bill pulled up the bush and walloped the medicine man on the head with it. We then were formed three to three, back to back. We had refused all along to give up our guns and revolvers. The old chief drove the other Indians back with a whip. They had a council which lasted from noon till midnight. In the meantime we were sentenced. If we proceeded they would kill us. If we turned back and relinquished our horses we would not be harmed. It was Hobson's choice. I received for my three horses an old horse, blind in one eye, and a yearling colt. For my three pairs of Oregon blankets a buffalo robe and a half, and for my grub, consisting of flour, bacon, coffee, beans, etc., a dozen dried buffalo tongues. Simmons remained with the Indians.

"We came back on the north side of the Yellowstone, after one day's travel. We met an old squaw, who warned us not to cross the river. We took up into the mountains and camped there until morning, fearful of the Indians. We then saw thirty or forty of them looking for our trail. We remained until night and then crossed to the south side of the river. We came up pretty near to Shield's river or Twenty-five-Yard creek, where we crossed to the north. There we found the Indians were ahead of us and had gone over the hills toward West Gallatin. We came on over the pass where the city of Bozeman now lies, and saw the Indians coming up the valley. We concealed ourselves in the brush along the creek and exchanged shots with them. There was a parley. They agreed that if we came out they would not harm us, but we wouldn't trust them. We waited until dark and then struck for the Madison river, crossed it and went into the hills between the Gallatin and the Madison. The following day we crossed the Madison river and came up what is now known as the head of Wigwam gulch. We camped beside a lake at the foot of Bald mountain. We killed an elk there, and remained during the afternoon and over night to dry and smoke the meat.

"The day after we came down by the lake and over the bridge to Alder gulch. That was on May 26, 1863, about 4 o'clock in the afternoon, and the sun was shining brightly. Fairweather and I were to make camp and stand guard. The other four proceeded up the gulch, to what is now Highland, prospecting. About sun down Bill went across the creek to picket the horses.

" 'There is a piece of bed rock projecting,' said Bill, 'and we had better go over and see if we cannot get enough money to buy a little tobacco.' So Bill took the pick and shovel and I took the pan and we crossed the creek. He dug the dirt up and shoveled it into the pan. I went down to the creek to wash it. While I was washing the dirt he scratched around in the bedrock with his butcher knife and picked out a piece of gold and called: 'I've found a scad.' I had the pan about half washed down and I replied: 'If you have one I have a thousand.' And so I had. That first pan weighed about $2.30. We washed three pans before dark and the three aggregated twelve dollars and some cents. As we finished, the other four returned tired and hostile because we hadn't taken care of the horses. They had only found a color. I showed Sweeney what we had and asked him what he thought of the pan. 'Salted, by G-d,' exclaimed Sweeney. 'You know well enough if you pike me down and run me through a sluice you couldn't get a color,' said I. Then all were in good humor. We had dried elk meat for supper.

"The next morning, as soon as daylight, we were all out. Sweeney's first pan weighed five dollars. Hughes and Cover went up the gulch. Fairweather, Rogers, Sweeney and I went down. We staked two claims apiece, two hundred feet to the man, all connecting. We took fifty feet adjoining the claims on each side of the creek.

"We obtained about $180 that day altogether. We were tired and hungry and all out of provisions. As we panned the last gold we saw five antelope on the hill. Bill said to me: 'Old man, if you ever looked straight for your supper, look straight now.'

"He went around one way and I went up the hill the other side, and each of us secured an antelope. We had neither coffee nor bread. Our supper consisted of antelope straight and visions of gold. We spent the next morning measuring the ground and staking it off. I wrote out the notices. The first I wrote was for Barney Hughes.

" 'What shall we call the gulch?' I asked. 'You name it,' he said. So I called it Alder Gulch on account of the heavy clump of alders along the banks of the creek."

Mr. Edgar was born in Dumfries, Scotland. He came to the United States when eighteen years of age. In 1850 he was in the Michigan lumber region; in 1857 he lived at Fergus Falls; in 1858 he was at Fort Geary, in the British possessions; in the fall of 1862 he was mining in Bannock and the following spring joined the party that discovered Alder gulch. Mr. Edgar is now past seventy-four years of age, and lives with his wife in a cozy mountain home near Plains, in Missoula county, in this state.

ROBERT VAUGHN.

SEPT. 25, 1899.

The James Stuart Prospecting Party.

This expedition had the most desperate experience of any party of men in the Rocky mountains. They were chased by hostile Indians for hundreds of miles, endured untold privations, perils and hunger, some being killed; and during all this time they were in an unexplored region where assistance could not be obtained.

The first part of the history of this expedition has been given in the foregoing letter. The day the Fairweather party discovered Alder gulch the James Stuart party was being chased by Indians. The following are extracts from Captain Stuart's diary, which he kept on that eventful prospecting trip in the "Yellowstone Country" in the spring of 1863.

"April 28, 1863.—We have traveled twenty miles today. About an hour before sundown, while lying around camp resting from the fatigues of the day, we were startled by hearing several guns fired from a clump of cottonwoods across the river, and immediately afterwards we saw about thirty Indians fording across. They came on a run, vociferating 'How-dye-do,' and 'Up-sar-o-ka,' which latter means 'Crow Indians,' in their language. By the time they were fairly in camp we had our horses all tied up, and every man prepared for emergencies. They first inquired who was our captain. I told them, and asked which was their captain. They showed me three, one big and two little ones. The large chief told me to have my men put all our things in the tents, and keep a sharp lookout or we would lose them. I then gave him a small piece of tobacco to have a grand smoke, and I also found that one of them, a very large man with a big belly, could talk the Snake Indian language, and he was at once installed as interpreter. They (the interpreter and chiefs) sat down in a circle and requested the pleasure of my company. I accepted the invitation, and our party soon stood guard over our horses. Meanwhile the other Indians began disputing with each other about who should have our best horses. I requested the chief to make them come from among the horses and behave themselves, which he did. At eight p.m. I put on double guard, and at ten p.m. all except the guard retired to rest. The Indians wandered around camp all night, like evil spirits; and somebody would have to rush out of his tent and capture something which the Indians would steal from under the tents, in spite of the guard, and this, too, when it was bright moonlight. At daylight I aroused the party, and we proceeded to ascertain our losses; each had lost something. As soon as we began to pack up they at once proceeded to forcibly trade horses, blankets, etc., and to appropriate everything they wanted. I saw that the time had come to do or die; therefore I ordered every man to be ready to open fire on them when I gave the signal. With one handful of cartridges and my rifle in the other, I told the Indians to mount their horses and go to their camp. They weakened, mounted their horses and left. Two of the chiefs, however, very politely requested to accompany us, which we refused, but they came along. After the Indians fed on the fragments of the breakfast, the chiefs and five others offered their robes, which we refused, I saying to keep them until we met again. After breakfast they went back and we traveled on down the river. After sundown we saw two Indians.

"April 29.—Started at sunrise accompanied by the two chiefs and six others. One of them had a letter from Agent Schoonover of Fort Union, which stated that the bearer was 'Red Bear,' one of the principal chiefs of the Crow nation. We gave them some supper, etc. He then presented me with a black horse; said he was all right; friend of ours, etc. Had a long talk with him, in the course of which he asked about old Jim Bridger, and also Peter Martin, desiring to know where

JAMES STUART.
Courtesy Montana Historical Society, Helena

they were and why they never came to see the Crows. The other Crows had told me that the Sioux had attacked the Fur Company's express boat from Fort Benton, near Fort Union, and some said they had taken it, and others said they had killed some of the crew, but had not captured the boat. I asked Red Bear if it was so, and he replied that a rumor to that effect was current among the tribes, but he did not know whether it was true or not. When we retired to rest I gave orders to the guards not to kill, but take prisoners, any Indians which they might discover prowling around after our horses, and sure enough, about eleven p.m. they discovered one crawling up to two of our best horses that were tied to the same tree. They watched and waited until they got dead wood on him, and then captured him and called me up. I introduced him to Red Bear as one of his good Indians, who, he had just been telling me, would not annoy us any more, as he had told him not to, etc. He said the man was crazy and had not ears, etc. The old story, anything to excuse him. We had already had a practical illustration that stealing or attempting to steal is far from being considered a crime by even the best of them. We turned the thief loose, and early in the morning they all started back, leaving us alone in our glory. Traveled eighteen miles.

"April 30th.—Traveled all day down a valley between terraced table lands and buttes; valley about eight miles wide; snowy range to the west about eighty miles distant; no other snowy mountains in sight; low, open country around base of mountains. Camped three miles below the mouth of a large stream coming in on the south side; suppose it to be Clark's Fork. I accepted Red Bear's black horse last night and presented him my white mare in return. I thought at the time I had a little the best of it, but I found, during the day's travel, that I was mistaken. We are so far away from any high mountains that all the party feel discouraged and lonesome. Give me the mountains in preference to plains, where one can see more level ground than he can ride over in a day. The ground is literally covered with young crickets. Between them and the grasshoppers I am afraid the grass will soon be used up. Course of river, six degrees north of east. Traveled fifteen miles.

"Friday, May 1, 1863.—About one o'clock last night Bostwick had his roan horse stolen while he and Greery were on guard. It was taken by two Indians, one of whom showed himself, but not plain enough to shoot at; while the guards were both watching to get a shot at him, his companion crawled into the other end of the camp and cut the horse loose and got away with him without attracting their attention; and this, too, when the moon was nearly at the full and without a cloud. Verily, the Crows are world-beaters, and words cannot do the subject justice. Fortunately, Bostwick was on guard himself, so he cannot charge anybody with carelessness. Course of river nearly northeast."

The summary of the journal for the next eleven days is as follows: May 2d they saw large herds of buffalo and elk. May 3d they camped a few miles from Pompey's Pillar. Arriving at this natural monument, they found the names of Captain Clarke and two of his men cut in the rock with the date, July 25, 1806. There were also two other names inscribed—Derick and Vancourt—dated May 23, 1834. On May 6th five men were detailed to cross the Big Horn river and survey a townsite and ranches, and another party of four was sent out prospecting for gold. On this day James Stuart and four others engraved their names on a sandstone up the river. On the 7th the party went up the west bank of the Big Horn, traveling eighteen miles that day. On the 8th they traveled fifteen miles through a desolate country. On the 9th the remains of an Indian were found buried up a tree. On the 11th a party of three white men was observed a little ways across the river; they would neither answer nor halt. It proved afterwards that this party were J.M. Bozeman and John M. Jacobs and his daughter, eight years old. They were on their way from the Three Forks of the Missouri river to Red Butte, on the North Platte river and were then selecting a route for a wagon road, which was afterwards located and known as the "Jacobs and Bozeman cut-off." This party had been chased by a party of Indians a few days before, and when they saw the Stuart party they at once mistook them for Indians. But two days afterwards they met about eighty mounted Indians. Knowing that they would be plundered of everything they had, if not murdered, Jacobs dropped his rifle and ammunition into a bunch of sage brush. Sure enough, the Indians did capture and stripped them of nearly everything they had and many were for killing them on the spot, but, after holding a kind of council, they let them go after giving them three miserable ponies for all their horses; most of their clothing and what provisions they had were taken away from them. They started off slowly until the Indians were out of sight, then returned and got Jacob's gun and ammunition, but unfortunately, there were but five bullets. Soon these were exhausted, and when they got through to North Platte they were in a famishing condition.

Again Mr. Stuart says: "May 13, 1863.—Last night Smith and I had the first watch, and about eleven o'clock the horses at my end were scared at something, but it was very dark and I could not see anything. I thought it might be a wolf prowling around the camp. A few minutes before eleven o'clock I sat up and lit a match to see what time it was, and also to light my pipe, but at once lay down again; we were both lying flat on the ground trying to see what made the horses so uneasy, and to this we owe our lives. Just then I heard Smith whisper that there was something around his part of the horse herd and a few seconds later the Crows fired a terrible volley into the camp. I was lying between two of my horses and both were killed and nearly fell on me. Four horses were killed and five more wounded, while in the tents two men were mortally, two badly, and three slightly wounded. Smith shouted, 'Oh, you scoundrels!' and fired both barrels of his shotgun, but, as far as we could tell next morning, without effect; he most probably fired too high. I could not fire, for the horses were in the way. I shouted for someone to tear down the tents to prevent their affording a mark for the murderous Indians a second time. York rushed out and tore them down in an instant. I then ordered all who were able to take arms and crawl out from the tents a little way and lie flat on the ground, and thus we lay until morning, expecting another attack each instant and determined to sell our lives as dearly as possible. When, at last, day dawned we could see a few Indians among the rocks and pines on a hill some five or six hundred yards away watching to see the result of their bloody work.

"An examination of the wounded presented a dreadful sight, C.D. Watkins was shot in the right temple, and the ball came out at the left cheek bone; the poor fellow was still breathing, but insensible. E. Bostwick was shot in five different places—once in the back of the shoulder, shattering the shoulder blade, but the ball did not come out in front; three balls passed through the right thigh, all shattering the bone, and one ball passed through the left thigh, which did not break the bone; he was sensible, but suffering terrible agony. H.A. Bell was shot twice—one ball entered at the lowest rib on the left side and lodged just under the skin on the right side; the other entered near the kidneys on the left side and came out near the thigh joint. D. Underwood was shot once, but the ball made six holes; it first passed through the left arm above the elbow, just missing the bone, and then passed through both breasts, which were large and full, just grazing the breast bone. H.T. Greery was wounded in the left shoulder blade with an arrow, but not dangerously hurt. George Ives was shot in the hip with a ball—a flesh wound; S.T. Hauser in the left breast with a ball, which passed through a thick memorandum book in his shirt pocket and lodged against a rib over his heart, the book saving his life. Several others had one or more ball holes through their clothes."

Mr. Stuart continued his diary until they arrived at Bannock on June 22, 1863.

As the "Standard" man always camps on the trail of the pioneers, again, November 5, 1899, he met John Vanderbilt, who was with the James Stuart expedition of which I have spoke. During his conversation with the "Standard" reporter, Mr. Vanderbilt consented to give an account of the historical event. He said:

"We left Bannock on April 9, 1863. Our principal object was to explore the Wind, Big Horn, and the Stinking rivers. We got down among the Crows on the Yellowstone, when our troubles began. As we went into camp they tried to rob us of this thing and that, whatever happened to strike their fancy. We had a parley, but it did no good. They became so desperate that we had to show we were ready for action. There were probably thirty or forty Indians in the party, but they all gave in after we showed fight. That was in the latter part of April. They put down their bows and arrows and retreated. We immediately packed our camp and moved on. They followed along some distance behind. It was this band of Indians who turned back the Edgar and Fairweather party, which was just one day behind us.

"After that trouble we followed on down the Yellowstone, keeping guard at night. We frequently saw signs of the Indians, but had no more trouble for a few days. We camped seven days at the mouth of the Big Horn and laid out a townsite which we called Big Horn City. It still bears that name. We merely took a survey and platted the town, but took up no land. On May 3d we camped at Pompey's Pillar, where we were much interested in reading the inscription bearing the names of Captain Clarke and two men, and the date, July 25, 1806.

"Then we started up the east side of the Big Horn river, crossed the Little Horn and went further up as far as the canyon. That was probably seventy-five miles from the mouth. On that night—the night of May 12th to 13th—took place our great fight with the Indians.

"It was just about midnight when the Indians attacked us. Stuart and Smith were on guard. They didn't hear the Indians until they began firing on us. They first fired one or two shots and then a volley. Bostwick was the first one wounded. Then Watkins was shot through the head. Bell was shot in the side. A ball went through Underwood's arm and into his breast. Another ball struck a memorandum book in Sam Hauser's pocket and glanced onto a rib, saving his life.

"After this attack the Indians withdrew. Stuart told us, however, to lay low, as it is a common custom with Indians to attack again just before daylight. Some of our men were groaning, and in the darkness we could not tell the full extent of our casualties, nor could we tell at what moment the attack might be renewed. It was, indeed, a terrible night.

"Morning came without any further attack. Watkins died just about daylight. We found that three or four of our horses had been killed. Bostwick was badly wounded in the side. Bell was also severely injured. We held a consultation. To remain meant the certain extermination of the entire party. Yet we were reluctant to leave the wounded behind, and it was impossible to take them along. Sometime before we had all agreed that, in case we had a battle, each man would reserve one bullet for himself, so that he could not be captured and tortured. It was also agreed at that time if any were wounded he would not permit the others to remain behind to help him, but would end his own existence. It was, however, decided that if a man's wound was not mortal the others were to stay with him. It was decided that Captain Stuart should be sole judge as to whether a man's wound was mortal or not.

"That being the previous agreement, it was decided to wait until noon to see how serious the wounds of Bostwick and Bell might be. It was not considered possible to delay longer and save any of the party. All the forenoon the Indians were in sight on the side of the canyon. Stuart approached them and challenged them to come out and fight, but they made no response. As noon approached x asked us to go on and leave him, as he could not live long. We did not want to leave him while life was left in his body. He then asked Greery for a revolver, and at the last moment it was given him. He put the revolver up to his head and killed himself.

"We started at noon, leaving all our camp except provisions for eight days. Bell said he couldn't travel and didn't want to kill himself, so we left him on the ground. We got about a quarter of a mile away, going toward the east, when we saw Bell motioning us to wait. We went back, put him on horse, and he kept along with us. He got through all right.

"That same evening Greery accidentally shot himself with his rifle. We made the practice of laying our guns in the same place. His rifle, as he picked it up, became entangled in the sage brush, exploded and shot him. After fifteen or twenty minutes he begged us to kill him, as he said that he was suffering intensely and could not live. We refused, however. Finally, when it was necessary for us to go on, we let him have his revolver. He asked Stuart where the surest place for him to shoot himself was situated, and Stuart told him in the ear. All bade him good bye. I was the last to see him alive. I pleaded with him not to, but he said he couldn't live long anyway. I stood a little on a little raise. He was behind it. He was very weak. He pulled the trigger, but it didn't go off. Then he pulled a second time and killed himself. We dug a hole in the ground and buried him in his blanket. The Indians were constantly in sight during this time.

"We then packed up and continued that long and terrible journey. We traveled nights and rested part of the day. In that way the Indians following our tracks would almost overtake us, but we would get ahead again during the night. We suffered hardships that can never be told. We took only eight days' provisions along after the battle, and that was soon consumed. One night we had nothing to eat. Then Stuart killed an antelope. The next day we had nothing but a fawn two or three days old, which made us all sick. After we had nothing else, and only alkali water to drink. For a long distance we traveled through snow two or three feet deep and would sometimes sink down into pools of ice water. While crossing the Big Horn range we were wet nearly all the time. We hadn't been able to buy boots or shoes at Bannock and had nothing on our feet except moccasins. Crossing the Big Horn mountains we were guided by the stars, changing our course a good deal.

"We struck the Wind river above the canyon and followed it up, going in a southerly direction. Bell complained of pain all the time, so we could only go at a walk. When we crossed the divide we saw emigrant wagons on the road twelve miles away. Hauser felt so overjoyed he tied his handkerchief to a stick and hurrahed. Then we traveled rapidly along towards the road, which we soon reached. The emigrants thought we were Indians; we were so black and dirty, and they came out to fight us. We soon convinced them that we were all right. They let us have flour, potatoes and everything we wanted.

They didn't want to charge us, but we had plenty of money and so paid for what we obtained. We went on to Pacific Springs, on the California road, by the Snake river to Bannock, which we reached sometime in June. We left Bell at a soldiers' station, where the bullet was extracted, and he remained until he had recovered.

Mr. Vanderbilt has made his home for several years past in New York state, but recently he returned to this state, where he has met many of his old-time friends. He says that the changes made in the "Rockies" by "Then and Now" are great, but that the old mountains that he used to climb in search of gold are the same; and that the high peaks that reached to welcome him back to his old camping ground are the same "now" as they were "then," otherwise he would have thought that he was still in the East.

ROBERT VAUGHN.
Nov. 14, 1899.

From Alder Gulch to Last Chance.

Having remained in Alder Gulch all summer working in the mines for Boon and Vivian at ten dollars per day in gold dust, in December, 1864, four of us made a bargain with a man who had two small Mexican mules and an old spring wagon, to take us and our baggage to the new gold mines called Last Chance (now Helena). It was understood that we were to walk, and help the mules (or "Jerusalem ponies," as one of the boys called them) up the hills. The little animals were not over thirteen hands high, and would weigh about 400 pounds each. We came down the Prickly Pear creek, where now the Montana Central railway is. "Then" there was no town of Clancy, nor a quartz mill nor a smelter on the creek; not a sound could be heard there, except that of the pick of the prospector on the mountains, hunting for gold. We kept on the trail until we got to the new Eldorado, where several hundred miners were at work; many were taking out gold in great quantities, others were prospecting their claims.

Before going any further we will stop a minute and listen to "Now" telling a short story in connection to the creek referred to. "A few days ago I was invited to go to the round-house at this place to see two new locomotives which had just arrived from the East. They were the largest in weight and dimensions ever built in any country up to that time, each weighing one hundred and fifty-four tons. Mr. Bruce, the master mechanic at the railway shops, informed me that they were to run on the Montana Central railway from Clancy, on Prickly Pear creek, and over the Rocky Mountain divide. Although this is one of the heaviest pulls in the country, the big engines each are to draw six hundred and seventy tons. Several hundred passengers are drawn over this divide every twenty-four hours, besides about seven thousand tons of freight, principally coal from Cascade county to Butte and Anaconda, and copper ore from the Butte mines to the copper smelters and refiners at the falls of the Missouri river, near Great Falls, and lead and silver ores to the East Helena smelter.

When looking at those two great locomotives I could not avoid thinking of the contrast between them and the two Mexican mules, and of the motive power on the old trail, and the motive power on the new. The little mules were thirteen hands high and drew one thousand pounds; each of the big locomotives is fifteen feet, or forty-five hands, high, and draws six hundred and seventy tons. It is to me like a dream to think of the great changes that have taken place since that time.

Then Helena was but a mining camp, consisting of but a few log cabins. There is where I helped to run a drain ditch, commencing at Discovery Claim, near where now stands the Montana Club building. We reached bed rock in the upper end of the city. Among the gravel in this drain ditch, about forty-five feet from the surface and near where the Helena fire department building is, a mastodon tooth was found; it was a grinder, three inches on top, six inches deep and eight inches lengthwise; it was as perfect as it was when it came from the monster's mouth, when this northern country was a tropical region. In another claim a tusk was found like that of an elephant. Many other remains of animals have been found in mines and rock formations in the Rockies, showing that the Rocky mountain region has, at one time, been the home of animals that are not now in existence, at least not in the western hemisphere. It is estimated that thirty millions of dollars have been taken out of Last Chance gulch and its tributaries, and most of it from where the streets of Helena now are.

Miners' wages were then ten dollars per day; common laborers seven dollars. During the winter of 1865 eatables of all kinds were very dear, except meat, for game was plentiful;

"SULLY'S CROSSING"—PAINTING BY J.K. RALSTON.
Courtesy Montana Historical Society, Helena

flour sold for one hundred and twenty-five dollars per one hundred pounds. "Then" my friend Charley Cannon was an humble baker, and was selling dried apple pies that were not sweetened, with crusts as thin as a wafer, for one dollar a piece. "Now" he is an honored and respected citizen and one of the wealthiest men in the state. "Now" Helena is a city of twelve thousand inhabitants and the capital of the state. The capitol building is in course of construction, and when completed, will be one of the finest in the West. Where the log cabins stood, handsome business blocks and pleasant homes are everywhere visible.

Besides the Montana Central, which runs north and south and through Helena, the transcontinental line of the Northern Pacific connects the Atlantic and Pacific by extending east and west. Their freight and passenger depots are located on the old mining claims, where husky miners, in their overalls and flannel shirts, swung the picks and tossed the shovels with their brawny arms and contributed thousands of dollars to the world's treasury. Today railroad conductors and other officials are skipping over the same ground in broad cloth with pen and pencil behind ears that are braced up by high collars attached to boiled shirts.

And so it goes—the miner, the mechanic, the herdsman and plowman, the conductor, the railroad official and the man with the pencil, yes, the tie ballaster and the newsboy, all are linked in the endless chain of Western progress. And now a commerce is created which brings a revenue to our government amounting to millions of dollars annually, besides many millions more to the laborers and those who furnished the money to carry on these industries and enterprises that are continually developing and adding to the wealth of the nation.

Thus the wheel of progress has moved forward with tremendous speed since my first arrival in Helena in 1864 with the man who had the two "Jerusalem ponies."

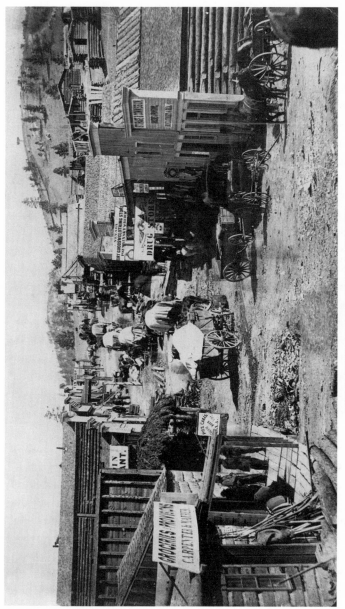

BRIDGE STREET, HELENA, MONTANA TERRITORY.
Courtesy Montana Historical Society, Helena

From Helena I went to Nelson gulch, where there were some very good diggings. The richest was that owned by the Maxwell & Rollins company, near the head of the gulch. In July, 1865, this company had a crew of ten men running a set of sluice boxes in very rich gravel. The man who used the fork to throw the stones which were too heavy for the water to carry out of the boxes, noticed that one small stone that he cast away was very heavy for its size. Wishing to know what kind of a stone it was, he went to the pile and examined it. To his astonishment it was a nugget of gold worth two thousand and seventy-three dollars. All hands quit work to see the big nugget, and the men on the adjoining claims came also to view it. Finally three cheers were given, and repeated several times until the echo went up and down the canyon. I was about a quarter of a mile down the creek at the time. Hearing the yelling, many thought that a serious accident had occurred. Soon the men came down the gulch with the big nugget suspended from the center of a pole, with the crowd following, and, as they marched down the gulch, everybody joined the mob; and when they reached the town which was near the lower end of the gulch where there were two stores and as many saloons, besides several miners' cabins, the crowd numbered three hundred or more. From two to three hundred dollars was spent by the Maxwell & Rollins company in treating the boys. The nugget was pure gold with no quartz. It was the shape of a hand with the thumb turned under. In 1877 another nugget worth one thousand and fifty dollars was found in the same gulch by Mr. Rogers. The gold of the Nelson and Highland gulches is the purest of any ever found in Montana.

The largest nugget was found in Snow Shoe gulch in 1865, which weighed one hundred and seventy-eight ounces and was worth three thousand two hundred dollars; there was some quartz attached. This nugget was long in shape, more like a foot than a hand. Snow Shoe gulch is located on top of the main range of the rockies, and near the Mullen tunnel on the Northern Pacific railway.

Deitrick and Brother found a nugget on their claim in Rocker gulch in 1867 worth eighteen hundred dollars. Many other large nuggets were found in different gulches, but these were the largest. The placer gold varies in size from microscopic powder to the monster slugs spoken of, and in quality from 600 to 990 in fineness.

Several hundred bars and gulches were in operation in the years 1865–1866, and were producing thousands of dollars daily. Those mines extended through a region one hundred and twenty-five miles square. The greatest producer of all was Alder gulch, with thirteen miles of pay ground. It is estimated that from seventy to eighty-five million dollars have been taken out of this gulch. Last Chance ranks next. Many other gulches were as rich, but not so extensive. It is safe to say that Confederate gulch produced more gold from the same number of square yards and in less time than any other placer mine ever found in the state. In the summer of 1866 a party of men took out of this gulch two and one half tons of gold worth one and one half million dollars. Early in the fall of the same year it was hauled by a four-mule team, escorted by fourteen armed men, to Fort Benton for transportation down the Missouri river. Mr. Lindiman and Mr. Hieediman, the two men who were the owners of most of the gold, accompanied the outfit.

ROBERT VAUGHN.
DEC. 18, 1898.

From the Mines to the Farm.

I remained in Nelson gulch over three years; during this time I did some mining, afterwards kept a meat market.

I had not the least idea of establishing a home in Montana, and, in truth, the field was not, just then, an inviting one for the homeseeker. All of us then were seeking gold and nothing else. Nearly everyone had made up his mind as to the specific amount he wanted, after which he was ready to return to the states to enjoy the same. Many made fortunes and carried out precisely this programme, but others were not so successful—among the latter myself. I was not ready to return at the end of the first or second year. I observed, with others, that our ponies and work cattle fattened readily on weathered bunch grass, and would live on this provender through the winter without care or shelter; that the meat of the deer, elk and buffalo was in prime condition, even in the dead of winter; and that experiments on a small scale in growing vegetables and grain in the valleys were very successful, and that the climate of the country gave health and vigor to both man and beast. In view of these observations, I concluded that Montana was a good enough country for me to live in.

In the fall of 1869 I came to the Sun river valley and located a ranch on the north side of the river, nine miles down the valley from Sun River Crossing, and near the Leaving Stage Station (now Sunnyside), on the Helena and Benton road. I remember well when I made the entry in the land office at Helena, that the register said to me: "Well, Vaughn, this is the first entry made in Choteau county."

A few weeks later Colonel Baker made a raid on the Indians on the Marias river. During the years 1867, 1868 and 1869 the Blackfeet and Piegan Indians caused a great deal of trouble by attacking freighters, killing settlers and stealing their horses. These outrages became so frequent that the war department finally decided that those bands of bloodthirsty Indians must be taught a severe lesson.

General Sheridan was in command of the military division of the Missouri, which embraced Montana. Direct telegraph communication existed between General Sheridan's office and Fort Shaw. In December, 1869, all the minutiae of the campaign were worked out at the division headquarters, and the necessary details sent to the commanding officer at Fort Shaw. Cavalry from Fort Ellis and infantry from Fort Shaw were detailed for the expedition, and the forces were under the command of Colonel Baker of the Second cavalry, with Joe Kipp, Henry Martin and Joe Cobel as guides. Every effort was made to keep the destination of the troops secret. It was late at night when they marched to the point where the guides intended to take them. On account of frost in the air and a few inches of snow on the ground they had some difficulty in keeping the right course. Finally the command arrived at the bluffs overlooking the Marias river; the tepees of the enemy were hardly observable, but the scouts had located the Indian villages, and, before daylight, they were completely surrounded by the soldiers. At an early hour the firing commenced and before the bugle called a halt nearly two hundred Indians had joined their ancestors in their happy hunting grounds. Two soldiers were killed in this terrible battle. When the news reached the stations along the Helena and Benton road, there were a few who became alarmed for fear that retaliation would be made by the Indians. But they did not retaliate; the battle was the best thing that ever happened to Northern Montana at that time. For several years afterwards the Indians were very shy, although some roving war parties of different tribes would cross the country and kill people and steal horses and cattle.

William Sparks and myself were only farmers in Northern Montana for several years, although some farming had been done in Sun River valley as early as 1858, by my namesake, Colonel Vaughn, who built the first agency for the Blackfeet Indians, which was located on the north side of the Sun river, about one-half mile above the crossing, and was known as the "Government Farm." Here is where Colonel Vaughn, as an experiment in behalf of the government, cultivated a number of acres of land, several acres of which were sowed in wheat. It proved to be a grand success. The colonel estimated that the wheat crop would average seventy-five bushels to the acre, and so reported to the department at Washington. A story is told on the colonel that, in addition to his agricultural report, he also reported that the beavers were so numerous that the wheat crop was in danger of being destroyed by them, and to send him immediately five hundred beaver traps. The traps were sent at once by the fastest express then in existence and arrived at the "Government Farm" after the wheat was threshed and put in the granary. The traps were used during the following winter by trappers, as they were intended in the first place. It was a good joke on the officials at Washington, for who ever heard of a beaver eating wheat.

In 1861 Mr. Sam Ford settled and located two miles above where now stands Fort Shaw. In 1862, also, the following named people were living on the government farm: J. H. Vail and family, a sister of Mrs. Vail's, Miss O'Brien (who, in 1863, married Henry Plummer, the only sheriff then in what is now Montana; but he was a traitor, for at the same time he was the leader of a gang of desperadoes, although unknown to the young lady). The following is from a letter written by Judge F. M. Thompson of the probate court for Franklin county, Massachusetts, to a friend in this city:

"It would give me great pleasure to visit your city, the site of which I first saw June 5, 1863, under somewhat interesting circumstances. I was at that time stopping with my friends, Mr. and Mrs. Vail, at the 'government farm' on Sun river, awaiting the arrival at Fort Benton of the St. Louis steamers. Besides us at the farm were Joseph Swift, who had wintered there, my partner, Mr. C. E. Wheeler, Henry Plummer, Miss Electa O'Brien, two Vail children, and a hunter-herdsman. I quote from my diary: 'June 5, 1863.—About 3 p.m., with Mr. and Mrs. Vail, Miss O'Brien and the two children in the government ambulance, and the remainder of the party on horseback, we left the stockade in charge of the hunter and started for the 'Great Falls' of the Missouri river. The Indians are very saucy and are cleaning out small parties of the whites, whom they can intimidate and steal from. We feel somewhat the risk we run in taking the women and children on the trip. Near sundown we had a scare, as Plummer, Wheeler and Swift in advance climbed the top of a knoll and suddenly stopping made signs of Indians, but, fortunately, the moving figures proved to be antelopes. Arriving at the lower falls after dark, we camped in a ravine, so that the light of our campfire might not be seen by the Indians. The next forenoon was spent in fishing and viewing the falls and building a large stone cairn, in which we deposited a paper claiming that the ladies of our party were the first to view the falls. (In this I think we were mistaken, as probably Mrs. La Barge and a friend visited the falls in the summer of 1862.) After dinner we started upon our return to the Fort, and, coming within sight of the farm, we found that the bottom was covered with a large number of Indian ponies grazing, under the charge of a guard.

Recognizing them as Spokanes, and friendly, we found a large party of their warriors visiting the farm. Finding that only one man was in possession, and he having locked the gates, they parleyed with him at the front, while some young bucks scaled the walls in the rear and took possession of the premises, compelling the hunter to cook from the stores of the station dinner for the whole crowd.

After a full discussion of the situation, by aid of the little 'Chinook' I had picked up, and a vigorous exhibition of sign language on our part, we finally persuaded the chief that it was best for him to 'clatawaw,' which he did much to our relief. (Clatawaw means go away.)

On the 20th of June, 1863, at Sun River, Henry Plummer and Miss Electa O'Brien were married by Rev. Father Minatre of the mission of St. Peter, Mr. Swift acting as best man, and, for the only time in my life, I acted as "bridesmaid." The happy couple immediately left the farm in the government ambulance, to which were attached four green Indian ponies.

A few months later Henry Plummer had ended his career upon the gallows at Bannock."

There was no farming done by those settlers except gardening on a small scale. In 1867 John Largent bought a cabin from a trader named Goff, and built another one near where now stands his fine residence. The same year Joe Healy built a cabin where now is H.B. Strong's residence. Those two men were the first settlers of the town of Sun River.

In 1872 Ed Dennis, Hod Maine, James Strong and Charley Femeston farmed in Sun river valley. John Largent had then a store and blacksmith shop at Sun River Crossing; J. J. Healy and Al Hamilton kept a trading post on the north bank of the river, near the bridge. They had a large trade with the Indians.

In 1871 R. S. Ford and Thomas Dunn brought the first range cattle to the Sun River country, and, for that matter, to Northern Montana. They had 1,100 head. The following year O.H. and D.H. Churchill brought eight hundred head. These cattle were turned out on the range north of Sun River, between the Leaving and the falls of the Missouri river. The following winter thousands of buffaloes came from the north and we had to cross all domestic stock to the south side of the Sun river, and herd them, to some extent, to keep the buffaloes away. A few years later two brothers named Rock settled near the mouth of the Sun river and were engaged in chopping wood. Near where now stands the Montana Brewery plant was an empty cabin which had been built by hunters (the same cabin, which is made of logs, has been removed and now stands half a mile southwest of its first location, and is the property of the Great Northern Railway company). One morning, as one of the brothers was going to his work, twelve Indians, who had been secreted in the old cabin, rushed out and murdered him. The other brother was on the opposite side of the river, the present site of the city of Great Falls, and saw the Indians perpetrate this cold-blooded murder, but could render no assistance. After shooting him, they all made a rush to see which one would get there first to secure his scalp. Just then the brother, who was across the river, fired several shots. This scared the Indians and they fled before reaching their victim, who was killed instantly by eleven bullets, ten through the body and one in the head. "Scalping" is a cruel practice that these savages commit after capturing an enemy. They take off the crown of the head; sometimes they do this first and the killing afterwards. They preserve the scalp, and the one who has the greatest number to his credit is considered the bravest and is promoted in his tribe, and often obtains the chief's daughter in marriage. It was not long after the killing of Rock that an Indian, while in the act of skinning a young domestic cow, was shot by one of the settlers. At this point on the Missouri river, where now stands the railroad bridge, there was a good ford. Here the Flatheads, Pend d'Oreilles, Nez Perces, Bloods, Piegans and Blackfeet crossed to get to the Judith and the Musselshell country en route to their winter hunting grounds; returning in the spring laden with dried meats, buffalo robes and pemmican. It was also a lurking place for the Blackfeet warriors when on their way to steal horses from the Crows. In returning the Crows would follow them up and commit all sorts of depredations upon the settlers along the line of their forays. As the buffaloes were getting scarce and more cattle were being put on the range the Indians became more troublesome by killing cattle. Once, as a party of Sun River settlers were crossing the country, they met eight young warriors on foot and among the cattle. They were on a horse-stealing expedition and well equipped with lariats and guns. The settlers, all well armed and mounted, made a swoop on the Indians and rounded them up. They took their arms and marched them out about five miles on the prairie towards the agency; then they gave back their guns and released them, telling them to make quick tracks for the reservation. As the Indians expected to be shot, they lost no time in getting away. This put a quietus on their cattle killing, and from that time they became more peaceable.

As more mines were discovered and operated, the population of the territory rapidly increased. The traffic on the Helena and Benton road was very great during the boating season on the upper Missouri, and before there was a railroad nearer than Ogden, Utah, consequently more settlers came into the valley. There were twelve locations between the Sun River Crossing and The Leaving. We joined together and constructed an irrigation ditch. We succeeded in growing a large crop of oats, wheat and barley; as high as eighty to one hundred bushels to an acre were raised by the writer and others. Also the largest and finest crops of potatoes I ever saw were raised there.

Now the Sun River valley and its tributaries have developed into some of the most extensive and wealthy settlements in the state. It has several towns with populations ranging from one hundred to thirteen thousand, having schools, churches, railroads, telegraph and telephone lines, flouring mills, refineries and smelters, electric lights and power and many public works.

The once hostile Indians have been subdued and are now on their reservations cultivating the soil by following the plow, running the mower and self-binder, raising horses, sheep and cattle, and are fast becoming civilized. Fort Shaw military post has become an Indian school. The parade ground, where the soldiers used to drill and prepare for Indian wars, is now used for picnic grounds and for the young Indian students to hold their Fourth of July celebrations.

ROBERT VAUGHN.

JAN. 29, 1898

A Letter to My Little Babe.

My Darling Little Babe—Your mother died January 13, 1888, when you were but thirteen days old. Today you are seven weeks old. Your tongue and communicative powers are tied with the tie of infancy. You can't tell papa how dear mamma was loved and how sweet her last kiss was. You can't tell papa that mamma said, "Take good care of darling babe," and how she embraced you to her bosom and blessed you for the last time. Neither can you comprehend papa telling you how happy papa and mamma lived together. You are now sleeping in the cradle, and I am sitting alone by your side thinking of your dear mother and how she loved you before you were born, and the pleasure she had when making your little clothes during the last four months, before she was confined to her bed.

But she has gone to that land where rivers flow over golden sands; where pearls and many a gem deck the shores. Last night as I was mourning over her and thinking of her loving companionship and her kind words, a still voice came to me saying: "Tell our darling babe that we lived happy." This set me to thinking that I may have passed through the "valley" before you will be old enough for me to tell you this happy tale. But, by the grace of God, I comfort myself with the hope that you and I will be companions to each other for many years to come, and that I will have the pleasure of listening to your reading me this letter which I am now writing. God bless you, sweet angel!

Your dear mother was born near Toronto, Canada, March 19, 1855. She was the daughter of Matthew and Jane Donahue. We were married August 25, 1886, at the home of Uncle and Aunt Spencer (where also she made her home), by Rev. J. H. Little. The same morning we left for Helena. We arrived there next day. It was fair week. We remained five days and met many friends. Here we had our photos taken and purchased our household goods—the organ, sewing machine, etc. And this is the time I had her ring made out of a nugget of gold I had taken from the mines twenty years before. We came home happy and went to work and organized our little home, and in about three weeks we had it—to us, a little palace. And oh! Such a welcome she always gave me when I came home! What a heart she had! So large and pure, so kind and womanly! She always kept everything so neat and nice. She made me love home and gave me new thought—how very little happiness depends upon money. Often in the still hour of the evening we would stroll away through the meadows, sometimes down along the banks of Sun river, and carelessly hold each other's hands. She walked closely at my side, telling me some sweet words and sometimes rhymes, and often we sang some favorite hymn. And now it seems to me how beautiful those happy days were. They are like dreams.

Your dear mother was always pleasant. I never left the house to be away all day without her giving me a kiss before I left, and she never failed to meet me at the door to give me a kiss and a welcome on my return. We truly loved each other. No wedded couple ever lived happier. Whatever I would do I could not improve. It was impossible. Anything in the house, if it was moved from the place she had for it, I could preceive it at once. Even a picture on the wall could not be moved anywhere else to look as well as the place she already had selected for it. She was a perfect mechanic. She was genial. She was gentle and polite in her manners. A more faithful partner never lived. A more true, affectionate wife and more loving mother never existed. Your dear mother was a Christian. She lived and died as such. The first time we met in our little chamber to go to rest for the first night together, your dear mother knelt by the bedside and prayed to God to give us grace and bless us as we started on the voyage of life together. She asked Him to give us grace to live a happy life, to live so we could die happy. And many, many times I have thought of her prayers during our happy life, and of her sweet words, "Tell the folks I die happy." From that time until she went to her final rest she always prayed before she retired at night. Also in the morning she kneeled before the Throne of Grace and thanked the Lord for his loving kindness. She always had her bible on the dresser or on the table in our bed room and perused it with care. She said one day: "If we can't attend church regularly in this country, we can be good by prayer to God and read our bible regularly." And her motto, in her own handiwork, is now over our bed-room door, chosen by herself years ago. It is this:

```
*   *   *   *   *   *   *   *   *
*           Simply            *
*      To Thy Cross I Cling   *
*   *   *   *   *   *   *   *   *
```

She illustrated on her death bed how this beautiful motto was engraved on her heart, for among her last sayings was: "Blessed be the Saviour who died on the cross, and I cling to that cross." Oh, what a treasure she was! Our short life together was but a holiday, and a happy one. And here now, I ask you, my dear babe, let your creed be the bible and your example your dear mother. If your father is not with you, ask some one to teach you to pray when you are young, for He said: "I love them that love me, and they that seek me early shall find me." "The same God who moulded the sun and kindled the stars watches the flight of an insect. He who balances the clouds and hung the worlds upon nothing notices the fall of a sparrow. He who gives Saturn his rings and placed the moon like a ball of silver in the broad arch of the heaven, who gives the rose leaf its delicate tint and makes the distant sun to nourish the violet, the same being notices the praises of the cherubim and the prayers of a little child."

It is He who is the father of the orphan; He whom your dear mother placed her trust in and who comforted her through life and death.

The following is her testimony on her death bed of a happy life ending in a happy death. She said to your sorrowful father: "My dear, do not let this worry you. Trust in the Lord and he will support you. I have trusted in Christ through all my life; now I trust in Him and He comforts me, for the Lord doeth all things well. I am ready to meet Him. I am ready to die. Take good care of our darling babe and tell her that we lived happy. God bless the little angel. It seems hard to us that we must part after living but a little while together, but it is God's will; it is well. Do not be sad! be happy. The ring you made for me in Helena I will take to the grave with me. Call my loved ones to my side and let me kiss them and bid them good bye. Tell the folks I die happy. Blessed be the Saviour who died on the cross. Oh Lord! I am ready—take me, Oh Lord! Take me at midnight or in the dawning of the morning. Dear Lord, take me. Let me go home in peace. The valley is lighter. I see the great white throne. I want to go home." She frequently said: "I want to go home" or "Take me home," during her last hours on earth. Thus your dear mother passed away in peace, prepared to meet the God in whom she had placed her trust. I imagined hearing the soft wings of the angels fluttering in the room when they came to take her home and their soft whisperings saying: "She is dying happy. She is clinging to the cross;" then a voice: "Open the gates of heaven; she is coming home." Her remains are sheltered safe from sorrow in the cemetery at Great Falls. Dear is the spot where she sleeps. "Though I walk through the valley of the shadow of death, I will fear no evil, for Thou art with me."

Now, my dear little daughter, I am about to close this joy-mingled-with-grief letter, hoping that you and I will be loving companions to each other to scatter flowers over your dear mother's grave for many decoration days to come.

Remember dear mother's words, her Saviour's cause extend—
Live pure and holy here, as through life's way you wend—
And when the journey is over and you come to the valley
May her words be your words: "Tell the folks I die happy."

The grace of our Lord Jesus Christ be with you. May He be your guide. Put your trust in Him. And that He will comfort you in life and in death is the prayer of your affectionate father,

ROBERT VAUGHN.

P. S.—This letter and your mother's jewels, which she willed to you, I will deposit in the First National Bank of Great Falls for safe keeping for you.

R. V.
SUN RIVER, MONT., FEB. 18, 1888.

From the Farm to the City of Great Falls.

In the year 1889, after meeting with my great loss in the death of my wife, I sold my farm in the Sun river valley and came to Great Falls, and built the "Arvon Block," and the "Vaughn Building," in which I now live, in rooms fifteen and sixteen, with my dear little ten-year-old daughter. Like the man who chased his shadow, I have chased myself from place to place for the period of sixty-one years, and for the distance of six thousand miles, and at last have caught up with myself. Now it is in order to give a sketch of my first visit to this spot where I now reside. It was in the winter of 1870, and it was rather a cold day, when, mounted on my gray mustang and looking down from the summit of the hill on the west side, where now stands the residence of Hon. T. E. Collins, I first saw the beautiful landscape, the site of the city of Great Falls. As I bent in my saddle to view the panorama before me, I longed to be an artist, that I might portray it. It was a picture that I shall never forget. On the south side of Sun river lay an Indian village, two tepees were on the north side, and one on Indian hill. The latter, I was afterwards told, sheltered a lookout who watched for the approach of an enemy and to observe in what direction the buffalo herds were moving. On Prospect Hill was a band of antelope, and through the low divide, west of J. P. Lewis,' a herd of buffalo were slowly moving in single file towards the river. In the grove some of these monarchs were rubbing against the trees, and, I should judge, were enjoying themselves immensely. Further east, on what is now Boston Heights, several hundred more were feeding on the grasses of the bench lands. While viewing the open plains, stretching on to where the Highwood and Little Belt ranges rose, covered with the first fall of snow, the winding rivers, the confluence of the Sun and the Missouri, following the latter in its course

GREAT FALLS, MONTANA—CENTRAL AVENUE.
Courtesy Montana Historical Society, Helena

until lost to view between high bluffs, I forgot all save the scene before me, hearing only the roaring of the waters as they rushed over the Missouri falls further down the river. Just then I saw an Indian about half way between myself and the two tepees; he was on foot and coming towards me. As I had not lost any Indians, I put the spurs to my horse and headed for home. When I had gone about a mile I looked back and saw the Indian standing where I had been but a few minutes before. Today I once more looked down from the summit of the same hill, but what a changed picture was spread before me! The plains that were "then" dotted with buffaloes are "now" covered with pleasant homes and imposing business blocks. Where was once an Indian village, today the stock farm of Hon. Paris Gibson is located. The two tepees are replaced by The American Brewing and Malting company's plant, and at the foot of Prospect Hill, where the antelopes were, a water plant for a city of fifteen thousand inhabitants is in full operation. On the commanding bluff, "then" occupied by the lookout tepee, "now" the lofty smokestack of the Boston and Montana copper smelter stands in bold relief against the blue background of the sky, a landmark for hundreds of settlers for many miles around. The Missouri river is spanned by several steel bridges which carriages and locomotives cross at will. The buffalo trails have given place to electric railways, and the grove, where these shaggy-looking animals used to rub their coats, is now a beautiful park echoing with children's laughter. But the greatest change of all has been wrought at the falls of the Missouri. Its mighty voice "then" paramount, "now" has been overpowered and well nigh silenced by the humming of dynamos and the sound of the great ore crushers as they labor on day and night, the slaves of the white man's civilization. A brief sketch of these falls is proper at this time. The falls of the Missouri river were first made known in 1805. Thomas

Jefferson, the third president of the United States, was a leading figure in the purchase of Louisiana, which embraced the country west of the Mississippi from its mouth north to the forty-ninth parallel at the Lake of the Woods. The forty-ninth parallel constituted the northern boundary to the Rocky mountains; the western line was the summit of the Rockies to the Arkansas river, to the one-hundredth meridian, thence south to the Red river, thence down that river to the ninety-fourth meridian, thence southerly along that meridian to the Sabin river, thence down the Sabin river to the Gulf of Mexico.

In 1803 Jefferson sent a message to congress, asking for an appropriation of $2,500 for the exploration of the Missouri and Columbia rivers. The result was that the amount was granted. Lewis and Clark were chosen to take charge of the expedition.

The expedition spent the winter of 1803–1804 near the mouth of the Missouri river. The Northwest was then a wilderness. The expedition ascended the Missouri river to Fort Mandan north of Bismarck, where they laid over during the winter of 1804–1805. Their means of transport were several rowboats. July, 1805, they arrived at the falls of the Missouri river, where they spent two weeks surveying and making a portage. Lewis and Clark were the first white men who visited the falls of the Missouri river, or at least they were the first to make its existence known to the world.

The lower falls, known as the Great Falls, is a perpendicular fall of about ninety feet. The river at this point is estimated to contain a volume of water about three times greater than that of the Ohio at Pittsburg. This immense volume is here confined between rocky walls on either side, from two hundred to five hundred feet in height and about three hundred yards in width. Next to the right bank nearly half the stream descends vertically with such terrific force as to send continuous and always beautiful clouds of spray sometimes two

COPPER SMELTER AT GREAT FALLS; INSET: GREAT FALLS OF THE MISSOURI RIVER.
Courtesy Montana Historical Society, Helena

YORK, WATERCOLOR BY CHARLES M. RUSSELL.
Portrays Mandan Indians examining the one African-American member of the Lewis and Clark Expedition.
Clark sits at extreme right; Lewis wears officer's hat.
Courtesy Montana Historical Society, Helena

hundred feet or more in the air. The other side of the river is precipitated over successive ledges of from ten to twenty feet, forming a magnificent view some two hundred yards in breadth and ninety feet in perpendicular elevation. A vast basin of surging, foaming waters succeeds below, its deep green color and commotion betraying a prodigious volume and depth.

Five miles above are the Crooked and Rainbow falls, the latter fifty feet in perpendicular descent. Here the entire river, one thousand two hundred feet wide, hurls itself over an unbroken rocky rim, as regular in its outline as a work of art, into a vast rock-bound amphitheater, where when the sun is shining a rainbow spans the river from bank to bank. This with the sprays, the roar and commotion of the water make a fascinating scene. From this rainbow the falls received its name.

Another two miles up the stream is the Black Eagle Falls. Here the entire river takes a vertical plunge of twenty-six feet. On an island, and just below this falls, there formerly was a large cottonwood tree, in the branches of which a black eagle had built its nest. It is from this that the Black Eagle Falls received its name.

The river where these falls are located flows through a grand natural canyon, where in its ceaseless flow, has cut a path for itself through the rock of the plains, sometimes to a depth of five hundred and fifty feet. The series of falls and cascades add a wild beauty to the scene.

In no place has there been found so great a water power. Within a distance of ten miles, including falls and cataracts, there is a descent of five hundred and twelve feet.

Robert Vaughn.
June 27th, 1899.

Montana's Pioneers.

Who were the pioneers of Montana? They were the brave men and noble women who came here first; they were descendants of many countries, and were the most courageous of the nations from which they came. They were the heroes who rescued this beautiful mountain land from the hands of the savages and laid the foundation and moulded the destiny of this great state.

The cut-throats, robbers and murderers who were here in the early days were not worthy of being called pioneers, for they made a desperate effort to demolish what the real pioneers were building up. To expose their kind, I will refer to two of this class who were hung at Virginia City in the presence of several hundred citizens. They belonged to a gang of highwaymen and murderers. Each stood on a separate box with a rope around his neck, which was attached to a crossbeam, and, while in this position, one was using the most profane language and cursing every one present; just then a friend of the victim whom he had robbed and killed shoved the box from under his feet; while this one was dangling in the air the other one looked at him, and with an oath said: "Kick away old boy, I will be in hell with you in a minute," then jumped off the box himself and into eternity. Though these men were human beings, the wicked and vicious habits they had contracted had destroyed all the humanity they possessed. Now, in consequence, nothing was left of them but the brute, for they neither feared God nor respected their fellowmen. Between those ruffians and the Indians the pioneer had his hands full. He had to work for himself, and at the same time he was ready at a moment's notice to defend the right and his fellowman with as much pluck and bravery as any soldier ever displayed.

Many think that most of the early settlers of Montana were of the rough element, but this impression is wrong. Most of the old pioneers were of the best law-abiding citizens that could be found in any country, men of culture as well as courage. Many of them afterwards helped to frame the constitution and the laws that govern the state at the present time (1899). Edgerton, her first governor, was here before the name "Montana" was thought of.

Ex-Governor S. T. Houser is now carrying a scar which he received at the time the James Stuart party, of which he was a member, had that terrible battle with the Indians on the Yellowstone in 1863. W. A. Clark, recently elected United States senator, and Ex-United States Senator Wilbur F. Sanders, and others who have already represented Montana in the halls of congress, also have worked in the prospector's hole. Granville Stuart, who was appointed Envoy Extraordinary and Minister Plenipotentiary to Paraguay and Uruguay in 1894, and served a term of four years, were here among the first comers. Nathaniel P. Langford (now of St. Paul, Minn.), the author of "Vigilante Days and Ways," and who at one time was bank examiner for Montana, Idaho and Washington, was one of the first pioneers. Ex-Chief Justice W. Y. Pemberton was one of the pick and shovel brigade.

Judge Knowles, Judge Hedges, and many others who are now holding high positions were with us. Judge Frank H. Woody is a Montana pioneer, for he came to what is now Montana in 1856, when the western portion of this state was a part of Washington Territory. Many of the leading lawyers that are now pleading at the bar of the state also have spoken in those "miner's courts which were held in the open air." Jack Fisk, Will H. and Robert N. Sutherlin and others who are to-day among the leading journalists of the state, were here before a single type was set. And there are scores of the veterans of early days, who, when the opportunity was given, have ranked themselves with the best business men of the state. When the roll is called of the self-made men of Montana, her pioneers will head the list.

And there were men who held divine services wherever the opportunity was given them; they were no cowards, either, for it took a pretty good man to fight the devil on his own half acre and whip him, too. I am glad to state that there are some of these old reverends "still in the ring."

Peace be to the memory of those who have gone to receive their rewards for the good work they have done. With all respect to the Christian people, Catholics and Protestant alike, they did considerable for Montana in the early days and more than anyone knows, for a great deal of their work was done in the "Sacred chamber" without making any noise. I now recall two old prospectors who were up in the mountains searching gold. After delving all day, they cooked and ate their supper, and then sat by the camp fire. One was telling about the dear ones at home, and that he was almost certain that they were thinking of him that very night. The other one spoke of his wife and three little children whom he had not seen for four years, but that he was writing to them constantly and he was receiving letters in return, and said he was in hopes of "striking it" soon and then he would go home. They sat up rather late that night; the moon had gone down, and the shade of the dark green pines made it still darker. It was in autumn when the leaves were falling. As the fire was getting low, they both went to bed side by side. It was a calm, still night; the rustling of the dead leaves that were strewn on the ground could be heard as some wild animal was passing their silent chamber, with occasionally the rumbling sound of a piece of rock which had broken loose from some distant cliff and went rolling down the mountain to the canyon below,

SONS AND DAUGHTERS OF MONTANA PIONEERS.
Courtesy Montana Historical Society, Helena

re-echoed by the screeching of night birds, while the cataracts of many ripples swelled the midnight melody. Not a word was spoken for some time, each thinking that the other was asleep. But one began saying his evening prayers in a low, murmuring voice, which was as follows:

"Near the camp fire's flickering light
 In my blanket bed I lie,
Gazing through the shades of night
 At the twinkling stars on high;
O'er me spirits in the air
 Silent vigils seem to keep,
As I breathe my childhood prayer
 Now I lay me down to sleep!

"Sadly sings the whippoorwill
 In the boughs of yonder tree,
Laughingly the dancing rill
 Swells the midnight melody;
Indians may be lurking near
 In the canyon dark and deep,
Low I breathe in Jesus' ear
 I pray the Lord my soul to keep.

" 'Mid the stars one face I see,
 One the Saviour called away,
Mother, who, in my infancy,
 Taught my baby lips to pray,
Her sweet spirit hovers here
 In this lonely mountain brake,
Take me to her, Saviour, dear,
 If I should die before I wake!

"Fainter grows the flickering light
    As each ember slowly dies,
Plaintively the birds of night
    Fill the air with saddening cries;
Over me they seem to cry,
    'You may nevermore awake,'
Now I lisp, if I should die,
    I pray the Lord my soul to take!"

"Now I lay me down to sleep,
    I pray the Lord my soul to keep,
If I should die before I wake,
    I pray the Lord my soul to take."

These things that I have mentioned indicate that there was much of the better element here in the early days, and also a great deal of intelligence among those who wore the buckskin shirt, and to them a large portion of the credit should be given that Montana is today one of the brightest gems in our star spangled banner.

ROBERT VAUGHN.
MARCH 4, 1899

The Dark Side of the Life of the Pioneer.

In another letter giving an account of Indian depredations, I stated: "I will not attempt to follow their war path, for it is too long," but allow me at this time to vary a little from that assertion. My object in doing so is to add to the already written history of this portion of the Northwest, where I have lived from my early manhood, and this portion of the country which was then in its infancy as far as civilization and settlement were concerned, therefore, to use a common expression, "we growed up together."

Though a frontier life is free and fascinating, still, like everything else, there is a dark side to it, and this letter is principally intended to show the "dark side" of the life of the pioneer.

As a frontiersman, I, myself, may not care to again experience what I have passed through, yet, with all its perils and dangers I would not give my pioneer days in the West for all the balance of my life.

The following events occurred in Northern Montana. All are facts, and some of them I know of my own personal knowledge. Some of those whose names appear hereafter were killed by Indians, others died from exposure. I have often thought of the many victims that have fallen in the West; even their death never has been known nor heard of by anyone. Many remains of white men have been found without a trace of anything to lead to their identification.

Once there were three of us in the mountains prospecting. In a sheltered place under a projecting cliff there lay the skeleton of a man. It appeared that he had laid down to rest or to sleep. Nothing could be found to indicate whose remains it was. The clothing was weatherbeaten and torn, and an old silver watch and a gun laid on the ground with the scattering bones. The hair was light in color. It was one of those instances of "somebody's boy" dying without even a stranger to record his last words.

By examining the following list the reader will find that the identification or names of twenty per cent of the unfortunate victims herein mentioned were not known, and that all included in the list, except six or seven, were killed in what was then Choteau county. They are but few in comparison to all that were killed in what is now the state of Montana.

First on the list is Little Tex, who was killed in 1866 by Blood Indians at the agency on what was then known as the government farm, on Sun river; then Indians set fire to the buildings. There is no certainty as to the number that perished.

Early in the spring of 1866 three men were murdered by Blackfeet not far from old St. Peter's mission, which was then located on the Missouri river near Ulm on the Montana Central railroad. April 6th of the same year John Fitzgerald, an employe of the mission, was killed almost in sight of the buildings by Bloods. His grave and that of a man by the name of Johnson, a blacksmith, who was formerly at Fort Benton, and about fifteen other graves, mostly of Indians, are at the foot of the hill and near the Montana Central track, about half a mile from Ulm. The next day after the killing of Fitzgerald, Father Giorda, and all the inmates of the mission left for Helena, fearing that more trouble might come.

Lagree and Hunicke were murdered by Blackfeet and Bloods at Three Tree Coulee, Jan. 9, 1866. James Chembers was killed by Blackfeet at Dearborn in 1866, and old man Thebeaw killed at Dearborn the same year.

The murder of the builders of the town of Ophir occurred in May, 1865. Ophir was a new place located at the mouth of the Marias river, twelve miles below Fort Benton. At this period there had been only one or two houses built. The men, eleven in number, were about one mile above the location cutting logs and some of them were chopping wood for the steamers that were coming up the Missouri to Fort Benton. They were at work when the Indians killed them; not one escaped. When the news reached Fort Benton a party went and buried the unfortunate victims on the bank of the Missouri river near where they were killed. Thirty-four years have passed since then and the gradual cutting of the bank by the swift current has washed away that little graveyard, and now the resting place of these founders of states and builders of cities has been swept from the face of the earth and its occupants swallowed up by that mighty stream.

Six men were killed by Bloods on Old Man's river early in 1865. The victims came from Fort Garry (now Winnipeg), and were reported to possess a large amount of money. Their leader was an old white-haired man.

William Berry was killed by Bloods on Elbow river and Joe Monroe was killed by Bloods on Old Man's river in 1874.

Miller was killed by Bloods on Old Man's river in 1872.

McMillan was wounded by Assinnaboines, near Bow river, in 1874.

Two unknown men were killed by Assinnaboines, near Milk river, in 1874. The bodies were found tied to trees and riddled with bullets. Cottle and another man were killed in their house on Flat creek in 1877. The Nez Perces were supposed to be the murderers, as a few stragglers of that tribe were seen in the vicinity about the time the deed was done.

A party of men, women and children were killed by Bloods near Porcupine mountain in 1865. Their identification could not be obtained.

A soldier was killed by Piegan Indians on Marias hill, not far from Fort Benton, in 1873.

Wey and Mitchell were killed by Piegans on Badger creek in 1875. Five days before they were killed, both stayed over night at my ranch and bought some oats to feed their horses while on this unfortunate prospecting trip.

Joe Day and Howard were killed by Piegans, near the Marias river, in 1875.

John Rock was killed by Blackfeet, at the mouth of Sun river, in 1875. An account of him I have given in my letter "From the Mines to the Farm."

Jack Gorman and Frank Keisser were killed by Assinnaboines, on the Milk river, the same year.

Frank Robinson was killed by Gros Ventres Indians, near Cow creek, in 1877.

Joseph Spearson was killed by Bloods, on Belly river, in 1870.

Nelse Kyse, George Huber and one man, name unknown, were killed by Sioux Indians, on Squaw creek, near the mouth of Musselshell river.

Andy Harris was killed by Assinnaboines on Milk river in the winter of 1867, and a soldier was killed by Piegans at Camp Cook in the spring of that year.

Bozell A. Bair was wounded by Piegans on Eagle creek in 1867.

Paul Vermette was killed on the Teton river in 1866.

Champion was killed by Arrapahoe Indians at Fort Hawley in 1867.

Malcolm Clark was killed by Piegans in 1869. Clark had been a classmate of General Sherman's at West Point. The former, after finishing his term, instead of entering the army, came west as an employe of one of the fur companies which operated in the upper Missouri river country. After following the Indian trading business for many years he located in the Prickly Pear canyon, about twenty miles north of Helena, and kept a stage station. The place is now known as "The Mitchell Ranch." Once a party of Piegan warriors came to the premises. One of the Indians, who was well acquainted with Clark, approached the door and asked for the latter; just as Clark stepped into the door he was shot and killed by this Indian. Several shots were fired into the house. A bullet struck Clark's wife, and one of his sons was shot in the nose; in course of time both recovered from their wounds, but the tragedy caused the mother to go insane and she died a few years ago still in that condition. Clark is buried near the house, and now his resting place is marked by a railing crowning the grave. A few months later the "Col. Baker Indian Massacre on the Marias river" occurred. And when the firing commenced on the Piegan camp the murderer of Clark was there sick in bed; when he was told that the soldiers had come there to kill him, he took a long knife and plunged it into his heart.

When General Sherman passed through this section in 1875 on his tour of inspection of the government posts at Fort Shaw and Benton, he stopped for dinner at Clark's old ranch. The general inquired for Malcolm Clark. He said that Clark had been a schoolmate of his at West Point, but had gone west to trade with the Blackfeet Indians while he was yet but a young man. When the story of Clark's career and of his death had been told, and the grave of his early associate shown him, he had been but a few moments on the spot when he showed signs of grief and requested to be left alone for a while. He stayed for some time and when he came away traces of tears could be seen on the cheeks of the brave old warrior.

Charles Carson was killed by Piegans, near Dearborn river, in 1866. He was a nephew of Kit Carson, of frontier fame. He was killed and buried near the ford on the Dearborn.

Mrs. Jennie Smith, who at one time lived in Helena, was scalped alive by Sioux Indians at the mouth of Musselshell river in 1869. The unfortunate woman recovered and was still living in 1879.

Jack Leader was killed by Sioux at the mouth of the Musselshell river in 1869.

A man named Lowe was killed by Blackfeet. His remains are buried on the old Helena and Benton road at the crossing of what is now known as "Deadman Coulee." The place received its name because it is the place of the death and burial of Mr. Lowe.

Macgregor and Tabor were killed by Sioux, and another man wounded, near Fort Peck in 1868. Also two unknown men were killed by Sioux near the same place and in the same year.

Ross and McKnight were killed in 1868, by Sioux, at the mouth of Musselshell river. McKnight was a brother to the Hon. J. H. McKnight of this city. At the time the tongue of their wagon had broken, and, while they were cutting a tree to make a new one, they were killed.

Nat Crabtree was killed by Piegans, near Camp Cook, in 1868.

Old man Lee was killed, and Charley Williams and Drew Denton wounded by Sioux, near Carroll, 1870. Denton's life was saved by the bullet striking his pocket in which he had a plug of tobacco and some letters.

A Frenchman was killed by Piegans in the summer of 1868 on Sun river, south of where stands Pressle Rowls house.

McArdle and a comrade were killed by Crow Indians near Benton in 1869.

Tom Ross was killed by Sioux near Fort Peck in 1873.

Michael Thebault was killed by Piegans on the Teton in 1868.

James Quail was killed by Piegans, near Silver creek, in 1869. He was killed only half a mile from where I was mining at the time, and about nine miles from Helena. He was getting his horse, which was grazing on the slope of a hill near his cabin, when he was shot and killed by an Indian who robbed him of his horse and of a gold watch on which his name was engraved. The watch was seen afterwards in the possession of an Indian in a Piegan camp on the Marias river.

Clark was killed by Piegans on Sun river in 1868, of whom I have given an account in my letter, "Indian wars and tragedies on Sun river."

Dauphant was killed by Sioux near the mouth of Milk river in 1865.

Charley Desronin was killed by Indians near the Bear Paw mountains in 1870.

Little Frenchie was killed by Assinnaboines on Milk river in 1869.

A man who was taking care of some cattle for Carroll and Steell was killed by Indians on Milk river in 1869, and Sam Rex was killed by Bloods the same year on Eagle creek.

Fifteen men and one woman and two children were killed by Sioux in 1863. They were returning from the mines, and on their way by the Missouri river route in a Mackinaw boat, which they had built at Fort Benton. Their names I cannot give, except one whose name was Thomas Mitchell, and who joined the party at one of the trading posts further down the river.

It was plain to be seen that the Indians did not kill them for their gold, for it was spilled on the shore where the mutilated bodies of the men lay. The woman was hanging to a limb of a tree, the limb being driven through her chin; the two children, one on each side of the mother, were hanging in the same manner, and the bodies were full of arrows.

Jim Matkins was wounded by Piegans, near Benton, in 1868. Mr. Matkins was one of my best friends. At the time he was shot by the Indians he was an employe of the "Diamond R. Company," a firm that had several ox teams engaged in hauling freight from Fort Benton to various towns and points in the territory. He related to me the following particulars of the chase he had with the Indians at the time he was shot. He said: "One day at Fort Benton I loaded sixteen of the company's wagons with freight for Helena. Tom Clary and J. C. Adams had charge of the outfit. They pulled out that day and camped the following night at Eight Mile spring. I was clerking for the company at the time. I could not get the bills of lading ready at the time they left; so, late in the evening, after dark, I got on my saddle horse and started for their camp. After I had gone about three miles I heard the clatter of horses' hoofs, and, looking back, I saw eight Indians coming as fast as their horses could carry them, and bullets began whizzing by me; but what frightened me the worst was their fearful "Indian yell." I put the spurs to my horse and rode for dear life towards Clary and Adams' camp, which was five miles further. I had a Winchester rifle that had sixteen loaded cartridges; I fired several shots at the Indians. In this way I kept them at bay for a while. But there was one who had a very fast horse and he was the only Indian that could keep pace with me, for mine was a good runner; but this redskin could run up to my side whenever he wanted to. After running in this way for about three miles, and in a shower of bullets, I discovered that I was shot in the hip. I could see but one Indian and he had slacked up his pace to load his gun. I dismounted and took as good aim as I could in the dark and fired four shots. I believe that I wounded him or his horse, for he came no further. I could feel that my boot was filling up with blood and I was getting very weak; it was as much as I could do to mount my horse. When I arrived at the camp I told all that had occurred. I was put in a wagon drawn by two yoke of oxen, and Clary and Adams, with two other men took me back to Benton that night, and my wound was dressed. The bullet is still in my hip."

Mr. Matkins afterwards died from the effects of this injury. He is buried in the Highland cemetery at Great Falls.

This recalls one Decoration day when the Grand Army

veterans were on their way to the cemetery with beautiful flowers to cover the graves of their comrades. I spoke to one of them: "Say, comrade, I am a veteran pioneer. An old comrade of mine is buried in that cemetery. He was shot by the Indians and died from the effects. I have a few wild flowers with me and I am going to decorate his grave. Won't you 'take me in' and let me march with you?" I did not march, but the wild flowers were placed on poor Jim Matkin's grave.

Old man Ling, Foster and Jordan were killed by Sioux near the mouth of Pouchette creek.

Henry Simpson was killed near my ranch on Sun river in 1870. He was shot twice.

A shepherd by the name of Hunt was killed near Grassy Lake, eight miles north of my home, in 1883. He was found with several bullet holes through the body.

Bill Morrison and John Hughes were killed by River Crows on Arrow creek in 1877.

Antelope Charley and Cook were killed by Piegans at the mouth of Eagle creek in 1873.

Little Rock was killed by Sioux on Judith mountain in 1874.

Buckshot and Poulett were killed by Assinnaboines at Rocky spring in 1871.

Joseph Gipperich was killed by Bloods on Saint Mary's river in 1872.

E.B. Richardson and Charles Steel, James Downey, Charles Buck, J. J. Barker and an African were killed by the Nez Perces in October, 1877, near Cow creek, during the tour of Chief Joseph through the country.

One man, name unknown, was found dead near the Marias in 1875. He was killed by some of the Northern Indians.

One man, name unknown, was killed by Piegans on Sun river in 1868. No clue to the murderers could be had.

Seven unknown travelers were killed by Sioux on the Missouri river, above Fort Peck, in 1868. It was supposed that they were on their way from the East to the gold mines, for they were well equipped for a long journey.

Two men, names unknown, were killed by Sioux at the mouth of the Musselshell in 1873.

One man, name unknown, was killed by Piegans on Warm Spring creek, near the Judith river, in 1874.

The remains of a man were found a few miles up the Missouri river, from the mouth of Sun river, in 1887. His identification could not be had. The opinion was that death had come from exposure.

The above are a few of the shadows that darkened the life of the pioneer.

It is human nature that every person is pleased to hear others saying something good about him. Joaquin Miller said of the pioneers of Montana that some fell from overtoil, others in battle with savages; some died even as they sat for the first time by the new-laid hearthstone waiting for wife and babes to arrive with the first flowers of spring; and that the world does not, perhaps, understand what it cost to come here in the early days.

And, as Mr. Miller says, the Pilgrim fathers set forth in the ship and landed on Plymouth Rock; the Cavaliers of Virginia sailed pleasantly up the James river and scarcely knew what a camp in the wilderness was until they sat down in their future home; the Argonauts of California, many of them, merely sailed from port to port; but Montana was a thousand miles from any ocean, a wilderness in the center of an untrodden country with savages in her every pass and valley, and so, necessarily, every man that came here among the first was in some way a soldier, yes, a veteran soldier, who had mustered, camped, marched and battled, endured hunger and exposure to all kinds of weather—all that the bravest soldier endures—

before he ever came within sight of the Mecca that he was toiling to reach. He truly says that there was a great difference between the Montana veteran and the bravest of the brave in any war that has ever been; that the soldiers Caesar, Napoleon and Grant had their governments to clothe, feed, pay and pension them, but the hero of Montana stood alone.

I have just given the names of seventy-six of those heroes who fell victims to the wrath of the redskins, and of several that were wounded and died afterwards. The names of the fourteen men, the woman and the two children, I have not, but their relatives were informed of their sad death. Of the other party of men, women and children no further account of them but the finding of their bodies could be obtained. And, in addition to all, we have twenty-two unknown who were killed; not a trace of their identification could be found—no one knew either their names or where their homes were— therefore, an account of their death could not be given to friends or relatives, who may never know what has become of their dear ones who went West years before.

Think of the affectionate sister who had ceased receiving letters from her brother who had gone to the unsettled West to try and better his condition in life. She said: "My brother John used to write to me often, but now, for a long time he has not written. It may be that he is in the mountains prospecting, and that he has no way to send a letter to me. I expect the next letter, when it comes, will be full of good news." Month after month has passed and she is patiently waiting for that newsy letter to arrive. Poor girl! She does not know the fate that has befallen her brother. And thus of a loving wife, with a babe on her arm, and with her other arm embracing her kind and loving husband when he left home to go to the gold fields of the "Rockies" to hunt enough of the yellow metal to pay off the mortgage that was on their little home. She said that her husband had been gone nearly four years; that during the first three years he wrote every month, and, in every letter there was some money for her, and that in the last letter he stated that he had good prospects and hopes of "striking it" before she would get another, and would be home with enough money to pay off everything. And she, too, is waiting, waiting. It has not entered her mind that her beloved husband has been——————————.

Again a fond and loving mother, bent with age, and who parted with her only son several years before. For a long time after he left for the gold regions, she said: "He used to write to me very often and always send me some money, and one time he sent me a nice specimen from the mines, but now I have not heard from him for a long time and I am afraid something has happened to him. I am getting so I can't sleep at night thinking of my darling boy." He was advertised in the newspaper nearest where his last address was, and the editor of the paper, for the sake of a broken-hearted mother, left the advertisement in double the time the contract called for, besides inserting, "other papers please copy." But no one responded. All this time an unheard voice was saying: "He is one of the unknown that were killed by the Indians in an isolated place in the Rocky mountains a long time ago." It may be that some of the relatives of those unfortunates are still hoping that the lost son, brother, husband, or father is yet alive; but the fact is, their remains are resting in an unmarked grave on the plains, or, may be, far in some lonely gulch in the mountains, and the once little mound is now leveled by the elements and the secret spot robed with herbs and wild grasses, so that even his fellow pioneer who buried him cannot designate the place where the remains sleep and rest forever.

One night, when lying in my blankets under the spreading bows of a pine tree, thinking of those lonely graves that are

scattered here and there through the west, in which lay the
"unknown," the following lines occurred to me:

> Slain by Indians a pioneer was found,
> > His home or his kindred nobody knew;
> Over his cold form bendeth
> > The grasses in tears of dew.

> A fellow pioneer, as best he could,
> > Laid the body in a newly made grave;
> And after the task was done, he said:
> > Here's where lies one that was brave.

> Many memorial days have passed:
> > But no mother, no sister has ever come,
> To lay beautiful flowers
> > On the grave of the unknown one.

> There is a broken heart somewhere,
> > Bleeding from a terrible wound;
> A hope that has nearly perished,
> > For the dear one that cannot be found.

> There is a grave—in those grasses,
> > A pioneer's grave—and lo!
> Him whom those green sods cover;
> > His name no one knows.

> But the name of the unknown
> > In the Great Book is recorded,
> As well as those of the world's rulers,
> > Kings, princes and potentates.

> And, when comes the last day,
> They, too, will be gathered
> The same as those rulers—
> Not one neglected.

Some people, after reading this letter, may say that it was wrong for those daring men and brave women to go into such a country, occupied only by savages. Well, that may be so, but the unexplored West never would be developed were it not for the immigrants, miners and prospectors who had the ambition, courage and pluck to commence to conquer. They are the "John the Baptists" of civilization, and the founders of states that are represented by stars in our banner and of those yet to come.

I came to Montana when a young man, now I am old, enjoying excellent health, but I may be robbed of this greatest gift to man, and I may, like "Job," be reduced to poverty, but there is nothing that can rob me of the pride and glory of being a "hero of Montana," one of those who stood by its cradle.

ROBERT VAUGHN.
MARCH 4, 1898.

The Indian Praying.

The winter of 1869 and 1870 was my first winter in Sun River valley. For a while I boarded with Mr. and Mrs. Armstrong, who kept the Leaving Station adjoining my ranch. This place was so named because it was at this point the road leaves (Leaving) the Sun River valley to Fort Benton. (This was the winter that Col. Baker made a raid on the Indian village on the Marias river.) Also this same winter and spring the smallpox caused many deaths among the Indians. Several whites died also from the same disease. Two stage drivers who drove from Benton to the Leaving died; and as they stopped at the station where I boarded, I took the smallpox in a mild form and was very sick for two weeks, but it left no marks. About this time I concluded to fence the farm. Early in the spring I went to a bend in the Missouri river about ten miles south to cut posts and poles for this purpose. Here there were several log buildings that had been erected sometime in the early sixties by some of the Catholic missionaries and used as an Indian Mission (old St. Peter's Mission). In 1868 it was abandoned for missionary purposes. After that it was occupied in winter by Indians. In the same bend is now what is known as "The Churchill Ranch." During the time I was chopping I lived in an old empty cabin that had been built by some trappers; it was in the edge of the woods about a quarter of a mile from the old Mission buildings. There was neither a door nor a window, but it had a good fireplace; I hung a blanket for a door, and cut lots of wild rye-grass for my bed. Although alone, I was very comfortable and slept well at night, for I worked hard all day. There were in all about thirty Indians in the old buildings, many of whom were sick with the smallpox; and a great many had died of the same disease. Their mode of burying the dead was to wrap the corpse in a buffalo robe and lay it under a tree in some secret place in the woods and cover it with leaves and branches off the trees; others were placed on a scaffold in trees, as heretofore described. There were a great many buried in this way in the woods where I was working. One Indian buried his wife and two children two days before I came. The female relations showed great grief by hacking their legs from the ankle to the calf into many small cuts barely through the skin; and they would sit alone with a robe over their heads and mourn and sigh. Once in the dead of the night, when I was asleep, some unearthly noise awoke me. It was at my cabin door. I raised on my elbow in my bed which was on the ground. As usual, when danger came, I grabbed my old gun which was under my head and pointed it at the door where the blanket hung. I listened, and finally decided that it was a human voice. It was a kind of chanting talking and in the most mournful tone, with now and then a deep, pitiful sigh as though it came from the bottom of the heart. It was the most mournful and pitiful utterance ever made by a human voice. It was kept up for at least twenty minutes. There was living with the Indians a half-breed who could speak English. His name was Simpson. (Afterwards he was killed by the Indians on the hill across Sun river from my ranch.) Next morning I told the half-breed of what took place at my cabin the previous night and he interpreted to me that it was an Indian, "the husband and father of the woman and two children that died the other day," and that he was praying, and asking me to ask the Great Spirit to stop the smallpox. A few minutes later the Indian and the half-breed came together to see me; the Indian said to me that his wife and two of his children were already dead and that more of his relations were sick. He firmly believed that I could do a great deal towards preventing the disease.

I told him that the Great Spirit was listening to his praying last night and heard every word, and as soon as the "warm

winds" came the smallpox would be no more. This appeared
to be of great consolation to him. It was plain to be seen that
the poor fellow loved his family. He was the Indian that saved
Mr. and Mrs. Kennedy's lives only few months before at the
Kennedy ranch near the mouth of the Prickly Pear canyon when
the Indians took them out of their home and were going to kill
them, but this Indian came forward and stood between Mr. and
Mrs. Kennedy and the other Indians that would be murderers.
He raised his gun and spoke in a firm voice: "If you kill this man
and woman you must kill me first." He stood them off and
saved the lives of two good citizens. He was well known by the
whites and was always friendly and honorable. He went by the
name of "Cut Lip Jack." This kind and brave Indian is dead, but
Mr. and Mrs. Kennedy are alive and live in Missoula county,
Montana. Will Kennedy of this city is their nephew.

ROBERT VAUGHN.

JAN. 14, 1898.

Indians Stealing My Horses.

In the month of August, 1871, I went near the mouth of Sun river to make hay. John Traxler, the man I had hired, was with me. I had a very fine span of gray mares which were brought to Montana from the State of Missouri, and they had cost me three hundred dollars. We pitched our tent on the open prairie and away from the brush for it was a safer place in an Indian country, beside the mosquitoes were very bad. Each of us had an old army needle gun with several rounds of ammunition. When night came we picketed the horses about five hundred yards off where there was good grass; the picket pins were iron and the ropes were new, so we had the horses well secured. We went to bed and covered our heads to keep the mosquitoes from biting us. When morning came I went to change the pickets for the horses so that they could get fresh grass, and John went to prepare breakfast. But to my surprise the horses were gone, and on investigation I found that the ropes had been cut near the picket pins, I decided at once that they had been stolen and so reported to John. He could see that I was feeling very badly over losing my fine team. "Well," he said, "I will let you have all the money I've got to get another team." After breakfast and discussing what was best to do, we went to see in what direction the horses had been taken. We found moccasin tracks near where the horses had been picketed, and we tracked them going north. It was plain to be seen that Indians were the thieves. John went up the valley and I took the direction the horses had gone, each of us taking his gun and ammunition; we soon lost sight of each other. After I had gone about four miles, and on the flat north of Alkali springs, I found the tracks of the horses and they were very plain, for the gray mares were shod. Going a little further I discovered where they had been changing saddles, for there were pieces of buffalo robes and old Indian blankets that were full of horse hair and wet with sweat from horses; no doubt there the change had been made from the Indian ponies to the gray mare. I followed the track crossing the Benton road and in the direction of the Teton river. After traveling in a northerly direction for fifteen miles I changed my course and headed for the ranch. I was eight miles from home. I got home in the afternoon and found John there. Early next morning I went to Fort Shaw and told my story to the commanding officer, who was General Gibbon. He at once called for Bostwick, the interpreter, and asked him what Indians were camping up the valley. Bostwick replied that they were Gray Eagle's party. "Go and bring Gray Eagle here to me," the general said. Bostwick, with six mounted men, went after the old chief, and in about three hours they had him and two of his staff in the general's headquarters. The general told Gray Eagle (through Bostwick, the interpreter), that some of his men had stolen my horses and if they were not returned immediately that he and his people would be severely punished, and he further said that he was in this country with his soldiers to look after such thieves as they. The old Indian listened eagerly, and said, that he was very sorry that my horses had been stolen; but he assured us that there were none of his men out that night, and said in the most emphatic manner that none of his men stole the horses; but that he would do all in his power to find them and bring them back to me. After considerable discussion about the matter, the general told the chief that if he would get those horses and bring them to the fort that he would give him a sack of sugar, and I said that I would give a sack of flour. Again the general said: "If you let me know who stole Mr. Vaughn's horses, I will give you a sack of coffee and a sack of bacon."

The old Indian promised faithfully that he would do all in his power to find the horses. However, after eleven days from the time the horses were stolen, the morning of the twelfth, the first thing after opening my cabin door was to see the two gray mares feeding on the grass only a few yards from my door. And I was a happy man. No one asked for the reward. That was the only time the Indians ever stole anything from me.

Robert Vaughn.

Jan. 25, 1898.

The Great Sun River Stampede.

In the years 1865–66 there were from fifteen to twenty thousand people in the various mining camps of Montana, and its mountains were swarmed with daring prospectors. In those times nearly every day had its new discovery, and the slightest whisper of a new "find" would create a stampede, in which instances the most extraordinary endurance and courage were displayed. There is no animal on earth that will stampede quicker, keep on going with the same stubbornness and determination, as a fortune hunter; they are worse than Texas cattle. For one instance, I will relate the following: McClellan, an old mountaineer and prospector, and who was the discoverer of the "McClellan Gulch," but sold his claim in that renowned mine for a song, and after having two or three weeks' good time in town, he began laying his plans for another prospecting tour.

In the following fall (1865) he decided to go to the Sun river country, that was about one hundred miles north of Helena, and hunt for more mines. He was considered a lucky prospector in finding gold, and when a report came from him it could be relied upon.

After having prospected for two or three months the cold weather began to set in, and, as he had already found some gold, he decided to build a cabin and keep on prospecting till spring. In a week or so he had his house up and everything in apple-pie order, except one thing, and that was, to have some one to have his meals ready after returning from the hills where he had been working hard all day. As there was a Piegan camp not far off he went there one day and engaged a squaw to come and cook for him. As the new employe had many relations, who became her frequent visitors, it was not long before the proprietor discovered that a few extras in the line of groceries

MRS. JAS. BLOOD (A PIEGAN WOMAN).

had to be gotten, an extra sack of flour, a few pounds of soap, and so forth; besides some calico, beads, brass ear rings and bracelets for the new housekeeper, who was trying her hand for the first time in her life at house-keeping.

One day, Mc mounted his pony, and, with another pack horse, struck for Helena to get the goods. On his arrival he met many of his old friends, and of course they were anxious to learn what success he had prospecting. He said that so far he had not discovered anything that would pay, although he had found what he called good indications. For all that a close watch was kept on the old prospector during the few days he was in town, and a suspicion was aroused among many that on account of the fact that he was buying considerable goods he must know of something greater than he wanted to tell. To one of his confidential friends he told of the pleasant home he had in the Sun river country, and, in a whisper, his last sentence was: "I have as got as good a thing as I want," meaning his new housekeeper and the household outfit that he had just purchased. Two of the anxious ones stood near and overheard him saying, "I have got as good a thing as I want." They decided at once that a new find was meant. The news spread like wild fire to every camp in the vicinity, and, like the story of the "three black cows," something was added to the first report as it went from camp to camp. A tremendous stampede followed, and, although it was in the month of January and the thermometer stood thirty-five degrees below zero, and there was over a foot of snow on the level, this did not check the rush. From twelve to fifteen hundred rugged miners participated in this stampede; some went on horseback, others on foot, and, after traveling about one hundred miles, the new Eldorado could not be found. Before returning home several suffered severely from cold and hunger and two died from exposure. Some threats were made against the one giving the false report, but no foundation could be found that McClellan had said that a discovery of gold had been made, but to the contrary it was proven that he had said that no diggings had been found. And, when the particulars of what started the stampede were learned, no further complaint was made. All returned home except a few who had supplied themselves with enough provisions; they stayed and prospected.

Mr. Thomas Moran of St. Peter, who was on this stampede, told me only a few days ago that at least seven hundred men were one night in camp in a bend of the Missouri river and near where the St. Peter's Mission was then. He said that Father C. Imoda, who was in charge of the Mission, treated them kindly and gave assistance to many that were suffering from cold and hunger. Mr. Moran said that the thermometer registered forty degrees below zero that night.

All of the old timers remember this event, and it is known at the present time as the "Great Sun river stampede in the winter of 1866."

ROBERT VAUGHN.
APRIL 21, 1899.

A Trip from Virginia City to the Head of Navigation on the Missouri River in 1866.

It was about the 20th day of April, 1866, that the first wagon train drawn by oxen pulled out of Virginia City and down the famous Alder Gulch bound for Fort Benton, the head of navigation on the Missouri river; and this train was the property of Sutherlin Brothers, of whom the writer hereof was a member. The train was not a large one, for our firm was not rich and had all it could do to equip four teams. Work cattle were then worth from $130 to $160 per pair, and they could be bought only for gold. One feature of this little train was the coupling of wagons together which had never been in practice before, so that one driver could handle five or six yoke of oxen pulling two wagons carrying from seven to eight thousand pounds. This was the first train of the kind to go on the road, a view to economy caused its invention. Our firm had some wagons of four thousand pounds capacity and could secure lighter ones for trails, while to buy big "Prairie Schooners" was out of the question. We had tried the plan of coupling wagons together for the saving of drivers the year before and found it practicable, hence no risk was taken in outfitting upon a more extensive scale for general freighting. The usual freighter had but one heavy wagon to a team, but it was noticed that our little train hauled as much per team as they, and made better time, consequently many adopted the same plan, and in a few years rich firms had gone into the freighting business, with teams of from nine to twelve yoke of oxen, and four wagons; each team hauling from sixteen to twenty thousand pounds. Eight to ten teams constituted a train. One driver to a team, a night herder and wagon boss, was all that was necessary to make a full crew.

At the time we made this trip to the head of navigation there were no stage coaches, except the lines to Salt Lake and

Helena, and there were no liveries, the principal means of travel being on horseback, the traveler taking his bed in a roll behind his saddle or upon an extra horse, together with frying pan and coffee pot.

The large number of steamboats which had left St. Louis for Fort Benton, laden with merchandise, seemed to offer an easier means of going east and south, then fifteen days and nights of stage coaching via Salt Lake to Denver, then to Omaha or Kansas City; and, as a great many people had already made quite a fortune, passage on a freight train to Fort Benton was acceptable, even with our ox train, which was among the first to leave Virginia City. The mule trains had the preference until reports came of the Indian raids and danger of loss of mules when the business was quite evenly divided. An ounce of gold dust was the customary fare from Virginia City to Fort Benton.

Our crew was fairly well armed and the passengers were generally provided with revolvers; as many of them carried considerable gold dust weapons of defense were considered essential to safety.

From morning until night our little train moved along, fifteen miles being the usual extent of a day's drive. Down the valley by Pete Daly's station, then to "Garney's," across the Jefferson, up White Tail over the boulder range, the Boulder valley and into "Last Chance." I remember my first glimpse of Bridge street, then the principal thoroughfare of the new metropolis, Helena, for the greater part of Main street was a winding wagon road over piles of tailings, around sluice boxes and miners' huts; and I remember, too, the winding road out into the unsettled and apparently valueless valley that spread out as we proceeded northwestward and the large herd of antelope that scampered away as we approached, disappearing in the virgin meadows which hid them. The little town of Silver City, where a few people were placer mining, lay to the

FREIGHTING IN THE EARLY DAYS—CATTLE TEAM BETWEEN FORT BENTON AND VIRGINIA CITY.
Courtesy Montana Historical Society, Helena

left of our road. The head of Prickly Pear canyon, the home of the brave Malcolm Clark, has a place in my memory, for it seemed to be the sunniest spot in the wilderness. Lyons Hill, Medicine Rock, and other somewhat mountain-like high places were passed, and then the crossing of the Dearborn river, which was made between showers when the stream was so deep that the water came into the wagon beds, I do not forget.

At "Bird Tail Rock" some of our party took their first hunt. Mountain sheep in considerable numbers were seen at the base and far up the rugged sides of that great landmark, and a taste of the rare mutton in the mountain wilds they longed for before getting back, as they said, to "God's country, America," but the jaunt was a long one, further to the game than they had anticipated, and the ramble was abandoned, the party reaching camp long after camping time satisfied to go home without the taste of mountain mutton.

At Sun river an unexpected halt was made; we called it a "layover." There had been copious rains, together with the melting snow, and the river was booming, out of its channel in some places. The ferry boat, a small craft built of whip-sawed lumber and capable of carrying only one wagon and one yoke of oxen, was intact, but the cable had to be stretched. In doing this, after several efforts the end was landed on the opposite shore, but in drawing it up out of the water the strong current parted it. This was repaired after much exertion, but, in cross-ing, the first wagon of the Bullard train, which was among the number in waiting, the trail rope again parted, and it was with difficulty that the boat and contents was landed. J. J. Healey, the ferryman of the boat crew had already departed for Benton to secure a new cable, and there followed several days of waiting before his return. During the days of waiting a number of trains arrived. Finally the ferryman came with a new cable and then followed the task of placing it in position, a job more difficult than the first, owing to the continued rise of the river. Effort after effort was made, each proving a failure. The end of the cable was brought across the river, but it was not possible to draw it out of the water, and when, with a long team of oxen, it had been drawn across from the east shore J. J. Healey and many freighters had almost despaired of placing it in position. Ben Anderson and his three associates volunteered to perform the task. These Indiana boys had for years followed the business of rafting saw-logs down the Wabash river and proved to be the right men in the right place on this occasion. They made several rafts out of dry cottonwood logs, and, locating them at intervals up the bank of the stream, the cable was stretched on them in such a manner that it was held above the water, then starting with the upper end the rafts were swung around, the further one reaching the opposite shore, when it was easily raised to the proper height without touching the rapid current. It did me good to see the hats go up and hear the round of applause that echoed out upon the beautiful Sun river valley as the cable was anchored—"hurrah, hurrah, hurrah for the boys, the Indiana boys." This feat gave our little train the first right of way over the ferry, and we crossed in time to drive as far as the "Leavings," a nine-mile pull down the river bank.

I almost forgot to state that Mr. Healey, besides bringing the big rope from Benton, brought the report that a large body of Blackfeet Indians were camped on the Teton river not many miles away to the north, and that their mission was to steal horses, pillage and murder. This was not pleasant news to the passengers who, though well armed, felt that they "might be taken in." It was sundown when camp was made at the "Leavings," and I cannot forget the anxiety manifest as I went around to the several campfires. Up to that date we had no night watchman, but it was easy to see the necessity of a night sentinel, therefore I volunteered to perform that duty. It was not a new duty by any means, for I had seen weeks of it in crossing the plains to Denver in 1863 and coming to Montana in 1864. To make the night easy my friend, Joe Lacky, volunteered to take the first half of the night and went on his beat at nine, all rolling into bed about the same time.

It was 12:30 when I was awakened by a whisper, to which was added: "The camp is all right." With my revolver in my belt and Ballard rifle in hand I was soon on duty. The oxen were lying down, broken clouds hung over head, and all was quiet except the hooting of owls in the hills across the river and who seemed to be keeping company with their neighbors located some distance away. So far away were these that they were but faintly heard. At first I paid little attention to the hooting, but as the hours began to grow longer and the clouds thickened, the hooting became more interesting. These hootings came at intervals, while between them the stillness seemed almost unbearable.

There is much that I might write of that night of picket duty at the "Leavings," but least I may tire the reader the same is passed. Writing at this time, thirty-three and a half years later, my thoughts go back to more recent scenes of the place, and I cannot pass on without recalling just one or two visits there quite as distinct as the first. The Sun river tour of 1879, when introducing the "Rocky Mountain Husbandman," comes fresh. It was then I rested a day with my friend, Robert Vaughn, who had cultivated on that lonely spot a fine farm, built a good home, and owned herds of horses and cattle. We talked of the early days gone by, of Indians and Indian hunting, and wound up the day of pleasure in a hunt among the feathered tribes—geese, ducks and swan. Mr. V. showed not alone his marksmanship, but his skill in selecting young birds of which it was less than an hour's sport on the river to capture a dozen. But this is digressing from my subject.

The morning of that lonely night in 1866 dawned, the oxen arose to feed and the expected attack by Indians did not materialize. We were on the road early, for the drive to the lakes was a longer one than we had usually made. Without especial incident the day passed and we reached the head of the lakes about sundown. The wagons were corralled—drawn up in a close half circle, cattle turned out to graze, supper cooked, etc. No Indians or signs of Indians had been seen and our passengers were buoyant with hopes, for it seemed that the head of navigation would be reached in safety, there being but two more days' travel before us. Having the lead from the ferry we were a day's travel ahead of the other trains, and realizing this added somewhat to the anxiety and I might say fear. The night passed quietly, particularly the latter part. We were too far away from the cliffs to hear the hooting of the owls, and the only charm I can remember was when a breeze came up from the southeast which brought with it the roar of the great Missouri river falls, some twenty or more miles away.

The following day's travel was also long on account of the scarcity of water. Getting an early start the journey was made, arriving at Twenty-eight-Mile Springs about sunset. Just before turning the summit of the ridge west of this well known place we were overtaken by a large mule train, probably forty wagons, four to six animals to each wagon, and they were well loaded with passengers—probably about one hundred and forty persons. This train pulled by, and, passing the springs, turned south and went into camp on the summit of the elevated lands six or seven hundred yards away, while our little train halted for the night close to the springs. Soon after turning out our teams several visitors came from the big train. Nearly all were from Virginia City, and among them there were few ladies. Several of the passengers carried large amounts of gold dust, the estimated amount in the train being

THOMAS FRANCIS MEAGHER.
Courtesy Montana Historical Society, Helena

over $400,000. This train had been making fast time, having that day come from the "Leavings," a distance of twenty-five miles. Fresh stories were told us of the large Indian camp and the probable raid, for at this time we were near to their camp. We were solicited to join the big party, but our teams were turned out and we had to decline. This request came several times, and lastly in the shape of a message from his excellency, Acting Gov. Thomas Francis Meagher, who was among the passengers. This brought our firm and friends together for council, at which it was decided to remain where we were. If an attack was made by the Indians the object would be to secure the mules and horses, as they could not expect to drive our cattle away, and if siege was made we would be better off in reach of water than on the hill. Further summing it up, we considered our people better off camped as we were, and as the mule outfit was placing a strong guard for the night we could all turn into our beds and sleep. Soon after dark the lights were put out and quiet reigned. The night was cloudy, and in getting into my bed under a wagon it was surmised that I might be driven out by rain before morning. We had but one horse and he was tied with a long lariat to a wheel of the wagon under which I slept. That horse was my body guard. I knew that if Indians appeared he would snort and try to pull away, which would awaken me.

It was perhaps 3 o'clock in the morning when a single report of a gun rent the air south of the mule camp, and following close on this I heard in the distance the sound of many hoofs. Then a general commotion ensued at the mule camp. General Meagher was among the first to rise and his strong voice could be heard giving orders. He was the self-constituted commander on this occasion, and I could hear him knocking on the sides of the wagon and commanding every one to get out and prepare for an attack. A messenger came down to inform us that Indians had attempted to stampede the mules, but the guards had succeeded in rescuing them and driving them into the corral, and an attack was expected. General Meagher sent us word to leave our wagons and join the mule camp, and for a few moments it seemed that some of our passengers were willing to do this, but better judgment prevailed, and all decided to remain with their wagons and protect, if possible, their own valuables, which could not well be removed at that hour. Our men were all up and in readiness, but the night was too dark for one to shoot with any degree of accuracy, and it seemed hardly reasonable that the "Redskins" would make an attack until the beginning of daylight. There was, however, no let up to the racket in the mule camp. General Meagher got his fellow passengers out in line and marched them in regular soldier form around and round the big corral in which the mules were secured. This corral was composed of wagons drawn up in a circle and ropes so tied between that the mules once inside could not get out. I could hear the commands given and I listened with interest to the exchange of words with some of the men who attempted to evade the duty. "I have but a small pistol and can do no good if I come out there," said one of the men. "Yes, you can do good," said Meagher, "these helpless women and children must be protected and I beseech you to come like a man to their rescue." "Fall in line, shoulder arms, forward, march!" "Why, sir, do you dare disobey orders?" "Oh, why, I was just looking into the wagon to see if things were all right."

The truth of the matter was that those fellows who protested had little pets in their wagons in the shape of sacks of gold dust which were unhandy to carry and they were afraid of losing the treasure. But the energetic general appeared to take more interest in the safety of those women and children than of those gold sacks, and his strong voice echoed for nearly three long hours, as he gave commands to keep in line ready for action and protect the camp. Quite an episode when, after marching for more than an hour, the general chanced to find a little Jew covered in his blankets and crouched down in one end of a wagon. Loud calling did not seem to disturb him—all this time he was playing that he could not hear—but by prodding he was aroused, and the general, thinking him deaf, shouted very loudly trying to arouse him to action in resisting the enemy. It was said that the fellow could hear as well as anybody, but took that plan of evading the general's orders, preferring to keep closer watch of his treasures which, it appears, were too heavy to be handily carried, but the general kept on urging until he got the Jew into line. Perhaps the most laughable incident that occurred during the scare was when the general's messenger returned from a visit to our camp and reported that "them folks with the ox train are Missourians and won't get up." It was a mistake, however, as our party did get out and were ready for the fray, and afterwards one of them remarked that it was really too bad that the "Redskins did not give us a fight, that we were entitled to have some fun after so much preparation."

Early next morning our train was on the road, and the mule train, at the general's suggestion, fell in and kept company. Plenty of evidences were seen to establish the fact of the near approach of the Indians that night, and I attributed their failure to attack to the action of General Meagher and men in the mule camp. Forty wagons and teams added to our little train, with from eighty to a hundred armed men marching by their sides and about thirty mounted on horseback scouting in advance on either side, made up a pretty formidable procession. I had the honor of accompanying General Meagher on horseback as an advance picket during most of the day, and it was rare enjoyment listening to sketches of his early life adventures, his leave taking of the "old country," and incidents of his connection with the war of the rebellion.

The general was en route to meet his wife who came up on the "Josephine." Our trip of the day was without material interest, and it was cheering to my soul to see the glad faces of our passengers as our caravan hove in sight of the quaint little fort and city, nestled beneath the rounded hills, and three Missouri river steamers, the "St. John," the "Waverly" and another moored at the wharf discharging their cargoes.

WILL. H. SUTHERLIN.

WHITE SULPHUR SPRINGS, MONT., NOV. 12, 1899.

By request the above letter was written for publication in this book. Mr. Sutherlin has been a resident of Meagher county ever since June, 1865, and has contributed much to the upbuilding of the county and the state. He was elected and served two terms as sheriff, also filled the office of county clerk and recorder one term, and was ex-officio probate judge during the same time.

He was elected in 1886 to the office of territorial councilman, and served two sessions. A number of the laws remaining on the statute books of Montana were originated and passed through his efforts. He was chairman of the committee on agriculture of the State World's Fair Board and erected and had charge of Montana's agricultural exhibit at the World's Fair at Chicago in 1893. He was the commissioner for this state and had full charge of the state's exhibit at the Trans-Mississippi Exposition at Omaha in 1898. He was one of the founders of the Rocky Mountain Husbandman, November, 1875. His brother, R.N. Sutherlin, was and still is associated with him in its publication. Mr. Sutherlin is one of the best authorities on agriculture in the Northwest.

ROBERT VAUGHN.

GREAT FALLS, MONT., JAN. 7, 1900.

My First Buffalo Hunt.

I do not think that there is anything more exciting, combined with fun and enjoyment to a man, than a buffalo hunt, or, as some call it, a chase, especially the first. I well remember my first experience along that line. It was on the lake's flat, between Sun river and Fort Benton. John Argue and James Armstrong were with me. We could see for several days buffaloes in the coulees on the Muddy. The weather had been cold and snowing for some time. The first clear day we mounted our horses and prepared for a chase.

After we arrived on top of Frozen Hill we could see that the Lake flat and the region beyond was entirely covered with buffaloes. It was a sight to behold. Without exaggeration there were a quarter of a million buffaloes in sight; the main herd covered eight miles by three miles, and they were so numerous that they ate every spear of grass as they went. We rode slowly until we got near the herd, for they were quietly feeding. Soon we could see that the outside ones discovered us, and we made the charge with guns in hand. I had a dragoon revolver, the kind that the cavalry used the time of the war. I was riding a very fine horse. Soon we commenced shooting. It was not long before every buffalo was on the move. And now the fun began. Tens of thousands of these ponderous animals were running at a furious pace; the earth trembled, and the clicking of their hoofs could be heard for miles away. By this time my horse had me in the midst of the herd, for he could run like a racer, and I had two big buffaloes badly crippled and they fell to the rear. Now I had gone all of two miles and fired a dozen shots, with buffaloes in front of me and buffaloes behind me and buffaloes on each side of me; in fact I could see nothing but buffaloes. It takes some practice to load a gun while on horseback and on full speed. However, I was doing

HERD OF BUFFALO.
Courtesy Montana Historical Society, Helena

this with considerable accuracy. Now I had my old dragoon loaded the third time, and I took after a fat young cow. The chase began to tell on my horse for it was as much as he could do to keep up with this particular buffalo. Soon I had two bullets in her and one more in my gun; I was determined to make a sure shot with it. I now could see that the pace of the buffalo was slower. I spurred my horse and with a spurt he was at her side. As quick as lightening the buffalo whirled around and caught my foot with her crooked horn and came very near throwing me out of the saddle and as near goring the horse. This warned me to be more cautious. The buffalo started in another direction, but very slowly. I followed it; finally it stopped and turned, looking directly at me. I was fifty yards off. I took a deliberate aim at it and down she came. I shot it directly between the eyes. This cow buffalo netted nearly nine hundred pounds and it was as fine meat as I ever tasted. I was now in the center of the buffalo herd and all running like mad and going in one direction; the clouds of fine snow and dust making it very dangerous for a man, being liable to be run over by the buffaloes. At this juncture I had to stand in one place, hat in hand, yelling at the top of my voice to keep them from running over me and my horse. Once a big bull, coming on a terrific speed directly towards me, was in ten feet before he saw me, but made a dodge and at the same time gave a snort and passed me, brushing his shaggy coat against my buckskin suit. It was not long before the big rush had gone by and I had had my first buffalo hunt. A few miles west of me some Indians were chasing another herd. On my way back I found the first two buffaloes that I crippled; one was dead and the other could not get up. Armstrong and Argue had good luck. Next day we went back and brought home a wagon load of as good meat as anyone could wish.

The buffaloes are the most watchful animals that I ever saw. At the least disturbance in the herd they are all at once on the watch as if they had some way of telegraphing to each other; and their scent is remarkably keen. When getting away from the hunter they all run one way and invariably go north. They have remarkable lung power; it takes more than an ordinary horse to keep up with the average buffalo for a mile, and, if not in a mile, good bye horse, for about this time the buffalo begins to warm up and is getting ready for a race. This was in the winter of 1872.

ROBERT VAUGHN.
JAN. 23, 1898.

Tom Campbell Running the Gauntlet.

All of the old-timers of Northern Montana remember Tom Campbell (now dead). He was always jolly and a good fellow in general. Tom told me of what happened to him one time when out in the hills and alone. At the time referred to he was employed at one of the trading posts down the Missouri river. One day he was sent to get a deer for meat at the post. When he was about six miles from the camp he came in contact with four Indians. They at once captured him and wanted to know what business he had to hunt in their country. One Indian leveled his gun at Tom's head, while another one took his horse and gun from him. One of the Indians had seen Tom before at the trading store. This Indian told his comrade, who was threatening to shoot, to lay down his gun. And the four then held a kind of council to consider and decide what to do with their captive. Tom understood their language and overheard what they were saying. One wanted to tie him to a tree and all take a shot at him; another one wanted to scalp him first and then kill him; the other two were undecided. Finally, one of them, a strapping big fellow, said that he knew this man and that he did not want to kill him, but that he would take away everything he had and then let him go. Tom said that this Indian had a great deal of influence over the others. After having considerable talk about the matter with the other three, he turned to Tom and said: "I want that coat." "You can have it," said Tom. Again the Indian said: "I want that vest and shirt." "All right," said Tom. "And I want them pants and shoes you have on," said the lordly red man. "You can have them, too," said Tom. Tom was speedily divested of all his clothing. The Indian who made the demand had a rawhide lariat in his hand, and, with it, gave Tom a whack across the shoulders and a kick where his coat-tail used to be, and told him to go home. Tom, naked and barefooted, made a bee line towards the post. After he had gone a certain distance the Indians began shooting at him, and at the same time running after him, but, as Tom was in good condition and stripped for a foot race, he outran them; though the bullets whistled about him, he got home without being hit.

Tom said that it took him but a few minutes to cover the distance, and that when he arrived his feet were bleeding terribly.

About two years afterwards, on Front street, in Fort Benton, Campbell met the Indian who struck and kicked him and divested him of all his clothing. He seized the Indian by the arm and demanded that he should come with him. The Indian appeared greatly frightened and asked Tom what he was going to do with him. "Come with me and ask no questions," said Tom. The Indian obeyed, and in a few minutes they were in I.G. Baker's store. "Now," said Tom, "I want you to pick out the best shirt and the best pair of blankets in this store and I will pay for them." The Indian was greatly surprised at this and it was evident that it was the first time in his life that he ever was whipped with a golden rule, for all this time he thought that Tom was taking him to some place to receive punishment, or that he was going to be killed for what he and his companions had done to Tom when out hunting two years before. Tom said to the Indian: "You stole my clothing, you struck me, and the kick you gave me was a hard one, but all that, I owe you my life and I am glad to have the opportunity to return you this compliment." The Indian was much pleased and promised Tom his friendship as long as he lived. This Indian was prominent in his tribe, and this "golden rule" act of Tom Campbell's was made known to every Indian in that tribe, and not a hair of his head they allowed to be injured. And from that time he was always treated with the greatest kindness, and many trophies he received as a token of friendship from those Indians.

Mr. Campbell was well educated. For a long time he was in the employment of the American Fur company, and always occupied a post of trust. At the time I had the above conversation he was doing a prosperous business for himself.

ROBERT VAUGHN.

APRIL 7, 1899.

Edward A. Lewis' Early Days in Montana.

Having been acquainted with Mr. Edward A. Lewis, who lives on a thousand-acre farm in the foot hills near St. Peter's Mission, twenty-five miles southwest from this place, and, knowing that he is one of the earliest settlers in Northern Montana, one day last week I took a drive and had a very interesting interview with him in regard to his early days in the West. In the year 1869 he was married to a daughter of a Piegan war chief named Meek-i-appy (Heavy Shield). Father Imoda officiated. Mrs. Lewis had been baptized in the Christian faith previous to her marriage. She is an intelligent woman and speaks fair English; she is a splendid housekeeper, and, above all, a true wife and loving mother. They have three daughters who are well educated; the oldest is married to Mr. John Taber, a well-to-do farmer and stock raiser. When I arrived at the house Mr. Lewis, with his hired man, was in a field near by stacking grain. I asked him how many crops he had harvested off that field; he said: "This is the twenty-ninth crop." I should judge that forty bushels to the acre would be a fair estimate of the present one.

This beautiful mountain home is but a natural park, of a horseshoe shape, surrounded by high hills crowned with perpendicular cliffs to the height of several hundred feet, with here and there a low divide beyond which nothing is visible but the blue sky. One of the hills east of the house is called Skull mountain. When Mrs. Lewis' mother was a young woman, the Flatheads and Piegans had a fight in the little valley below, in which the Flatheads came out victorious. Eight of the Piegans fled to the top of this mountain, and there fortified themselves by building breastworks with stones and pitch pine logs. They held the fort for one day and a night, but the Flatheads greatly outnumbered them, and they were overpowered and killed; not one escaped. Many years afterwards Mr. Lewis and Mr. Moran, his neighbor, found the skull of one of those Indians and brought it home. From this "Skull Mountain" received its name, The little fort was standing until a few years, when some school children tore it down, and now nothing remains but the ruins.

Mr. Lewis, calling my attention to a clump of pine near the summit of Skull Mountain, said: "There is where there is a bed of oyster shells that are as perfect as those on the seashore." Pointing his hand at another high hill, he said: "And there is where there is another bed of the same kind of shells." On entering the house, and after I had asked him a few questions in regard to his early adventures in the West, Mr. Lewis said: "It was always my desire to go West. When but eighteen years of age, at St. Louis, Missouri, I hired to the American Fur company to go and work at Fort Benton on the upper Missouri river. I left St. Louis the eighth day of May, 1857, on the steamboat "Star of the West." I arrived at Fort Benton the twenty-second day of September of the same year. The boat was loaded with goods to pay the Indians their annuities for the treaty they had made with Governor Stevens in behalf of the government for the right of way for a wagon road through their country. The American Fur company had taken the contract to deliver the Indian goods. The boat came as far as about five miles below the place now called Culberson on the Great Northern railroad. There the goods were taken off the steamer and some of them were issued to the Indians at that place. We had brought with us from St. Louis enough lumber to build two Mackinaw boats, and we whip-sawed dry cottonwood logs into enough lumber to build the third one. With these boats we took the balance of the goods up to Fort Benton. We had to tow them all the way. There were seventeen men to the boat; sometimes we had to cross the river on account of the high banks and other obstacles. It was hard work, besides sometimes we were in the water up to our waists. It took us sixty-five days to come to Fort Benton from the place where the steamboat landed. In the fall of the same year I, with others, was sent to Fort Union with Mackinaw boats loaded with furs. For several years all the robes and furs belonging to the company were taken from Fort Benton to Fort Union in this way. The distance overland between the two places is three hundred and seventy-four miles, but much greater by the river route. When on these trips we often had to travel at night for the purpose of passing the many hostile Indian camps that were along the river. Notwithstanding all our precautions, many times we had narrow escapes from being robbed and killed by those Indians. Immediately after arriving from the trip referred to, I returned to Fort Benton overland in company with Bill Atkinson, a Frenchman named Rinober, and Henry Bosdwike, who, for several years afterwards, was an interpreter for the government. In 1877 he was killed in the Gibbon fight with the Nez Perces Indians at Big Hole. We had in our charge two carts that were loaded with Indian goods and were drawn by oxen, two to a cart. Then it was difficult to get enough goods to Fort Benton to supply the Indian trade. In the following spring I was sent down the river to Fort Union on the same kind of a trip. When we got there the agent wanted volunteers to take a dispatch boat to Omaha. Mr. Armel, Bill Fatherland and myself took the job. We went down the Missouri in a small cottonwood boat twelve feet long. For our provisions we had nothing but dried buffalo meat. We were happy and contented until we got to a Mandan Indian village; there we were informed that the Sioux chief, "Bighead," who was a bitter enemy of the whites, was in camp with five hundred lodges on the bank of the Missouri river near the mouth of Cannonball river. This was gloomy news to us, for we knew that

Chief Bighead was one of the worst Indians on the river. However, there was nothing for us to do but take the chance and to pass the village in the dead of the night. We glided along, stopping now and then to look for Indian signs in the sand on the shores. After coming near Grand Prairie we decided to cache our boat in the willows day times, and from there on run at night. One evening after an hour of hard rowing, we came where we could see the reflections in the sky from the fires in the Sioux camp, as from a good-sized town lighted by electricity nowadays. As we were getting near the village we stopped for a short time to lay our plans. It was decided that we would wait until the Indians were asleep, and then let the boat drift close to the high, steep bank next to the Indian's camp, for it would not do to use the oars for fear of making a noise. As we floated close to the bank, we could hear the Indians talking to each other. After we got past, one of the guards discovered us and gave the alarm, but as the lay of the land and the thick brush along the bank of the river were in our favor, and the way we worked the oars and made the little craft fly, we were soon out of danger. We hid ourselves and the boat in the willows on an island the next day, and the day after in a similar place, but after that we traveled day and night until we got to Omaha. There the company's agent paid our fare to St. Louis, and soon afterwards we returned back to the mountains.

It was in the year 1858 an agency was established in the Sun River valley where now Mr. H. B. Strong's ranch is. Here is where the annuity of Governor Stevens' treaty was issued to the Blackfeet Indians. Major Vaughn was agent to issue the goods.

In December, 1859, the company sent nine of us to the Highwood mountains, about twenty miles from Fort Benton to cut logs to make lumber to build Mackinaw boats, for the fur trade was doubling every winter, consequently a great many more boats were required to take the goods, consisting of fur robes and pelts, to Fort Union. After being in camp a few days we had everything running smoothly. Phil Barnes and I drove the ox teams. Some of the men were new hands who had come from St. Louis that summer and could not speak a word of Indian and did not understand their sign talk. One day when Barnes and I were about half a mile from camp we could hear from behind us the clatter of horses and the cracking of whips; on looking back we discovered thirty Crow Indians coming as fast as their horses could carry them, and were coming right towards us, all having their bows strung and their hands full of arrows, and as they approached us, they rent the air with their Indian yells. One pressed an arrow against Barnes' breast and demanded where our camp was; we told them and pointed in that direction. Twenty-seven of them left at once for our camp; the other three stayed to pilot us the same way the others went. The Indians soon could tell who the new men were and they stripped some of them, and then used the ramrods of their guns on them. They made us cook for the whole gang, and when night came they put us all together and stood guard over us all night, and until the evening of the next day, when one Indian named Red Bear, and who was the chief, told Barnes and I to get the oxen and go to Benton after more goods; and that they were going to take all we had, and he further said: "We have got all the horses your people had."

Barnes and I took an ox team, as Chief Red Bear had told us, and left for Fort Benton on that evening. We traveled all night, and when we arrived at Fort Benton, we were told that the night previous the Indians had stolen two hundred and fifty head of the company's horses. At the time they were holding us as prisoners the others of the party were stealing the horses that were on Pablow Island, near Fort Benton.

It was Chief Red Bear and his gang that robbed and plundered the James Stuart party on the Yellowstone four years later.

In 1860 Major Blake, with a detachment of troops, came up the Missouri river to Fort Benton and was bound to Fort Colville in the then Territory of Washington. Blake and his troops came on the steamboat named "Chippewa," and this was the first time a steamboat ever landed at Fort Benton. The same year Captain John Mullan was building a wagon road from Walla Walla to Fort Benton, which was afterwards known as the Mullan road. Major Blake, when on his way up the river, was very anxious to know the whereabouts of Captain Mullan, who was then somewhere west of the main range of the Rocky mountains. Malcolm Clarke, who had been in St. Louis attending to some business concerning the American Fur company, was on the same boat. When at Fort Union Clark volunteered to take a message overland to Fort Benton and from there forward it to Captain Mullan, saying that he would get to Fort Benton several days ahead of the steamer.

Clark mounted one of Major Blake's government mules and arrived at Fort Benton six days from the time he left Fort Union and five days ahead of the "Chippewa." From Fort Benton I was sent with the message to Captain Mullan, whom I met on the Hell Gate river. I traveled on the old Indian trail up the Prickly Pear canyon and crossed the main divide where now the Northern Pacific Railway crosses.

At the mouth of the Deer Lodge river I met a Flathead Indian who could talk a little English. I asked him where those soldiers were. He told me that they were a little ways down the river and on the other side. It was in the month of June; the snow was melting off the mountains, and the streams were very high.

The Indian came with me to show where Mullan was, and we followed down the banks of the Hell Gate river for a few miles until we came opposite where Captain Mullan's camp was. I told the Indian that I had a letter for Mullan and he said he would swim the river and take it to him. I gave the Indian the letter and he swam the swift current of that great river with the letter between his teeth and landed, after going down the stream nearly a mile. I was then a good swimmer, but I would not undertake to swim that river then for any consideration. Mullan, after reading the letter, wrote one to Major Blake, which I delivered on my return to Fort Benton, where I met Blake. It took me seven days and a half to make the trip. At the Benton Lake I met Captain W. H. Reynolds' United States engineer corps expedition, which was in camp there at the time. They had been viewing the Missouri Falls.

In the summer of 1861 the same steamer (Chippewa), when loaded with goods for the company, blew up somewhere near Fort Union, when on her trip up to Fort Benton. Mr. Sam Ford, who now lives at the city of Great Falls, was on the boat at the time of the accident. The cargo was lost, consequently they had to get another supply from Fort Union. The goods had to be hauled overland to Fort Benton. I, with others, was sent to bring the goods. We left Fort Union with several wagons and carts drawn by oxen and horses. Mr. Andrew Dawson, who was connected with the company, had charge of the outfit. One morning, when we were traveling, a war party of Crows came to us. They at once demanded some goods. Mr. Dawson gave them all a small gift, but, for all that, they kept troubling us by trying to stop our teams and they would get on the back of the horses that were pulling the wagons and climb on the wagon tongues and ride the wheel oxen. In this way they kept following and tormenting us. Sometimes they would go away, but only to return, and no doubt they intended to rob us when the first night came. One time they surrounded and stopped us and demanded more goods; some of them attempting to get into the wagons. Again Mr. Dawson gave them several blankets, a box of tobacco, a box of hard-tack crackers, and other small trinkets; this satisfied them then, but it was not long before they came again and acted meaner than ever. One Indian, while trying to get on the wagon tongue, was kicked by the wheel ox and he fell, the wagon wheel going over and killing him. The other Indians carried him away and we went on for several miles unmolested. But soon there came a large band of the savage devils, with nothing on in the way of clothing except a breech clout; they had their hands full of arrows and their bows strung ready to send an arrow on a moment's signal, and, in an angry manner, forbade us to go any further or there would be trouble, and with violent threats demanded pay for the killing of their man. Mr. Dawson reasoned with them, saying that it was the Indian's own fault that he was killed, but this would not satisfy them; they were bound to have goods and plenty of them, or scalps. Just then a Gros Ventres chief, with about fifty warriors, arrived, and, no doubt, was the cause of saving us from being massacred by the savage Crows. At this time a large camp of Gros Ventres was at Wolfe Point, about twenty-five miles up the river. Through some source they were informed that the Crows were interfering with our wagon train and came to see about it. It appears that about twelve months previous the Gros Ventres and Crows had made peace with each other, and, at this time, they were on friendly terms. It was but a few minutes after the arrival of the Gros Ventres that their chief, whose name was "Sitting Woman," called the Crows and whites together and had a council. Addressing the Crows, he said: "The Crows and the Gros Ventres have made peace with each other. That is good. The Crows and Gros Ventres smoke together. That is good. The Crows and Gros Ventres make presents to each other. That is good. The Crows and

WOLF VOICE, GROS VENTRE WARRIOR.
Courtesy Montana Historical Society, Helena

Gros Ventres trade horses with one another, and that is good. But these white men are our white men; the goods that are in their wagons are goods that they are bringing to trade with us. If you are going to fight these white men you must fight us." Not a word was spoken by the Crows, and they left in small groups of three or four at a time, badly disappointed and without a cent's worth of goods. The Gros Ventres escorted our train the balance of the day and camped with us that night, and traveled with us until we reached their camp the next day at Wolfe Point. And, after that, the whole camp came with us for over one hundred miles up the valley of the Milk river. Mr. Dawson paid them well for their kindness by giving them goods.

I well remember when the steamer "Gray Eagle" made her first trip with my friend John Largent on board, who now lives at the town of Sun River. He, too, left St. Louis after having hired to the American Fur company to work at Fort Benton. At this time I was in charge of several men repairing the outside wall of the fort, which was built with sun-dried bricks, or "adobes." One day Largent was on top of the wall laying brick; suddenly he came down, saying that someone was shooting at him. I asked him if he was not mistaken; he said he was not, but that he would go and try it again. He was not there but a few seconds before he came down again saying that a bullet whistled by his head. As I was anxious to have the wall finished that day, I went up myself, but I was not there more than a minute before a rifle shot struck the brick that was in my hand, and I also came down on the double quick. Some Indians were doing the shooting from under the bank of the river, about two hundred yards off. In 1864 I went to the mines. In 1865 I formed a partnership with Malcolm Clark and obtained a charter to build a toll-wagon road through the Prickly Pear canyon, which charter we afterwards sold to James King and W. C. Gillette.

In 1868 I located this place where I now live, and where I intend to stay the balance of my life.

Mr. Lewis told me of many adventures he had during the time he was in the employ of the American Fur company, of which I have made no mention. Fort Benton at one time was the greatest fur trading point in the Northwest, but, as the whites came and settled the country, the buffaloes and all fur-bearing animals disappeared like chaff before a hurricane, and now the fur trade at Fort Benton amounts to but a trifle.

ROBERT VAUGHN.

SEPT. 12, 1899.

A Brave Piegan War Chief.

At the time of my visit to the home of Mr. Edward A. Lewis, an account of which is given in the foregoing letter, Mr. Lewis asked his wife, who was at the time busy with her house work, to come to the room in which we were sitting and tell me of the fight that occurred between the Piegans and a party of Pend d'Oreilles Indians in 1868, and in which her father was engaged. She said that the Piegans were in camp on the Teton river, about eight miles above where now stands the town of Choteau, when the Pend d'Oreilles came and made a sudden attack on the Piegans and stole several of their horses. A desperate fight followed, both parties using guns, bows and arrows, and war clubs; many were killed on both sides. She said that thinking he was dead, the Pend d'Oreille in a hurry undertook to take the rings her father had on three of his fingers. Failing to slip the rings off, he jerked a large bowie knife out of a scabbard and chopped off the fingers. During all this time her father was unconscious, and it was after the fingers were cut off that he came to his senses. Many of the Indians believed that the cutting of the fingers was the cause of his coming to life again. The women dressed his wounds and the next day the plucky war chief, Meek-i-appy, with a party of his warriors, followed the Pend d'Oreilles and the following night recaptured the horses and returned home without firing a gun or a shot from a bow.

Meek-i-appy has been dead for several years. I knew him well. He was known among the whites as Cut-Hand, but I was never aware how it came about that he lost his fingers until this narrative was told by his daughter. She told me of another instance in which her father was one of the principal actors. This time—I relate the story as it was told to me—the Crows had been stealing some of the Piegan horses. Determined to play even, a war party of Piegans, of which Mrs. Lewis' father was the chief, prepared themselves to go to the Crow country. Each warrior was equipped with all that was necessary for a horse-stealing expedition. Those who did not have guns had perfect bows, and their quivers were filled with well-pointed arrows, and the chief had with him his medicine bag, which was a weasel skin stuffed with some herbs and the bark of a certain tree; to this medicine bag two small bells were attached; it was carried on the breast and tied to a string of beads worn around the neck. It was sometime after entering the Crow country before they could locate an enemy. Finally a camp of about ten lodges was discovered in a small valley between high hills in the Little Snowy mountains, the slopes of which were covered with pine. The Piegans worked their way cautiously through the woods until within a short distance of the Crow camp and there lay hidden the balance of the day, making their plans to get away with the horses that were grazing near the tepees. When night came they again began approaching nearer and nearer the camp of the Crows. After getting to the proper distance, which was about three hundred yards from the tepees, they halted and waited until they were satisfied that all the Crows were asleep. The Crows had their horses close to their tepees and many of them were picketed. The chief was to do the stealing and mount all of his warriors with the stolen horses, for he was considered the bravest and most expert performer in the party. The chief placed his warriors behind a small grove of willows that were thick with underbrush. Then he tied several long strings of rawhide together; this he attached to a bush in the center of the grove and on the same bush he hung his medicine pouch; then he stretched the rawhide, which was about sixty yards long, to the extreme edge of the grove and most remote from the Crow camp. Now everything was ready, and the time for

"ROPING BY MOONLIGHT"—PAINTING BY CHARLES M. RUSSELL.
Courtesy Montana Historical Society, Helena; gift of Margaret Sieben and the family of Henry Sieben Hibbard.

the fray had arrived. The warriors stood behind the bushes to receive the stolen horses, and the chief sneaked towards the horses with the lariats in his hands. The first haul that was made he brought three horses, and repeated this until he had a horse for each of his warriors, who mounted and drove away the balance of the herd. Not satisfied with all the horses, Meek-i-appy determined to steal the Crow chief's medicine pouch (to steal the medicine pouch from the chief of the enemy is considered the bravest act a warrior can perform). Knowing the chief's tepee, and knowing that, according to Indian custom, all chiefs hang their medicine pouches above their heads before going to sleep, again the Piegan leader crawled slowly but surely toward the tepee of the head man of the Crow camp and stole his way inside. The Crow chief was sound asleep. When retiring only a few hours before, and when wrapping himself in his gorgeous robes, he never thought or dreamed that there was an enemy anywhere near. The Piegan reached out his hand and took the trophy that hung on a tripoon and near the sleeping chief's head; he placed it under his belt and was quietly retreating when he stumbled and fell as he was getting out at the door of the lodge. This waked the Crow and he gave the signal war hoop, "enemy in the camp." All the Crow warriors were out in an instant and came very near capturing the Piegan, but he got into the brush, where he had placed his medicine pouch, only by a scratch. In a few minutes the willow grove was surrounded by the Crows and they all began shooting into the brush. It may be well to state here that an Indian never follows an enemy into a thick brush, especially in the night time.

The Piegan by this time had hold of the rawhide string; he gave it a few jerks and the bells that were attached to the medicine pouch rang. This drew the attention of the Crows that way, and thinking that the Piegan must be there, they all began shooting in the direction of the bells, and the more they shot the oftener the bells would ring. The firing was so rapid and the flashing of the old flint-lock guns was so blinding to the Crows that the Piegan killed three of them. They could not tell the direction the shots came from, still, after they ceased firing, the Piegan, who was at the other end of the string, would occasionally ring the bells. Finally all the Crows stood together near the brush, and opposite to where the bells were ringing, and asked several questions as to who was ringing the bells. One asked in a loud voice: "Are you a man or are you a ghost?" In reply the bells rang three times. Finally the Crows, who are a very superstitious people as a tribe, went away convinced that they had killed the Piegan, and that his ghost was ringing the bells. And Meek-i-appy came out of the willows without harm, and, with the medicine bag, which was a bad medicine to its first possessor. Soon the Piegan war chief was with his warriors, who were waiting for him in a coulee that was not far off. He was mounted on the best horse and the one the Crow chief was riding the day before. After a ride of over one hundred miles in one day and a night, Meek-i-appy and his warriors arrived home safe with all their spoils.

The warrior who displayed the greatest strength, good generalship and bravery, was elected or appointed by the head chief to the honor of war chief. On account of the prudence, bravery and good generalship Meek-i-appy had always displayed, he was elected war chief and was such at the time of his death, which was about 1878.

ROBERT VAUGHN.
SEPT. 22, 1899.

Bloody Battles and Tragedies
in the Sun River Valley.

The first printed records of the Sun river we find in the travels of Lewis and Clark, who, on June 14, 1805, viewed the lower part of this fertile valley, from the bluffs near the upper falls of the Missouri river. And Captain Lewis, on his way back from the Pacific slope, came down the Medicine river valley and praised its beauty and the purity of the waters in its streams.

The Sun river was then termed by the Indians the Medicine river. The valley is sixty-five miles long. Its course is nearly east and west, extending from the Missouri river to the base of the rocky mountains, while the river itself is twice that many miles, extending far into the mountains. On the south side the bench and tablelands, that are carpeted with luxurious grasses, extend for many miles; while on the north the same kind of landscape reaches to the British possessions, a distance of nearly 150 miles. The few old Indians that are now living admit that the Rosebud and the Sun river regions have always been their favorite hunting grounds; where game of all kinds was plentiful, summer and winter alike. And today the same ranges are the most favored by the herdsmen to graze their flocks and herds of domestic animals. It was no wonder that the Indians fought desperately before giving up this, "their favorite hunting grounds."

The first thirty years of the last half century the Sun river, Teton and Marias valleys were a great field for trappers and traders belonging to the various fur trading companies, who, to a certain extent, like our traveling men now-a-days, were soliciting trade for their respective companies; consequently, many Indians would collect at the same locality, bringing with them skins of different kinds, buffalo robes, and other trinkets; these articles they exchanged for Indian goods from the traders. These valleys had always been the home of the Blackfeet nation, of which the Piegan tribe was one of the most powerful.

The beautiful and fertile valley of the Sun river has been the scene of many tragedies and bloody battles between Indians of different tribes. On account of the shallow ford on the Missouri river, on the east, giving the Crows easy access to the lower end of the valley, and the Cadotte and Priest passes, in the main range of the Rockies on the west, through which the Flatheads, Pend d'Oreilles and other warlike tribes of the Pacific slope entered the upper end, the Blackfeet tribes were always prepared for war.

The following story was written by Father De Smet, the great Indian missionary, and who, I think, was the first to preach christianity in what is now the state of Montana. Besides showing his success as a missionary, it also shows the warlike character of the Blackfeet. Father De Smet says:

"In 1840 I visited the Blackfeet Indians, who, though they are a very warlike tribe, received me with a kind welcome. On this occasion I gave them a crucifix, merely explaining to them who Christ is, and how He died on the cross for them, to bring them to heaven with Himself. Again I paid them a visit in 1855, when I was still more warmly received and welcomed; in fact, with every mark of affection. This greatly surprised me, and I was going to ask the cause of it, when I was invited to a council of the warriors of the tribe. I went and soon found myself in the presence of their great men, and of the chieftain himself, who wore on his breast the crucifix I had given him years before. When I was seated, you may guess my surprise and delight when he began his harangue to me by begging me to send them black-gowns to teach them the way to heaven. 'Black-gown,' said he, 'we know that what you teach us is true;' and when I asked what had brought this conviction to their minds, he told the following fact: 'Three snows ago,

Black-gown,' said he, 'I and my warriors, thirty in all, went on the warpath against the Crow Indians, our enemies, and we entered their territory. We knew that the moment we entered their land we were beset with dangers, and therefore we took every precaution to prevent our track being discovered. Besides, when we camped for the night we built up a kind of fortress of dead wood to protect us, in case of a surprise, from their shots and arrows. Spite of all our care, the Crow Indians discovered our trail, and during the dead of night surrounded us with a body very much larger than ours, and then raised their wild warcry. We who were within the enclosure, giving ourselves up for lost, began to sing our death song, when I bethought myself of the crucifix which you, Black-gown, gave me, and of the words you said. I saw there was no hope but in it. Then I addressed my fellow warriors, and I said to them: 'Trust in Him who died on the cross for us!' and taking the crucifix I held it aloft in my hands and prayed to the Great Spirit to save us. I then kissed the crucifix and placed it on my head, and rubbed it over my arms and breast, and gave it to my companions. They all did the same. I took the crucifix in my hand and held it before me and told them all to follow. I burst through the palisade, right in the midst of the enemy, followed by all. Shots and arrows flew about us in every direction, yet, Black-gown, owing to the power of Him whom we invoked, we passed through unscathed, not even one of us being hurt. From that moment we all longed to see the black-gown again.'"

Some time in the early fifties a bloody and desperate battle was fought between the Blackfeet and Crows which decimated both tribes, nearly half of the braves on each side being killed. Some of the fortifications that were built by the Crows then are still visible.

An account of this bloody encounter was given by Little Plume, a Piegan chief, to three old frontiersmen of the Sun

REV. P. J. DE SMET—THE FIRST MAN WHO PREACHED
CHRISTIANITY IN WHAT IS NOW MONTANA.
Courtesy Montana Historical Society, Helena

river valley, James Gibson, Judge Burcher and S. M. Carson, who at the time was on the staff of the *Sun River Sun*, and in which paper the story was published December 25, 1884.

The chief says: "When I was a boy and had not yet gained a name for myself in the annals of war, I was witness to one of the hardest fought battles ever waged in this valley. The chief of the Piegans and a small party of his followers were encamped on the river near the mountains, when one morning a deputation of Crows came in, praying that a council be made, saying that they were tired of war and wished to make a treaty that would insure peace between them for all time to come. To the council the chief readily consented, and stated that on the morrow everything would be in readiness to receive the Crow chief, as their head men were not so far away but that they could be summoned by that time. When the morrow came, the Crows and Piegans feasted together for the first, and, as it proved to be, for the last time. The council had proceeded without even so much as a sign of hostility in the past, and as to the course to be pursued in the future, it was to be one that would make the Crows and Blackfeet as one nation. Everything had progressed to the satisfaction of all. The council had adjourned to give place to feasting and dancing during the night, and to give time so that Skoon-a-taps-e-guan, a medicine man who had not arrived, might be present at the final agreement. The feasting had been one round of pleasure from the first, and much good will had been shown by both parties. Still the feast went on and "The Strong Man" had not arrived. A few more stragglers from the Crow camp farther down the valley now and then dropped in.

"With the assistance of a dog, the prying eyes of a Piegan woman found among a bundle of moccasins that had been hidden in the snow a fresh scalp, which, on closer inspection, proved to be that of a Piegan. Fearing to cry out, lest they should but give the signal for a general massacre, they quietly informed their chief of what they had found, and the chief as wisely said nothing, but after a little he quietly went out from the lodge, and, to his astonishment, he saw dangling from the neck of a Crow the identical burning glass (sun glass) with which the 'Strong Man' was wont to light his pipe. He knew then that Skoon-a-taps-e-guan would never give his consent to a treaty of peace with the Crows. Going back to the council, he told the Crows that it would be impossible for him or his people to sign the treaty of peace until the "Strong Man" had given his consent, and further, that until such consent was given they would be considered enemies. Having thus delivered himself, he walked out, being followed by several of the leading men of both tribes, who inquired his reason for thus breaking up the council. His only answer was to the Crows, whom he told to go to their camp and prepare for war. The council having been thus suddenly broken up by the Piegan chief, it was deemed by the Crows necessary to put as great a distance between the two camps as possible. They therefore hastily moved their camp down to the breaks, some fifteen miles above where the village of Sun River now stands. Here they threw up fortifications and prepared to meet the Piegans if pursued. The Piegans, on the other hand sent runners to the different camps, informing them of the murder of their medicine man and of the turn affairs had taken. By the time night came on the peaceful camp was broken by the hurrying tramp of over a thousand war horses, each carrying upon his back the sworn enemy of the Crows. The particulars of the murder of Skoon-a-taps-e-guan had been learned by several of the outside camps about the same time the chief discovered it. It seemed that the "Strong Man" had received the summons and had immediately set forth, accompanied by his assistant, and when within a few miles of their destination they were suddenly attacked from behind whilst in the act of lighting their pipes. The "Strong Man" received his death wound from the first blow, but his companion was only stunned, from which he recovered in time to see the murderous Crows hastily making off with the scalp of his leader dangling from the saddle bow of a young brave. Knowing that to stir or show any signs of life would be to bring sudden death, he lay quiet for a long time, not even daring to raise his hand to his aching head, from which the scalp had just been torn. After lying in this position for a considerable time, he raised himself to a sitting posture, from which he cautiously took in the situation, and seeing no signs of the Crows, he immediately made off as fast as his legs could carry him. Having arrived at the camp from which he and his companion had so hopefully started in the morning, he told of the tragedy in as few words as possible, and then fell exhausted on the floor of the lodge. Runners were immediately sent to all the outlying camps, informing them of what had happened, and ordering them to at once repair to the camp of their chief. So rapidly does news travel in an Indian country, that before darkness came on, several hundred warriors were with their chief, as before stated.

"On the morrow the Piegan forces were largely augmented by these new arrivals and the chief deemed it best to immediately move against the Crows, who were reported by the scouts as being intrenched at what were then called the "Breaks." Every preparation having been made, the whole force moved forward in one vast column. Soon they fell in with the Crows and drove their outposts into their trenches, and then commenced one of the most bloody battles ever fought between two nations having a red skin. The Piegans, after fighting all that day and night, finally succeeded in dislodging the enemy, who, early in the morning, began to move off down the valley. After resting until evening, they again started in pursuit, and overtook the Crows at what the white men now call the "Middle Bridge," which is about two miles below the town of Sun River. Here, if you remember, a high point of bluff puts in close to the river, affording great defensive advantages. This is where the Crows made their second stand. Bright and early on the morning of the third day, the Piegans moved forward, and, against the most fearful odds succeeded, just as night was coming on, in driving the Crows out of their intrenchments; but, owing to the peculiar formation of the bluffs at this point, it was of no great advantage, as the ground immediately beyond was as well adapted to defense as that just lost.

"The Crows had again intrenched themselves, and when morning came, yells of defiance answered the taunts of the Blackfeet. Both parties had received such reinforcements that the combatants numbered 5,000 on either side, each bent on the extermination of the other; and so near did they accomplish this, that when the fight was over five hundred Piegan warriors marked the spot where the fight was made. For two days the fight continued, the Crows yielding but a little at a time. They seemed to still have some hope of victory, but fate was against them. Just across the river from where is now Robert Vaughn's place, they made their last stand. Here the hardest fighting was done, and when the last charge was made by the Blackfeet the ground was literally piled with killed and wounded of both tribes. The Piegans were so crippled by the continuous battle that when the Crows broke from their cover and retreated down the river and across the Missouri, they were satisfied and made no effort at further pursuit. Although," said Little Plume, "it took the Blackfeet nation over twenty years to recover their strength, Skoon-a-taps-e-guan was only partially avenged. As long as there remains a Crow and Piegan, so long will there be war. When the last Crow shall have been killed, then, and not till then, will the 'Strong Man' be avenged."

LITTLE PLUME (PIEGAN CHIEF).

Little Plume was one of the chiefs who were friendly to the whites.

In the fore part of July, 1876, when the Sioux war was going on, and soon after the Custer massacre, the chiefs of the Piegans, Bloods and Blackfeet were invited by the head men of the Sioux to an Indian council held at Cypress mountain. Among the attendants was Chief Little Plume. When the Yanktons and Santees, of the Sioux nation, proclaimed a war of extermination against the whites, Little Plume would not consent, thereby breaking up the council, thus saving the lives of many settlers. Judge Burcher and Mr. John Largent, of Sun River, who have lived in northern Montana since the early sixties, always speak highly of Chief Little Plume, and at the time of his last visit he was treated kindly by those gentlemen. Little Plume is now living on the Blackfoot reservation, in this state, and holds the honorable post of lieutenant of Indian police. He is about seventy-five years of age.

Several years later a great battle was fought where is now located the Floweree ranch. I am not able to state who were the forces, except that the Blackfeet and Piegans were on one side.

Some of the old employes of the fur trading companies, who are now living, state that the old Indians who were living when they came here about fifty years ago were telling them then that the Flatheads and Blackfeet were often having great battles in the valley of the Sun river. One of these long-ago encounters took place near where is now Allick Pambron's ranch; no one can tell who were the participants. All that the oldest Indians who are now living can say as to the time this battle was fought is that it was "heap long ago." It must have been in prehistoric times, for the arrows they used then had flint points, for many of this kind of arrow points have been gathered on this old battlefield. Mrs. McKalvy, who is one of Mr. Pambron's daughters, told me a few days ago that she and her little brothers used to pick up these points off this historic spot, filling several tobacco sacks for General Gibbon at Fort Shaw.

In 1858, and near where the Sun river irrigation channel is taken from the river, an agency for the Blackfeet Indians was built. In 1866 the same Indians killed its occupants and burned the agency.

In June, 1869, a party of Piegans had come to the Healy and Hamilton trading store at Sun river crossing, with buffalo robes, pelts and furs to trade. They had with them a great many horses. At the same time there was a party of Pend d'Oreilles, whose home was west of the main range, and who were on their way back from the Judith country, where they had been hunting buffalo during the previous winter, and at this time were in camp several miles down the river. One day many of the Pend d'Oreilles were at the trading store. The Piegans suspected that there would be trouble that night. They placed their horses in a corral that was near J. J. Healy's house. Sure enough, late in the night, the Pend d'Oreilles made an attack, and, when breaking down the corral where the horses were, a desperate battle was fought, lasting about twenty minutes or more. Next morning seven dead Indians were found. One, after he was shot, fell into the well. The Pend d'Oreilles stole all the horses. The bullet holes in Healy's old house can be seen at the present time. The following night, while the Pend d'Oreilles were in camp on Flat creek, the Piegans recaptured their own horses and many more besides.

Another time a white man named Clark was killed near the Middle bridge by two Indians; one of them was hung to a tree by the citizens, and the other was shot while trying to escape. Not later than one week ago Judge Burcher, of Sun River, stated to me that he and D. H. Churchill, in 1874, were across the Missouri river, opposite the mouth of Sun river, and on the slope of the hill near where now stands the south side school house in the city of Great Falls. There they found four dead Indians, lying not far from each other. By the beadwork designs on their moccasins, the judge recognized that they were Piegans. Likely they had been killed by the Crows.

A Frenchman was murdered by Indians on the Sun river, south of Presly Rowles' house.

"Little Dog," a Piegan chief, who was friendly to the whites and lived most of the time (up to his death in 1869) in the Sun river valley, had built a low log cabin for himself and family where now is located the Birkenbuell ranch. He was a man gifted with good sense and considerable intelligence for an Indian, and was as brave as a lion. But at last he was murdered by his own people.

The following was written by J. J. Healy and appeared in the Benton *Record* in regard to this noted warrior:

"It so rarely happens that an Indian is gifted with good, solid sense that when one of this kind is born into the world he soon becomes a prominent member of his tribe. Not that Indians as a race are wanting in intelligence, but there are few whose intellect is sufficient to overcome their brutish instincts or to understand that their habits and mode of life are slowly but surely wiping them from the face of the earth.

"Little Dog, the soldier chief of the Piegans, was one of the noted exceptions to this rule. He was braver than the bravest member of his tribe, a terror to his enemies, but always a devoted friend of the whites. No doubt he inherited the universal feeling of his race that the whites were his natural enemies and oppressors, but he had the good sense to understand and acknowledge that they were the superior of his people in all things and that entire submission to their rule could only be a question of time. And these truths he endeavored to impress upon the minds of his tribe, using arguments when his great oratorical powers were likely to prevail, but adopting force when, in opposition to his commands, the warriors committed the slightest depredation upon the surrounding settlements.

"Little Dog had a son who was the father's counterpart in personal appearance, and also possessed the reckless courage and remarkable intelligence of his parent. It is said, and I have personal knowledge of more than one instance in proof of the assertion, that these two men were, in deadly encounter, more than a match for ten of the best warriors of the tribe, and such was the confidence felt in their skill and prowess that a war party under their command would follow them into the very jaws of death. I will relate one instance to show the sort of stuff these two Indians were made of.

"A war party of Piegans, consisting of twenty well armed and mounted men, had encountered six Assinaboines. The latter had taken shelter in an Indian war house, a structure built of logs and affording a strong and safe defense to those within. After fighting hard all day, the Piegans were unable to take the fortifications, and would probably have withdrawn from the contest after the sun went down. But towards evening Little Dog and his son, attracted by the firing, came up, and learning that the war house was defended by only six men, they laughed at their own warriors, the Piegans, calling them cowards and squaws, and without a moment's hesitation dashed up to the fort in the face of a deadly fire from those within, leaped over the logs, killed four of the defenders, and dragged the remaining two by the hair out of the fort and turned them over to the squaws to be put to death.

"It was no uncommon thing when a war party returned to camp with horses or other property stolen from the whites for Little Dog and his son to turn out with pistols and tomahawks in hand, and kill every one of the thieves and then return the property to its rightful owners; but when the offenders were too numerous to be punished, the two men would leave the tribe and live together with the whites until the time the improved conduct of the tribe appeased their anger.

"But the depredations of the Piegans gradually became more frequent, in spite of the efforts of the chief to prevent them, and finding at last that his threats and punishments failed to have the desired effect, he came to Fort Benton to consult with the agent as to the best course to be pursued. Gad E. Upson was then agent for the Piegans and the agency was located on Front street. The chief told his story and was advised by the agent not to kill the offenders, but to arrest them and bring them to Fort Benton and that he would punish them.

"But however much the tribe feared the great chief and his son, they were not willing to submit to this sort of treatment, and no sooner had the prisoner been turned over to the whites than they concocted a scheme to rid themselves of these dreaded men.

"While returning to camp, after delivering up the prisoner, the party, who had provided themselves with a good supply of whisky, halted near the river bank to rest and have a social time. The plotters, headed by a half-breed named Isadore, suggested that as they were liable to get drunk, they had better put away their arms to provide against accidents. Little Dog and his son gave up their weapons without hesitation, and the boy left the party to indulge in a bath in the river.

The spree then began. After the cowardly plotters had nerved themselves sufficiently for the bloody work, they secretly recovered their weapons and then began to quarrel with the chief. The latter, with his usual intrepidity, replied to their sneers and insults with contemptuous epithets, and finally brought the quarrel to a climax by kicking three of them over the river bank. The cowards then opened fire upon the defenseless chief and he fell riddled with bullets. Meanwhile the son, attracted by the noise, left the water and came to the assistance of his father. He was shot down four times, but reached the spot where his father laid and fell dead upon his body."

Many other skirmishes have taken place between Indians of different tribes in this vicinity, of which I shall make no mention, and, as Chief Little Plume said: "As long as there remains a Crow and Piegan, so long will there be war."

One more instance to confirm this statement I wish to refer to. It was in 1874. There were six of us working on an irrigation ditch near the bank of the Sun river, two miles from Fort Shaw, and on the opposite side of the river. One day, when we were eating our dinner that was spread on the sod, and near to the edge of the woods which grew thick on both sides of the stream, suddenly twelve Crow warriors rode up on us. They wanted to know how far up the valley the Piegan camp was. It appeared that the Piegans had been stealing some of their horses. Not sat-

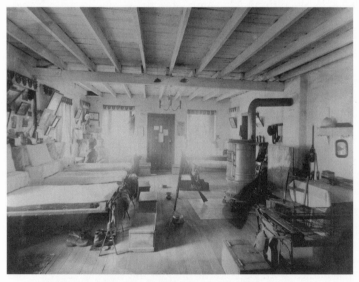

FORT SHAW, 1888-1901—INTERIOR OF ENLISTED MEN'S BARRACKS.
Courtesy Montana Historical Society, Helena

isfied with the information they sought for, they dismounted and began to take possession of our dinner. One of the Indians reached for my coffee, which was in a tin cup; just then I gave him a shove which landed him on his back on the ground but he took it in good humor. Another one grabbed Tom Cristy's tin plate which contained his dinner. Tom, being always a daring fellow, jumped to his feet and slapped the Indian in the face; it was no fun for this Indian. He gave a savage look, ground his teeth and tried to swear in English. His face, which was already red with war paint, began to get still redder. By this time indications were that there was going to be a general fight. At this juncture I invited the leader of the party to come with me, and told him I would direct him to where the Piegan camp was. He followed me up a steep hill, to the elevation of about two hundred feet, and in plain view of Fort Shaw, and, as it happened, a small squadron of soldiers were preparing for target practice. There, said I, pointing at the fort, is the Piegan camp. The Indian stared for a moment, then his jaw dropped like the lower half of a bellows, and I fancy that his complexion became nearer like that of a pale face than it ever was before. They spared no time in going down the valley as fast as their horses could carry them, and crossed the Missouri river at the ford near the place now spanned by the Great Northern railway bridge. They did not get any dinner either.

Evidently they did not know of the close proximity of Fort Shaw, for at this time they were away from their home and in the Blackfeet country.

All this goes to show that the Blackfeet nation and Crows were always enemies. Of course, "now" they are on their respective reservations, and are taught the principle of "Love thy neighbor as thyself."

ROBERT VAUGHN.
OCT. 20, 1898.

Charles Choquette Coming to
Montana in 1843.

The following sketch, from Charles Choquette, appeared in the New York Sun in the summer of 1899. Mr. Choquette says:

"My home was in the state of Missouri, near St. Louis. One day in 1843, when I was twenty years old, I went to St. Louis, and, against the will of my parents, hired to Pierre Choteau, who was the head man of a fur trading company that operated on the upper Missouri river. A few days after signing articles with the company I was put in charge of a crew to take Mackinaw boats loaded with goods to trade with the Indians. Our destination was Fort Union, which was a trading post belonging to the company to whom I hired. The distance from St. Louis to Fort Union is about two thousand miles. As oars were of little service, the big boat had to be towed nearly all the way. First on one side and then on the other, tugging on a rope, at times up to our waists in chilly water, and at other times forcing our way through brush that grew thick on the banks of the stream. After seventy-two days of hardships and dangers, we arrived safely at Fort Union, which was near the mouth of the Yellowstone river.

"It was not long before I and others were sent out along the various streams and into the mountains to trap fur-bearing animals that were very plentiful then. Many trappers had been killed by Indians, and others were continually robbed by them. It was not until I finally married a Blackfoot woman and traveled about with the tribe that I felt reasonably safe of getting my season's catch of furs to the company posts. For several years after I arrived at Fort Union I went with one or two companions each season up the Milk river to the Snowys or the Little Rockies, and about half of the time the Indians stole our furs. The first big catch I made was the time I met Jim

Bridger, the great trapper, hunter and scout, and one of the bravest men that ever lived. Now I will tell how it happened that we met.

"In the spring of 1848 we returned to Fort Union and we had only the few beaver we caught coming down the river. We had wintered up on the Fourchette, and the Assinaboines had raised our cache. We worked around the fort all summer, hunting for the company, and finally the time came for us to start out for another season's trapping. There were three of us—Antoine Busette, Louis La Breche and myself. All summer we had been trying to decide on the best place to go, where there would be plenty of beaver and where we would be likely to be safe from the Indians. We concluded to try the country of the Yellowstone. There many Indians to pass— Cheyennes and Crows and Snakes—besides the chance of war parties of other tribes, but once in the mountains beyond these people who always hunted on the plains, we felt we would be safe. We played Indian ourselves and traveled nights, hiding in some good place during the daytime.

"We left the fort late in August. Each of us had a saddle horse and two pack horses. Our outfit was simple; a couple of skillets and pots, a little bedding, an Indian lodge for shelter, a couple of axes, three dozen traps, and plenty of ammunition and tobacco. Having crossed the Missouri just below the mouth of the Yellowstone, we struck out over the rolling prairie, keeping far enough back from the latter stream to head its long coulees and breaks. None of us had ever been up the Yellowstone, but we had obtained a general idea of the country from the Indians who visited the fort. On every side there were buffalo and antelopes in countless thousands, from which we could have selected a fat one for our breakfast, but here was no water, and we were as thirsty as we were hungry; so we kept wearily on towards some wooded breaks a long ways ahead, where water as well as game was sure to be found. When we got within a mile of our destination, a dozen or more horsemen suddenly rose up out of the valley and came straight at us. Our hearts sunk; it seemed as if we had jumped out of the frying pan into the fire. Our horses were played out; we could not retreat, and were preparing to dismount and fight the best we knew how when we discovered that the strangers were white men. We had never expected to meet anything but Indians in that wild country. On they came, a big, strong, broad shouldered, flaxen-haired, and blue-eyed man in the lead, riding as fine a saddle animal as I ever saw. They were now quite close; they came within a few paces and stopped.

"'How?' exclaimed the big man.

"'How, how,' we exclaimed, shaking hands with him in turn.

" 'Who are you?' he asked, 'free trappers?'

" 'No,' I replied, 'we belong to the Company. And you?'

" 'My name is Bridger,' he said, 'Jim Bridger. Maybe you've heard of me.'

"We had. There wasn't a man west of the Mississippi river who did not know him or know of him, for he was the greatest hunter, trapper, and Indian fighter of us all. As we rode along with him and his men to their camp, we told of Indians we had seen the day before, and advised Bridger to move at once, as there was a big camp in the vicinity. He laughed, and just then we came to the edge of the valley, and, with a sweep of his hand, he said: 'Does that look much like running?'

"It didn't; around a number of small fires his band of white men—eighty in all, as we afterwards learned—were whiling away the time, smoking, cooking, cleaning guns, and mending clothes.

" 'No,' said Bridger, as he noticed our astonishment, 'we

only move when we get ready to, and God help the Indian outfit that tries to stop us. We've fought our way out here and we can fight some more.'

"This was Bridger's first trip into the Yellowstone country, he having before always trapped south of it. He told us that he left St. Louis in July and had fought his way through the country of the Sioux, the Pawnee, the Cheyenne, and the Crow, and that he intended to winter wherever he could find a good fur country. Well, we joined in with him and next day moved westward. It was on the Little Big Horn that we met him, and did not think that twenty-six years later our soldiers would be killed by the Indians there. We traveled on up the Yellowstone for a number of days until we came to the mountains, where, on a little tributary of the river, we built some cabins, got everything in shape for the winter, and then spread out over the country, each one for himself, in search of beaver and other furs. Bridger was sick nearly all winter, but kept doctoring himself with various roots he found and along towards spring recovered his health. He was unable to do any trapping himself, but his men got a big pile of fur, beaver, otter, fisher and marten, of which he owned a share. It was his intention to turn his furs over to the American Fur Company and get drafts for them on St. Louis, so when spring came we all packed up and started for the nearest post, which was Fort Cotton, situated on the Missouri river about forty miles below the Falls.

"We crossed the Yellowstone and swung up into the Musselshell country, trapping leasurely along the way, and by the time we reached the point of the Snowy mountains our animals, even the saddle horses, were so heavily loaded with furs and skins that they could carry no more. At that time of the year beaver trapping was at its best and they were so numerous that every one of us hated to quit. So we made a big cache of our furs, each one putting a tag with his name on his bundle. Three men were then sent to the fort to notify the company to come and haul in the furs, and the rest of us continued on our course, skirting the foot of the Snowy, the Judith and the Belt mountains. I never saw beaver more plentiful, and it was not long before our horses were again well laden. It was in the latter part of April that we came to the Missouri river, exactly where the city of Great Falls stands to-day. All the morning we had seen occasional Indians riding and dodging about ahead of us, and finally we came to the bank of the Missouri, opposite the mouth of Sun river and could look up that valley for quite a distance and we were not surprised to see a string of lodges scattered along the edge of the timber as far as the eye could reach 'Bridger,' says I, 'those are surely Blackfeet and we've got to fight them. Don't you think we had better find a better place to camp than this unprotected flat?'

" 'No,' he replied, 'this is good enough for us. If they come at us here I reckon they'll get their bellyful of trouble.'

"I said no more, and we went into camp beside the river, at the upper end of the flat on which the city is built. Night came on and the horses were all brought in, hobbled, and staked close to the river, and we made our beds in a circle about them, each one piling his furs, saddles, and whatever he had at the head of his couch as sort of breast-work. Double guards were put on and betimes the rest of us turned in. I don't think many of us slept much at first and the time seemed to pass slowly. At midnight the sentries were changed, Bridger himself taking a turn. It was just daylight when the air was filled with whoops, yells and the high-keyed war song of about 400 Indians, as they charged down upon us from all directions.

" 'Don't get excited, boys, and be sure of your aim. Take it easy, now,' Bridger hollered out.

"Well, 'twas good advice, and we did our best, but I tell

you the sight of 400 yelling, painted and feathered Indians coming down on you just as fast as their horses could run was mighty trying to one's nerves. I guess they expected to find us asleep and to stampede our horses in the first round. But when our rifles began to crack and some of them began tumbling out of their saddles, they were more surprised than we, and they turned and wheeled off. Some of them tried to pick up their dead, but we made it too hot for them. One fellow, who had his horse shot under him as he was trying this, lit out, running, and I guess as many as a dozen bullets struck him at once. He tumbled all in a heap. They had done some shooting, too, and two of our men were dead and one wounded. Besides that, some of our horses had been shot. We could count eleven Indians lying out on the plain here and there, and some of the boys started out to scalp them, and did get the hair off several of the nearest ones. But that brought the others back again, and for a while we had another exciting time, as some of the bravest came right at us. If the rest had followed them it would have been all day with us; but they didn't have the nerve, and of those who did attempt to close in on us few got away. One great, tall fellow had his horse shot from under him and when he struck the ground he made for Bridger, holding a wicked-looking war club in his right hand and a knife in the other. His gun was empty and he had thrown it away.

"Bridger just laughed as he saw him come, and he motioned us to let him alone. His gun was empty, too, but he had a pistol in his left. He wouldn't use that, though. When they met the Indian aimed a blow at him with his war club, but Bridger caught it on the barrel of his rifle and it flew away off to one side. Then the Indian tried to knife him but Bridger just punched him with his rifle barrel, so the fellow couldn't close in, and all of a sudden he hit him square in the forehead and smashed his skull just as cool and easy as could be. We all saw this out of the tail of our eyes, you may say, for we were pretty busy on our own account for a while. But our rifles and good shooting were too much for the Indians, and we made them draw off once more, having killed a lot of them and they only one of our party. We thought then that they had got enough of it and would go away. About 10 o'clock, however, they charged once more, but they didn't come with half the spirit they had previously shown, and in a few minutes they left us for good and recrossed the river at the ford below. That afternoon we saw them break camp and move up Sun river towards the mountains. They had left forty-seven of their number on the plains before us."

I have known Mr. Charles Choquette for twenty-nine years. He formerly lived in the Sun river valley and was engaged in farming and stock raising there for several years. He has always been considered one of our best citizens.

The home of Mr. Choquette at the present time is in Teton county in Northern Montana at the foot of the "Rockies," not far from the Great Northern railroad. He is still a prosperous farmer and stock raiser. He is seventy-six years old, but hale and hearty. Although having roughed it fifty-seven years in the "Rockies," few men twenty years his junior can keep up with him in climbing mountains and riding horseback. I do not know of one white person who is as old a citizen of what is now the State of Montana as Charles Choquette.

ROBERT VAUGHN.

GREAT FALLS, MONT., JAN. 15, 1900.

A Trip to the Twenty-Eight-Mile Spring Station.

In the fall of 1872 I made a contract with Gov. Pollinger, the manager of the Wells-Fargo stage line between Fort Benton and Helena, to furnish firewood to the Leaving and the Twenty-Eight-Mile Spring Stations. It was in the month of November that I delivered the wood to the latter place. My teams were six yoke of oxen and two wagons coupled together. The days were getting short, therefore I had to leave the ranch very early in the morning to get through in one day, for the oxen were very slow. Besides I had on the two wagons five cords of wood, which made a heavy load, and I had to travel through unsettled country all the way. I left home about two hours before daylight. The air was cold and frosty; I was watching anxiously for the sun to rise. Before long the eastern sky was colored by the beautiful Montana sunrise, soon the top of the mountains was the color of gold, and by the time I was crossing the first ridge the bright sunshine was at my feet. It was on this morning that I first saw the sun, moon and stars at the same time, for there was not a cloud in the sky. I stopped at the lakes for two hours to rest and graze the cattle, and to eat my lunch; then I yoked the oxen and started on my journey. After I had gone about two miles I discovered some Indians peeping over a small hill and apparently watching me, and as I came nearer they made their appearance for the second time and made a rush for the road a few hundred yards ahead of me. There were sixteen of them, all on foot; they had ropes and were well armed with bow and arrows and five had guns; apparently they were equipped for a horse-stealing expedition. Likely it was good for me that I had cattle and not horses. One Indian started towards me. I quickly got my gun ready and this one lifted up his hand and gave the sign that they were good Indians. He came and met me and offered his hand, at the same time saying, "Me good Indian," I shook hands with him, while at the same time I had my gun in the other hand. I did not stop the oxen, but kept them going and at the same time speaking to the Indian. He walked close to my side, and as we came to the other Indians he ordered them one by one to shake hands with me; after we got through shaking hands they all followed me. The first Indian still kept walking close to my left, as the cattle were on my right. I became suspicious of him that he might be waiting for an opportunity to grab my gun, which I had in my right hand; I kept an eye on this Indian and a firm grip on the gun. I had the whip in my other hand and now and then made a ringing crack at the oxen, for then I could use the "bull whip" to perfection. And as I was driving the oxen and calling them by their names the other Indians were walking promiscuously, some behind the wagons and others opposite to me and on the other side of the cattle. They would repeat the names of the oxen after me. It was not long before they knew the names of them all, especially Tom and Jerry, the leaders, and would laugh every time I would speak the name of the off wheeler, which was "Chief." I could not get them to tell why they were following me, but would make signs that they were going to cross the Missouri river to the Crow country. Some of them inclined to be ugly and spiteful, acting as if they wanted to make me angry. At one time one of them came from behind and gave me a shove and then ran; as he was getting away I gave him a crack with the whip; then the others would laugh and wanted me to run after him, but I stayed with the outfit, for I could see that they had some bad motive in view. Already they had traveled five or six miles with me, and by this time it was dark and I had several miles yet to go. It is true that I had lots of company to make the time short, but somehow at that time of the night, considering the complexion of my companions, I would rather have been left alone with but the cattle. When on top of the hill two miles from the station I stopped the oxen and told the Indians to get on top of the loads, for the balance of the way was down grade; in an instant they were on, and this was the first time that my left-hand bower deserted me; he was the first one to get on. When I spoke to the oxen and called on Tom and Jerry and the wagons began to move, all the Indians began to sing, and they kept up the concert until I stopped to unyoke the oxen at the station. It was fun for me to listen to their singing. Some of them humming, others barked like a fox or wolf, but they managed to keep good time and the chords were excellent; the ones that were humming would be half an octave or an octave lower than the barkers, or vice versa. I really enjoyed their singing as well they enjoyed the ride. By the time I had the yokes off the cattle I could not see an Indian. Now it was 9 o'clock and very dark, for the moon was not yet up. I had to drive the oxen to a spring, which was about a quarter of a mile off, for I knew they were very thirsty. In about half an hour I was back and got my roll of bedding off the wagon and went to the stable. Here I found the Indians peeping through the windows and cracks to see if any one was in. The stableman was there alone; the room where he cooked and slept joined the stable. He was scared nearly to death, for he had not been there long and had not seen many Indians; beside I was a stranger to him. It was some time before I could persuade him to let me in to spread down my blankets. Dutch Jake, the man who kept the station, was on the Teton, hunting buffaloes. The Indians were hungry, tired and cold. I took them to an empty cabin which was near by; the door was locked, but I took the window out. I went in and the Indians after me. Inside of the cabin we found six quarters of fresh buffalo meat with the hide on. The cabin had a good fireplace, and they soon had a fire. I told them to take a quarter of the meat; that it belonged to my friend, and that I would settle for it. I went back to the stable; the hostler had hot coffee, good bread, and plenty of fried buffalo steak for me, and I ate a hearty supper.

After supper we both went to see how the Indians were getting along, and they too, were eating broiled buffalo meat and having a good time. I got up very early the next morning, but the Indians were not to be seen. Several years afterwards I met some of those Indians, and they always remembered me.

ROBERT VAUGHN.

JAN. 28, 1898.

John Largent's Early Days in Montana.

Friend Vaughn: As per your request I give you the following sketch of my early days in what is now the State of Montana:

I hired out to the American Fur Company in the spring of 1862 at St. Louis, Mo., to go to Fort Benton at the head of navigation on the Missouri river. My pay was to be $19.50 per month, including board. I had a friend and companion by the name of Thomas Mitchell, who concluded to undergo the dangers and hardships of the three-thousand-mile trip and go with me. We took passage on a steamboat called the Spread Eagle and landed in Fort Benton ninety days afterwards; and I assure you these days were not spent in picnicking. The adventures had, the trial encountered, the hardships endured cannot be detailed in the limited space alloted for this sketch. I can only say that, while we took passage on the boat named above, it did not carry us all the way to Fort Benton by any means; in fact, the reverse happened; we tugged and carried it much of the distance. We stayed in Fort Benton during the remainder of the summer. There were no buildings in Benton at that time except the fort. Our time was occupied principally in repairing adobe buildings about the post. Andrew Dawson was chief in charge of affairs. Major Culbertson, who held some interest in the company, and who, with his wife, had made the trip from St. Louis with us, was here. About twenty-four white men comprised the entire force at the fort, and, as far as I could learn, it was fully half the white population of what is now known as Northern Montana. Matters and things had changed very materially since I had quit civilization in the "states," but I soon adjusted myself to the situation.

The Indian tribes who came here to trade were North Bloods, Mountain Crows, Blackfeet and Piegans. Coffee and tea were sold to them at one dollar per pint in trade; tobacco,

JOHN LARGENT, SR.
Courtesy Montana Historical Society, Helena

five to eight dollars per pound. Major George Steell, now so well known throughout Montana, and who was for several years the agent at the Blackfeet Agency, was then one of the trusted employes of the company. In the fall of 1862 he was sent to the mouth of the Musselshell river to build and superintendent afterwards a new trading post to be called Fort Andrews. Steell took me with him and was the means of having my wages raised from the before stated salary of $19.50 to $40 per month. I said Mr. Steell took me with him; this is incorrect, inasmuch as he sent me and my friend Mitchell overland with the horses while he himself and eight other men went down the river in a Mackinaw boat, carrying the goods and provisions. I remember the names of some of the men were as follows: W. R. Teasdale (Col. Spikes), James Chambers, William Oliver, Unica and John Wren; the three others I have forgotten.

In order that you may understand the hardships and privations endured by Mitchell and myself on this overland trip I will state that we were provided with a gun each. I had a muzzle-loading rifle; Mitchell had an old flintlock. In the way of provisions we had a few hardtacks and a small quantity of salt. There were no matches at that time to be had here. In place of them we used "flint rock," a piece of steel and gun powder. We reached our destination after being out four days and five nights. A detailed description of this trip would make an interesting sketch, but let us pass on to scenes more familiar to me.

After arriving we at once went to work building the post and other winter quarters. A house was first erected to live in, then a stockade surrounding it. Our provisions and ammunition ran short during the winter, and after that we subsisted partly on wolf meat; these animals we caught with traps; other diet I think of now was corn. A lot of this had been brought there to trade with the Indians; it was all disposed of, but the mice had carried some of it into their burroughs. This we found and dug out and ground it in a coffee mill into meal and made bread of it. The mice had eaten the kernel or heart out of this corn and it was strongly impregnated with mice pepper, but the bread fitted pretty well in our hollow stomachs. The Indians were very troublesome, and great care had to be taken to preserve our lives and property. Much of my time was engaged as hunter to secure meat for the men at the post. The post was enclosed with a stockade made of logs. At one corner there was a large gate. From the time I would be sent out to hunt, a man was placed on the outside of this gate to open it at once in case I should be run in by the Indians. I have had some close calls for my life on these occasions. One day I went out in the hills to slay some buffaloes, for we needed meat. I saw a large herd feeding and started to approach them when suddenly I heard and saw the whole herd stampeding. I rode up on a hill to better view the situation. I discovered that Indians were on both sides of me and buffaloes in front of me, and all running towards me. I saw that my only chance for life was to flee ahead of the buffaloes, and spurring my horse ahead of them, I went. The Indians discovered my intentions and tried to head me off, but by this time the herd had me surrounded and the Indians could not reach me. Finally I reached a descending bluff that separated the herd and over which myself and horse tumbled, but, again with myself in the saddle and the horse on his feet I kept going, the dust that was created had the effect of hiding me from view of the Indians long enough to reach the fort and get behind the gate. The horse that I rode on this occasion was the property of Charles Carson, one of the famous Kit Carson's family. Charles was killed some time afterwards by the Indians at Dearborn river.

I had another close call for my life by the Indians while at this fort. Bill Oliver (known as "Canada Bill") and myself went out one day to rustle for meat. Elk and deer were plentiful at that time. We had reached a point ten miles from the fort, and were on the lookout for game, also Indians. We saw Indians first and lost our interest in game. The Indians were on foot and we could easily have escaped from them on our horses, but Oliver mistook them for "friendlies" and would not run away. The Indians were coming towards us, running and yelling, when I said to Oliver "turn your horse and run!" He replied: "No, I shall not do it; these are friendly Piegans." I said: "Go to the devil, then; I am going to get out of this sage brush." I had an unbroken colt, and when I tried to move him I found he would not leave Oliver's horse. I struck at him with a small hatchet I had in my hand at the time; missing the horse my left hand caught the blow and it nearly severed one of my fingers. The Indians soon reached us, but they proved to be Bloods, a savage band, and out skirmishing for easy prey. Bill shook hands with the red devils and said "how! how!" but he was deceived, for they were on the war path and we were in imminent danger of being murdered by them at any moment. After taking my horse, gun and knife they held council for a few minutes, during which time they kept looking at me. I could understand by the signs they made that I was considered to be an important capture, while my partner Bill was not in it, so to speak. I well remember of ruminating on my chances of ever again being set at liberty. I observed upon counting that there were twenty-seven Indians of the party.

A movement forward was finally made. Three of the ugly devils had gotten astride my colt, and two on Bill's horse, he being allowed to ride with them, while I was made to walk. The party marched single file and kept me near the center of the column. My anxiety as to the object of our capture was quieted somewhat when I discovered we were moving up the river and towards the fort.

The Indians soon after got tired of packing my gun, fired

the charge out and made me pack it. Night soon came on and they camped near some dead timber and made a series of fires in one grand circle and one in the center. I was told that the center one was for me. I took a seat on the ground, and to all outward appearances was at home; but here was an inward awkward feeling that belied it. My friend Oliver was allowed certain freedom to move about, but I was carefully guarded; however, I was not roasted, as they threatened. During the evening no supper was eaten; and I must confess I did not sleep very well that night. The next morning an Indian brought me a small piece of raw meat and gave me a pointed stick to reach out over the fire and cook my meat on. My wounded finger was paining me some now, the excitement having subsided somewhat. Soon after daylight we started on the move again, the imps still keeping a close watch on me. During all this journey we were heading towards the fort, and there I learned that I was being held for ransom, and that the object in going there was to offer the American Fur Company my freedom for a certain consideration. The Indians sent Oliver with two of the party to the fort to state the terms, which were a quantity of blankets, coffee, tea and tobacco. George Steell soon came out and paid them what they asked and I was again at liberty. I thus became indebted to the company for quite a sum of money, for it must be remembered that these goods were very expensive here at that time. However, I was glad to get back to the fort once more; but I was mad at those Indians and have not yet forgiven them for the manner in which they treated me.

A Peculiar Incident.

In connection with this story, and while held here in the hands of the Indians, and about the time Steell arrived with my value in goods, another white man was captured and brought into the Indian camp. This man was none other than Nels Kies, the prospector, who is known to have discovered and worked a gold mine somewhere in the lower country, and but a short time after this occurrence, and who, to the disappointment of many, was killed by the Indians before the location of his mines was made known. Our honored citizen, John Leply, and others were interested in this discovery, but on account of Kies being killed the mines never have been found. It may be that the "Nels Kies lost mines" are in the vicinity of Fort Andrews. Kies was allowed to go to the fort with us, but remained only a short time when he departed alone, stating that he was going to his camp.

We had a number of scraps with the Indians at this post. They came in once ostensibly to trade, but in reality to clean us out. George Steell, who was in the trading house, discovered their intentions and calling the boys to arms checked them before they started to murder us.

At the time of which I speak the Gros Ventres and Mountain Crows were at war with each other, and their battle grounds were near Fort Andrews. In one battle fought here it was estimated that one-fourth of the warriors on each side were killed. One morning, just at daylight, an alarm was given, and someone shouted: "Hostile Indians in the corral!" All rushed out at once and discovered a party of Indians and one of them leading away my favorite saddle horse. I forced my way forward and took hold of the rope attached to the animal's neck and made a sign to the Indian that I loved that horse and would not part with him without trouble. He said that he was going to keep him and motioned me to let go of the rope. I refused. He then strung his bow and pointed the arrow at my breast. I still held on to the rope and told him that he might kill me, for I would not give up my horse. He then struck me in the breast with an arrow, cutting me quite freely, so much so that I felt blood running down my body. I then let go of the rope, mentally resolved that if I ever got an opportunity I would make a good Indian out of that fellow. He was killed about two years after this by one of a party of white men out hunting for Crows.

A Bear Story.

My friend Mitchell, having made up his mind to return to his home in Illinois, desired to kill a bear before leaving the West, and I was very anxious that his wish should be gratified and sought every means to aid him to get his bear. One morning a splendid opportunity came for this. I discovered a bear passing down a trail close to the fort. I hustled my friend outside the enclosure. A tree had fallen near the trail mentioned, and to it I piloted Mitchell, who, while in hiding there, was instructed to shoot the bear at close range and in a vital part which I pointed out was directly behind the shoulder. Watching Mitchell, I gave the word to fire and at the same time shot at the bear myself, fearing his shot might not be a deadly one. The bear fell, growling and roaring in the underbrush. I then asked Mitchell where he hit him, and he said in the heart. I then proceeded to reload my gun and requested him to do the same, and when he did so, he discovered his gun cocked and still charged—he had not fired it off at all. I was mortified over this because I wanted the boy to at least think he had killed a bear and be able to tell the story when he arrived home. The following sketch will show, however, that this was all useless, for he never again met the loved ones at home:

About the first day of August, 1863, there came a Mackinaw boat down the river from Fort Benton with a party composed of fourteen men, one woman and her two children. These people had come overland from the Frazier river mines, by the way of Bannock, and had in their possession a considerable quantity of gold. At Benton they built their boat. The party stayed with us for several days making some repairs. The men built breastworks on the boat for protection against Indian attacks. During this time the lady and her children stayed in the fort. My friend Mitchell, who, as before mentioned, being homesick, determined to return with the party. He used much persuasion to induce me to return with him. The risk of losing one's life in going or remaining was equally great, and I chose to stay where I was. So we separated.

One bright morning they bade us good bye and the little craft started on its long voyage down the Missouri river, with all on board jolly and happy. Five days afterwards we received news of the massacre of the entire party by the devilish Sioux Indians. It was never revealed to the whites just how it was done. A half-breed Indian reported at Fort Berthold the finding of the bodies horribly mutilated, the remains of the men laying on a sand bar with their feet in the water; having been placed there by the Indians; the woman was found hanging by the chin, hooked on the limb of a tree, and the children, one on each side of the mother, hanging the same way. The Indians apparently knew nothing of the value of gold, for they had cut the buckskin sacks containing it and strewn it all about the bar. Some of it was gathered up by half-breeds and taken into Forts Randall and Berthold some time afterwards.

Jerry Potts, a half-breed Indian, who lived and worked with us at Fort Andrews, started out with a companion one day to go to Fort Gilpin, a trading post at the mouth of Milk river. The Indians got after them and they retreated and came back to the fort. Potts was carrying a powder horn which was pierced by an arrow thrown by an Indian while they were retreating, the horn saving him from being killed. Some time after this we got orders from Fort Benton to move to this post and a boat was sent to us to transport our goods down the

Missouri river from Fort Andrews to Fort Gilpin. I had orders to take charge of the boat and send our horses overland in charge of two of the men. The boat crew was to be provided with firearms, including a small cannon, which were to be used in case of attack by foes. After we got the goods on board and ready to start, I found that none of the men would take the horses on account of the danger of being taken in by the Indians, so I was compelled to make the overland trip myself. I selected Chambers to accompany me, and Colonel Spikes to take charge of the boat crew and about seventeen thousand dollars' worth of goods, and he holloed "all aboard for Gilpin," and moved away. Chambers and myself soon after started for the same point overland. We traveled mostly by night, under cover of darkness, in order to avoid the Indians stealing our horses and killing us.

We succeeded very well until the last night out, when we left the hills about twenty miles west of Fort Gilpin to go to some timber near a point then called Dry Fork, now called Big Dry. I took the lead and Chambers brought up the rear. Soon I heard a dog barking, saw a dim light in the distance and in front of us, I concluded at once we were running into a nest of Indians. I gave Chambers the danger signal (a smothered whistle sound); this he returned, and, turning around, we retraced our route back to the hills and then made a circle around the Indians undiscovered by them, arriving at Fort Gilpin just at daybreak. While at breakfast, soon afterwards we heard the report of a cannon, and knew at once that our boat was near by; that the men on board were attacked by Indians, and that a fight was on. The very Indians that Chambers and myself avoided were at that time in hiding, waiting to capture this boatload of goods. As we subsequently learned they got these goods without much fighting, and, of course, all the blame for the loss of them was thrown on me, by the owners, just because I did not do as instructed or as was expected of me, which was to stay with the goods. It seems the party was attacked while moving along in the boat and the men ran it to land, took the cannon out and fired one shot at the redskins, then ran to the brush near by. The Indians, being satisfied with their capture of the goods, did not follow them, and they reached the fort unharmed, except a few scratches received in the scramble to get away from danger. I remember we all stood at the gate watching eagerly to learn the outcome of the fight, when, suddenly, a man came out of the willows; he was hatless and his hair stood pompadour, one foot shoeless and his clothes torn in strips. This was Colonel Spikes; following him came the six others before mentioned. They reported that a large party of Indians, probably a hundred and fifty strong, had attacked them with results as stated above. Our force was too small to go out and fight them, so we stayed in the fort until they left. We then went out and found that all there was left of seventeen thousand dollars' worth of goods was the cannon. The Indians had taken away, and otherwise destroyed, everything else. The robes and furs were thrown into the river and the other goods carried away. Major Dawson was coming up along the river from Fort Berthold with an extra wagon train of goods bound for Fort Benton. Chambers and myself went out and met him, and Chambers informed him of the loss of the goods. Dawson looked at me and said: "Where in hell were you, John?" I explained to him that I was compelled to bring the horses, as no one else would do it. He said: "That accounts for the loss of seventeen thousand dollars' worth of goods and not a man killed," and he added: "If you had stayed with the goods they would not have been lost."

We joined the men with the train here and went up the Milk river part of the way, thence to Fort Benton. This was about the last days of October, 1864. We had many Indian encounters on our way up to Benton, but reached there in safety. I stayed here about fifteen days, and then pulled out for Virginia City. This was a long trip to make, taken in the winter as it was, and at a time when the road agents were bad, a description of which would make interesting reading, but this was to be a short sketch of my first days in Montana, so I must quit.

Your friend,

JOHN LARGENT.

SUN RIVER, MAY 10, 1899.

There are not many men in the state that I am more familiar with than John Largent, having been neighbors for nearly thirty years. He is six feet two inches in height, rawboned, and of sanguine temperament. Though he is over sixty years of age, he has a good head of hair and not a single gray one. He is a Virginian by birth.

It is easy for those that know him to understand why the American Fur company depended upon and trusted so much to John Largent. It was because he was always honest, trustworthy, had good judgment to carry out the part of the work assigned him, and could stand any amount of fatigue, besides he feared nothing. In his earlier days he was a remarkably good shot with the rifle; few men equaled him in this respect. He became versed in the language of most of the northern tribes of Indians, and was feared and respected by them. It was a fact that many of the young warriors feared him because he was so remarkably quick and accurate with his old "Kentucky rifle."

ROBERT VAUGHN.

GREAT FALLS, MAY 15, 1899.

A Visit to Fort Benton.

It was in the early seventies I visited Fort Benton, the town at the head of navigation of the Missouri river. It was a busy place then, for it was in the summer and during the boating season, and the time the traders were bringing their collections of robes, pelts and furs, and shipping them, principally to Sioux City and St. Louis. Fort Benton, no doubt, is the oldest town in Montana. It was built in 1846 by Alexander Culbertson, who was the head of a fur trading company. The buildings were occupied by this company for many years. It was two hundred and fifty feet square and built of adobe. At one time since then it was occupied by the military; parts of the walls still stand (1898).

In the volume of 1876 of the Historical Society of Montana there is a very interesting sketch of the fur traders and trading posts under the title of "Adventures on the Upper Missouri," in which Fort Benton is spoken of. This sketch was written by the late James Stuart, after obtaining his information from the best authorities. I cannot think of anything more interesting or more appropriate at this time than to give the following extracts from Mr. Stuart's writings:

"Fort Union was the first fort built on the Missouri river, which is above the mouth of the Yellowstone. In the summer of 1829 Kenneth McKenzie, a trader from the upper Mississippi, near where St. Paul, Minnesota, is now located, with a party of fifty men came across to the upper Missouri river looking for a good place to establish a trading post for the American Fur Company. (McKenzie was a member of that company.) They selected a site a short distance above the mouth of the Yellowstone river, on the north bank of the Missouri, and built a stockade two hundred feet square of logs, about twelve inches in diameter and twelve feet long, set perpendicularly, putting the lower end two feet in the ground, with two block-house bastions on diagonal corners of the stockade, twelve feet square and twenty feet high, pierced with loop holes. The dwelling house, warehouses and store were built inside, but not joining the stockade, leaving a space of about four feet between the walls of the buildings and the stockade. All the buildings were covered with earth, as a protection against fire by incendiary Indians. There was only one entrance to the stockade—a large double-leaved gate, about twelve feet from post to post, with a small gate three and a half by five feet long, on one of the leaves of the main gate, which was the one mostly used, the large gate being only opened occasionally when there were no Indians in the vicinity of the fort. The houses, warehouses and store were all built about the same height as the stockade. The above description, with the exception of the area enclosed by the stockade, will describe nearly all the forts built by traders on the Missouri river from St. Louis to the headwaters.

"The fort was built to trade with the Assinniboines, who were a large tribe of Indians ranging from White Earth river, on the north side of the Missouri, to the mouth of Milk river, and north into the British possessions.

"In 1832 the first steamboat named the 'Yellowstone,' arrived at Fort Union. From that time, every spring, the goods were brought up by steamboats, but the robes, peltries, etc., were shipped from the fort every spring by Mackinaws to St. Louis. In the winter of 1830 McKenzie, desirous of establishing a trade with the Blackfeet and Gros Ventres (the Minatarees of Lewis and Clarke), sent a party of four men—Burger, Dacoteau, Morceau, and one other man in search of the Indians and to see if there was sufficient inducement to establish a trading post. The party started up the Missouri river with dog sleds to haul a few presents for the Indians. They followed the Missouri to the mouth of the Marias river, thence up the Marias to the mouth of Badger creek, without seeing an Indian, finding plenty of game of all kinds and plenty of beaver in all the streams running into the Missouri. Every night when they camped they hoisted the American flag, so that if they were seen by Indians during the night they would know it was a white man's camp; and it was very fortunate for them that they had a flag to use in that manner, for the night they camped at Badger creek they were discovered by a war party of Blackfeet who surrounded them during the night, and, as they were about firing on the camp, they discovered the flag and did not fire, but took the party prisoners. A part of the Indians wanted to kill the whites and take what the party had, but through the exertions and influence of a chief named 'Good Woman,' they were not molested in person or property, but went in safety to the Blackfoot camp on Belly river and stayed with the camp until spring. During the winter they explained their business, and prevailed upon about one hundred Blackfeet to go with them to Fort Union to see McKenzie. They arrived at Fort Union about the 1st day of April, 1831, and McKenzie got their consent to build a trading post at the mouth of the Marias. The Indians stayed about one month, then started home to tell the news to their people. McKenzie then started James Kipp, with seventy-five men and an outfit of Indian goods, to build a fort at the mouth of the Marias river, and he had the fort completed before the winter of 1831. It was only a temporary arrangement in winter, in order to find out whether it would pay to establish a permanent post. Next spring Colonel Mitchell (afterwards colonel in Doniphan's expedition to Mexico) built some cabins on Brule bottom to live in until a good fort could be built. The houses at the mouth of the Marias were burned after the company moved to Brule bottom. Alexander Culbertson was sent by

McKenzie to relieve Mitchell and to build a picket stockade two hundred feet square on the north bank of the Missouri river, which he completed during the summer and fall of 1832. This fort was occupied for eleven years, until Fort Lewis was built by Culbertson on the south side of the Missouri river, near Pablois Island, in the summer of 1844. Fort Brule was then abandoned and burned. In 1846 Fort Lewis was abandoned, and Fort Benton was built by Culbertson, about seven miles below Fort Lewis, on the north bank of the Missouri river. It was 250 feet square, built of adobe laid upon the ground without any foundation of stone, and is now standing (1875) and occupied as a military post. The dwellings, warehouses, stores, etc., were all built of adobes. The Piegans, Blackfeet and Blood Indians, all talking the same language, claimed and occupied the country from the Missouri river to the Saskatchewan river. Prior to the building of the winter quarters at the mouth of the Marias, they had always traded with the Hudson Bay Company and the American Fur Company. The Hudson Bay Company often sent men to induce the confederated Blackfeet to go north and trade, and the Indians said they were offered large rewards to kill all the traders on the Missouri river and destroy the trading posts. McKenzie wrote to Governor Bird, the head man of the Hudson Bay Company in the north, in regard to the matter, and Bird wrote back to McKenzie, saying: 'When you know the Blackfeet as well as I do, you will know that they do not need any inducements to commit depredations.'

"In 1832 McKenzie sent Tollock, with forty men, to build a fort at the mouth of the Big Horn river. Tollock built the fort named Van Buren, on the south side of the Yellowstone, about three miles below the mouth of the Big Horn river. It was 150 feet square, picket stockade, with two bastions on diagonal corners. In 1863 I saw the location. The pickets showed plainly that they had been burned to the ground, and several of the chimneys were not entirely fallen down. The fort was built to trade with the Mountain Crows, an insolent, treacherous tribe of Indians. They wanted the location of their trading post changed nearly every year, consequently they had four trading posts built from 1832 to 1850, viz.: Fort Cass, built by Pollock on the Yellowstone, below Fort Buren, in 1836; Fort Alexander, built by Lawender, still lower down on the Yellowstone river in 1848, and Fort Sarpey, built by Alexander Culbertson in 1850 at the mouth of the Rose Bud. Fort Sarpey was abandoned in 1853, and there have not been any trading forts built on the Yellowstone since up to the present time (1875). Kenneth McKenzie, after Lewis and Clarke, was the pioneer of the upper Missouri. He was a native of the Highlands of Scotland. When young he came in the service of the Hudson Bay Company, and started to explore the country from Hudson's Bay to Red river to Lake Winnipeg; thence to the Lake Superior country; finally concluded to locate on the upper Mississippi. In 1822 he went to New York and got an outfit of Indian trade goods on credit and established an Indian trading post on the upper Mississippi and remained in that part of the country until 1829, when he came to Missouri and established Fort Union. He was in charge of all the Northwestern fur trade until 1839, when he resigned to enter the wholesale liquor trade at St. Louis, Mo. He resided at St. Louis until his death in 1856 or 1857. Alexander Culbertson assumed his position as fur trader in 1839."

The town of Fort Benton was first surveyed by Colonel De Lacy in 1859. Choteau county was established by the legislature in an act approved Feb. 2, 1865, with the county seat at Fort Benton. The county was named in honor of Pierre Choteau, Jr., the president of the American Fur Company. Major George Steell, now of Dupuyer, Teton county, was one of its first coun-

ty commissioners. Fort Benton was named in honor of Thomas
H. Benton, United States Senator from Missouri.

In 1864 the American Fur Company sold their interests to
the Northwestern Fur Company. After that many other traders
erected posts throughout the territory. Those in the northern
part had their headquarters at the town of Fort Benton. Many
steamboats loaded with furs, pelts and robes left the wharf of
this old town during the period from 1860 to 1880. At the time
of the visit referred to there were many representatives of the
large fur companies on their annual visit from the East to in-
spect the business of their respective companies. There were
also Indian commissioners who had been sent by the government from Washington to close some deal with the Indians; of
course all the Indian chiefs were there, besides many other In-
dans, "ox-drivers" (bull whackers) and steamboat hands. One
day, when these Eastern visitors were in town, a pack train arrived from one of the trading posts. On the back of one of the
mules was a small brass cannan (mountain howitzer); it was
lashed on with the muzzle towards the rear end of the mule.
The government representative seized the opportunity to
show the Indians what a terrible weapon that was on the back
of the mule. The animal, with his burden, was led to Front
street, and a crowd of two or three hundred followed, half of
which were Indians. It was decided to fire a few shots from
the cannon while it was on the back of the mule at a high-cut
bank that was half a mile away and across the river. A certain
spot was shown to the Indians where the shot was supposed
to hit, and, to strike the spot designated on the clay bank,
which loomed up like some old castle, an extra heavy load
was put in. Finally the man in charge of the mule stood in front
of the quadruped with the rings of the bit in each hand. Now
he has the business end of the mule where he wants it; another man was adjusting the cannon, and taking aim, while

the third one took a match from his vest pocket, scratched it on the hip of his pants and touched the fuse. The hissing sound of the burning fuse made the mule lay down his ears and began putting a hump in his back; next thing he whirled round and round, in spite of his manager trying to get him back to his first position. By this time everybody was going for dear life, and the mule was making the circle faster than ever, and the gun was liable to go off at any moment. There was a perfect stampede; many went over the bank into the river, others were crawling on their hands and knees, while many laid flat on the ground, broadcloth and buckskin alike—the man held to the bridle and the mule held the fort. Luckily, on account of the bend in the mule's back, the shot struck the ground but a short distance from his heels. Many of the Indians never moved, thinking that the maneuvers of the mule were a part of the performance.

J. J. Healy (now Captain Healy, the manager of the North American Transportation and Trading Company) was there. Healy had fought Indians and assisted in arresting some of the worst desperadoes in the Northwest, who were terrorizing the country about that time But the mule was too much for him, as he was seen going for dear life over the bank into the river. It was the first time anyone ever saw Healy "take water."

The same cannon is now owned in Great Falls and was used to celebrate the Fourth of July, 1898. The mule could not be found.

It was a common occurrence then at Fort Benton to see six to eight steamers tied at the wharf at the same time and loaded for their return trips with robes, furs and pelts. The principal articles the traders had for traffic with the Indians were blankets, blue and scarlet cloth, calico, domestic goods, ticking, tobacco, knives, fire steel, arrow points, files, brass wire of different sizes, beads, brass tacks, wide leather belts,

"THE MULE AND THE MOUNTAIN HOWITZER."

silver ornaments for the hair, shells, axes and hatchets. Many articles were smuggled and traded to the Indians which the law prohibited. The articles brought by the Indians for trade were elk, deer, antelope, bear, wolf, beaver, otter, fox, mink, marten, wild cat, skunk and badger skins, and principally buffalo robes. At the time when the country was literally covered with buffaloes, and before the traders were in the country to supply the Indians with guns or even steel arrow points, the

Indians would move from place to place with two or three hundred lodges or tepees, with from five to seven people to the lodge. The tepees were made of tanned skins and a few small poles and so constructed that they could be taken down and put up in a few minutes.

With the poles, that were about fifteen feet long, they would make their travois by placing a number of poles on each side of a pony and tying one end of them to the girth of the saddle from which a strap reached across the breast of the animal. Then two cross-sticks, about four feet apart, were tied to each bunch of poles and close to the horse, and on these sticks a buffalo rawhide was stretched in a basket-like manner on which a stack of robes, pelts and furs was lashed. Each family had one or more of these simple conveyances, arranged as the one to the left in the illustration. In these they would carry their small trinkets, young pappooses, and the old people that were too old to ride a pony. In this way they would move from camp to camp with perfect ease and without delay, following the great herds of buffalo. When they needed meat the chief would give orders to make "a round." Under the direction of the war chief several hundred would turn out, some on horses, others on foot, and would quietly surround a herd of the buffaloes, and, closing up the circle, the buffaloes would run round and round in a circle, and as the outside ones would go by the Indians killed them with their arrows. The buffalo, the same as sheep, would follow the leaders, and, after getting them started in one direction, they would all follow that way. I know a place near where I used to live on Sun river where the Indians a long time ago used to surround the buffalo and run them over a precipice, and at a point where there was but room for one at a time to go in safety. The Indians would get a few to start, then close up on the big herd and rush them over the cliffs pell-mell; hundreds would be killed and many

GROS VENTRE WOMAN AND TRAVOIS.
Courtesy Montana Historical Society, Helena

crippled, and those they would kill with the bows and arrows. They called this manner of hunting "a run."

There are now on this spot great quantities of decayed bones, and hundreds of flint arrow points have been picked up by settlers. Professor Mortson, of this city, has in his cabinet now several hundreds of these points which he found. There is another place of this kind near St. Peter's Mission, where these runs were made.

Now the buffaloes are extinct. Where they used to roam, flocks of sheep and herds of cattle now graze. And the Indians' mode of living, since they are on their reservation, is entirely different. "Now" they live in houses, and the old Indian tepees made of skins cannot be found.

Until but a few years ago, the "Old Town at the head of navigation" was a great Indian trading post; her stores and warehouses were filled with Indian goods and their trade was exclusively with Indians. Today Fort Benton is a modern city with brick blocks, has a fine courthouse, public schools and churches, and many attractive homes. She has a railway depot, water works and many other modern improvements.

At the entrance of one of the main avenues of the city a steel drawbridge spans the Missouri river. And now her business houses carry the same kind and as fine goods as Eastern firms; her warehouses are filled with miners' tools, machinery, and all kinds of agricultural implements for the trade of hundreds of thrifty farmers, who are cultivating the land which was but a short time ago the red man's hunting ground.

ROBERT VAUGHN.

JULY 11, 1898.

John D. Brown.
A Narrative of His Early Experience in the West.

One day last December, when standing on the corner of Central avenue and Third street, Great Falls, I saw a lame old man coming towards me. Though his hair was white as snow, his cheeks were as rosy as those of a schoolboy, and, as he came to me and grasped me by the hand, he said: "Well, Mr. Vaughn, I came to town to pay my taxes, and as you have already asked me to come and stay at your house, I shall now accept the invitation and tell you the story of my early days in the West." The old gentleman referred to was John D. Brown, one of the first pioneers in the part of the country which now comprises the state of Montana.

That evening Mr. Brown related to me the following experiences:

I left St. Paul, Minnesota, in September, 1858, in company with George Wakefield, William Fairweather and others. We had decided to go to Colville, Washington territory, crossing the Rocky mountains through the Kootenai pass in the British possessions. At Sauk Rapids we met several Frenchmen, among them being the three Mauchoirs boys, the two Besoits, Shirlepeau and Felix Odell, all Canadian Frenchmen. On the eighth of October we crossed the Mississippi river at Crow Wing among floating ice, then we made a big campfire, and slept with our feet to the fire. Bill Fairweather was my bedfellow. We awoke in the morning to find a foot of snow on top of us. After breakfast we traveled through the deep snow and were overtaken by Tom McDonald, a Scotchman, an old fur trader, and with whom we camped at Otter Tail for a few days in order to rest our animals. There were but very few settlers at Otter Tail at that time. The Frenchmen had ox teams and we had horses. We had with us a year's supply of provisions.

The first night we camped after leaving Otter Tail the Chippewa Indians stole everything we had; then we were, of course unable to proceed on our journey, and so we returned to McDonald's place and remained there a week. There was a government surveying party making their headquarters there then. McDonald and the surveyors explained to the Indians that we were on our way to the Pacific coast, and the consequence was that we recovered our property; also the Indians gave us the right of way to cross their country the same as the Hudson Bay people had. Starting out again, one day we met an old half-breed carrying mail, who misdirected us as to the way we should go and, when it was time to camp, there was neither water nor fuel to be had, and a foot of snow was on the ground, and it was several degrees below zero. It was twelve o'clock at night before we found a place to camp where there was wood and water. We turned our animals out to eat rushes, which were plentiful. At daybreak the next morning, the oxen came running madly out of the timber with three moose after them, evidently the moose thinking that the oxen were of their own species. The oxen stampeded and the moose were right behind them, keeping them going through the deep snow, until all were out of sight. Two of the Frenchmen followed and were gone the entire day without having first had their breakfast, and it was about midnight when they returned with the oxen, after having followed them and the moose for at least thirty miles, and when they caught up with the outfit the moose were still with the oxen. On account of this chase it became necessary for us to stay in camp for a couple of days to allow the men and the oxen to rest themselves. Finally we arrived at Pembina, where Joe Rolette kept a trading post. He was pretty well fixed financially. After staying at Rolette's place for a few days, we crossed the Red river on the ice, destined for Fort Geary (now Winnipeg), which was supposed to be about sixty miles from Pembina, and which place we reached about Christmas. At Fort Geary everybody spoke French, with the exception of some English soldiers stationed there.

As by that time winter had set in and the snow was getting deep, we concluded to stay there until spring. Bill Fairweather and I went to work cutting logs for a man named McDonald. We hewed the logs on four sides, for which we received fifty cents for every ten feet, running measure. We worked there until spring (1859) and made considerable money.

Early that spring Bill Sweeney, Henry Edgar, Bill Fairweather, George White, Tom Healy, and others of the party, started on their western journey by the Kootenai pass. Larry Campbell (who used to keep a store at Diamond City, in Meagher county), Jack Brash, Sandy Gibson, Jim Wandel, Bill Smith and I decided to take the Milk river route, and thence down the Blackfoot river on the Pacific side of the Rocky mountains. After arriving on the Assiniboine river, we camped there for a few days. Here we met one of the Catholic fathers, with whom we signed an agreement to raft logs down the Assiniboine river and deliver them by the middle of May. As we were all good river men, we did very well. The logs were to be used to build the Palestine Mission. At that time there was an American named John Morgan who was a trader for the American Fur company at Fort Union, and who was married to a daughter of Chief Firewind of the Assiniboine tribe. Morgan had started another trading post on the Canada side, he being an American, having come from the state of Ohio. We bought what goods we needed from him. His mother-in-law came over frequently on a visit, and, as we stopped at Morgan's place during most of the winter, she got to know us very well, and, owing to the further fact that we were the very best of friends with Morgan, she naturally took a liking to us.

About the first of April I came to Morgan's trading post to

get a stock of provisions to use on the rafting trips. Morgan had gone to Fort Geary and the old lady was left in charge of the goods. Morgan had told her to let the American boys have anything they wanted. I remained there until Morgan returned, and during this time the old woman treated me kindly. Shortly after his return, he said to me, "Now, Mr. Brown, the old lady is going back home in a couple of days and, as you will be going that way, she might be of some service to you. It would be a good idea for you to make her a small present." I was pretty flush with money, so I bought her a couple of dresses and a Cree war blanket for her to give to the chief, and a lot of beads and trinkets, amounting probably to twenty-five dollars for the whole outfit. In a few days she left for her home camp on the American side.

About the first of May we got through rafting and started westward. Some days we would travel but ten miles. Buffalo were plenty and we killed fat ones and dried the meat to use on our journey. On the 25th day of May we espied an Assiniboine Indian coming towards us; he was on horseback. Presently we saw another, by and by another, and they kept on increasing. We had plenty of ammunition, but they were ten to our one. Well, they captured us, took us to their camp as prisoners and held a war dance over us and threatened to kill us. They stripped us of everything we had, clothing and all. Just then it happened that the old squaw to whom I made those presents was in the Indian camp, and when she saw me she ran and placed her hands upon my neck and kissed me and conducted us to the chief's tent, which was also her own, and she cooked dinner for us. Then she brought out the articles that I had given her at Morgan's trading post, and she held in her hand the Cree war blanket and the pipe that I gave her to hand to the chief, while at the same time she was pointing to me and telling him that I was the man that gave them. After that I was at liberty to

JOHN D. BROWN.
Courtesy Montana Historical Society, Helena

go around the camp and out hunting, and so forth, but my companions were put in a tepee and a guard kept over them night and day. At that time we did not know whether we were in the British possessions or on the American side. We were captured close to what is known as the Widow mountain. We were kept prisoners for six weeks and shamefully treated during this time. The poor old squaw worried a great deal on account of the condition we were in. She could talk a few words of English, and she did all she could to console us by telling us that we would not be killed, and so on. I am satisfied that she was the cause of our not being murdered at the time they stripped us.

When Major Schoonover, who was the Indian agent at Fort Union, heard of our being captured, he sent out his interpreter to tell Firewind and Antelope, both Assiniboine chiefs, to bring in the white prisoners to him, and that unless they did so they would get no annuities for that year. We were about two weeks getting in; we reached Fort Union on the morning of the 4th of July. We related to Major Schoonover all the facts in relation to our having been taken prisoners, and where we were from and where we were going. He took us up-stairs to his room and said, "Well, boys, this is the 4th of July." We had lost track of the day of the month, and did not know that it was the 4th of July until then. He treated each of us to a good drink of brandy. He asked me where my home was, and I told him that my parents lived in the city of Providence, Rhode Island. He asked the others the same question. Well, Bill Smith was from Baltimore, Jim Wendall from Piclo, Nova Scotia (he was killed in 1863 by Slade, a desperado, when on a freighting trip from Cow Island; Slade was afterwards hanged in Virginia City by the vigilantes). All the others were from Canada. The only true American in the lot was Bill Smith. I was born in Ireland, being three years old when my parents came to Providence.

The major sent for all the chiefs and had a council with

them, at which we were present. He told them that we were going across into Washington territory, and that he wanted them to give us the right to cross the country and not detain us again; and he further told them to bring everything that they took from us or he would have to give us goods out of their annuities. The Indians returned to us all of our property and promised not to trouble us any more. The old squaw, when we were leaving, came and shook hands with all of us and expressed gratification at our being safe. We came up the Milk river valley. At the big bend, near what is now Fort Browning, I first saw a grizzly bear. From there we came to Fort Benton and remained there until the spring of 1860.

Captain Mullan was then constructing the Mullan road from Walla Walla to Fort Benton. He wanted men to build bridges, and, as we were all good ax men, we hired out to him. Major Blake had command of several companies of recruits that came up the river to Fort Benton. They were on their way to Colville, Washington territory. The only houses I saw then between Fort Benton and Missoula were those of Johnny Grant, a half-breed who lived at Deer Lodge, and Bob Dempsey, an old discharged soldier, who lived between Gold Creek and what is now Radersburg. He had an Indian woman for a wife. That summer we built a bridge over the Blackfoot river and another over the Big Blackfoot. There were but few white people living there then. I remember Captain Higgins, Baron O'Keefe and old man Moues, who was running a kind of mill and grinding meal for the Indians, and Lou Brown, a Hudson Bay trader, who took charge of a ferry that Mullan built. There were few other white men who lived there then. We went clear through to the Coeur d'Alene; we got there in the month of September. From there we went to Wolf Lodge and crossed the St. Joe river and went down by where the city of Spokane now is; thence to Walla Walla, where we arrived on the 8th of October, 1860. There we separated, John Peterson, who was with me, working for Mullan, and I went to the Dalles in Oregon.

From there I went to the Cascade Falls on the Columbia river. That fall I voted for Stephen A. Douglas for president. When at the Cascades, I worked for the Oregon Navigation company, hewing timber for ship building, for which I received twenty-five cents per foot. At this place myself and two other men hewed a remarkable stick of timber, it being one hundred and thirty feet in length and four feet square. After the hewing was done, we sawed it lengthways into two pieces. The sawing was done by hand (whipsawing), there being no sawmills in the country at that time.

Those two huge timbers were used in the building of a steamboat that was to be operated on the upper Columbia river. I worked here until late in the spring of 1861. The following summer I went prospecting on John Day's river. Finding nothing that would pay, I went to Walla Walla, and remained there during the winter of 1861–2. That winter there was four feet of snow on the level. It was the worst and deepest snow I ever saw in my life. Mr. Gerald, a gentleman with whom I was well acquainted, had twenty-three hundred head of beef steers near Walla Walla; he was furnishing beef for the miners in the Salmon river and the Kootenay country. At that time you could buy five and six-year-old steers in Walla Walla for seven dollars per head. Gerald had several hundred tons of hay put up to feed during the winter; hay and grass were plentiful everywhere, but, for all that, most of the live stock in that country perished from cold and deep snows. You would see those big wild steers coming up the street and eating the cards that had been thrown out of the gambling houses. Gerald told me that out of the 2,300 cattle, and after feeding all the hay, he had but sixty-three cattle in the spring. Wood went up to $80 a cord in Walla Walla, and flour $30 per hundred pounds. Steamboats could not get up and there were no animals to haul the freight. Men used to go thirty miles to Walula to get a sack of flour and packed it on their backs.

In the early part of the winter I furnished a man named Fox with six month's provisions to go prospecting with John Peeterson on the North fork of the John Day river. In the spring of 1862 I received news from Peeterson stating that they had struck good diggings on Granite creek and for me to come at once. I went from Walla Walla to where Peeterson was. We mined there until fall and did very well, when we sold out for $1,500 to Eph Day, who at one time was the treasurer of the Oregon Navigation company. I suggested to Peeterson that we had better go next to the Fort Benton country, and we decided to do so and started our journey. Finally we got to Gold Creek. Jack Dunn was there, keeping a store. Jim and Granville Stuart were there. I remember giving Granville the Sacramento Union and he was very glad to get it, for newspapers were very scarce in the camp. They were the men that first found gold in paying quantities in Gold creek, and, for that matter, in the state of Montana, although "Gold Tom," an old trapper, had found a fair prospect in Gold creek before the Stuarts did. And there I met my old friend, Bill Fairweather, whom I had not seen since we parted at Fort Geary over three years before. A few weeks later I met Bill Sweeney at Bannock.

As I desired to go prospecting east of the Rocky mountain range, I left Bannock about the latter part of October, 1862, in company with John Peeterson and Thomas Thomas. On top of the main range, and where the Mullan road crosses, we met the old frontiersman, John Jacobs. He told us that Captain Fisk, in company with a lot of immigrants from Minnesota, were in camp in the Prickly Pear valley. I went to their camp, which was near to what is now called Montana Bar. James King and W. C. Gillette were there with a lot of flour; from them I bought a sack to go prospecting. With the same outfit came Jesse Cox, Jim Wiley, Albert Agnel, Jim Norton, Charles Cary, Alvin H. Wilcox, A. McNeal, James Fergus, Bob Ells, old man Olan and old man Dalton. They and others were in camp and had not decided where to go next. John Peeterson, Thomas Thomas, Jim and Bill Buchanan, Dick Merrill and I did some prospecting there that fall and got considerable gold.

Late in the fall, myself, a man named Thebeau, Nickolos Bird, and a fellow by the name of Gervais, who could talk the Flathead language, went off with the Flatheads and Pend d'Oreilles Indians to prospect the country they were going to travel through that winter. The Indians were on the way to the Musselshell country to hunt buffaloes. At this time the Flatheads and Piegans were at war with each other.

All the Indians, who numbered from eight to twelve hundred, went through what is now called Confederate gulch. We found good prospects there, but the Indians would not let us stay. It appeared that they had some kind of an understanding with the Crow Indians to go and hunt in that part of the country, but not to encourage any whites to go there, consequently we had to move whenever the Indians would move, and, by this time, they would not let us go back. We camped for several days on the little prairie at the head of Smith river, near where White Sulphur Springs, the county seat of Meagher county, now is. There the Indians had a buffalo hunt and killed many. After that we went down Shields' river and made three camps there. During all this time the Indians were killing buffalo and drying the meat. At the mouth of Shields' river we saw a large war party of Crows trying to capture some of the Flatheads and Pend d'Oreilles who were out hunting, and who belonged to the Indians we were with. We camped near

where there was a lot of willows. Moise, the head chief of the
Flatheads, came and asked me if I would fight; I said yes, and
he said, "That is good." I had a good rifle and two revolvers.
Soon our Indians got together and prepared for a battle, but
the Crows did not follow, and it was good for them, for the
Flatheads and Pend d'Oreilles were well armed and mounted
on good horses and were eager for a fight. That night they
placed their horses inside the camp and put pickets out in as
good way as I ever saw in my life, but the enemy did not make
an attack. From there we went east of the Little Snowys.
There we met a war party of Piegans coming around what is
called Wolfe mountain; there were about thirty of them. They
came to our camp to stop all night, and were received as
friends, and they played games during the evening with the
Pend d'Oreilles. About midnight the Piegans sneaked out and
stampeded many of the best horses belonging to the Flatheads
and Pend d'Oreilles and started away with them. Chief Moise
at once blew a horn and his son beat a kind of drum; this
aroused the whole camp. The Pend d'Oreilles and Flathead
warriors were in an instant on their best horses and went after
the Piegans and captured them all and recovered the stolen
horses and brought them to camp. The Pend d'Oreilles wanted to kill the Piegan thieves, but Chief Moise said, "No, we
will not kill them, though they are dogs. They came to our tepees as friends, but at the time they were deceiving us. They
are dogs; they came to our camp and we treated them as
friends, but they got up in the dark of the night and stole our
horses. No, we will not kill them, but we will mark them."
Then he ordered his warriors to bring the Piegans to the front
of his tepee. After this was done, he ordered them to take the
younger bucks and cut their hair short, and to cut a piece off
each ear of all the others. During the time this was being done,
the Flatheads and Pend d'Oreilles stood with their bows

CHIEF MOISE.
Courtesy Montana Historical Society, Helena

strung, and others with rifles in their hands, ready to shoot if anyone made a move to get away. After the marking was done, the Piegans were taken outside of the camp and were told to go home as dogs and never return or they would be killed as dogs. I witnessed all this.

On Christmas eve, 1862, we were in camp at Wolfe mountain. Chief Moise invited us to his tent to eat a Christmas dinner with him. He knew that it was Christmas day and respected it as such, for he had been taught what the meaning of it was by Father De Smet. His wife cooked dinner for us. She had fried doughnuts as good as any I ever ate, and excellent yeast powder bread; we had buffalo tongue and all kinds of meats. In all my life I never enjoyed a Christmas dinner better than I did that Christmas eve of 1862 in the tepee of the Flathead chief near Wolfe mountain.

Christmas morning I went on the top of what the Indians called Heart mountain. My object was to try and look in the direction of Fort Benton, for I knew we were not far from there, as I could see the Bear Paw mountains plainly. We decided to leave the Indians and go to Fort Benton. The Flathead chief sent six Indians to escort us through. It took us two days and part of a night. The second day out we traveled on a trail where the sage hens were as thick as I ever saw turkeys in a barnyard, but the Indians would not allow us to shoot, fearing that it might draw the attention of other Indians who were hostile to all of us.

Before the Indians started back we gave them tobacco and some matches, and a fancy pipe for them to take to the chief. It was the 18th of January, 1863, when we crossed the Missouri river at Fort Benton, and the river at that time was perfectly free from ice. There were only a few days of cold weather and but little snow that winter.

About the first of March, 1863, Thebeau and I started for the upper country and got as far as Sun river the first day. Vail had charge of the government farm, which was near where we crossed the stream. After going over the hill in the Prickly Pear canyon, and while we were in camp at a little spring W. C. Gillette came along with a cayuse pack train on his way to Fort Benton to get goods for Bannock. Tom Clarey and Jim Gourley were with him. Gillette had his sacks filled with gold dust, and as the road agents were very troublesome at that time, he mistook us for desperadoes; he went by and would not stop to talk with us. From there we went to Montana Bar. By this time the immigrants had nearly all left. Albert Agnel, Alvin H. Wilcox and John Peeterson were there yet, besides a few others. John Peeterson and I sunk a shaft twenty-five feet deep on the bar and found fifty cents to the pan on bed rock. After that Peeterson and I went and surveyed a ditch (it is the same big ditch that now conveys the water from the Prickly Pear creek onto the bench land). Our surveying apparatus was a triangle and a plumb bob which we made ourselves.

Alvin H. Wilcox, Jesse Crooks, Albert Agnel, and Jim Marston were also interested in the ditch. About the last of May I received word from Bill Sweeny of the discovery of Alder gulch and that he had staked a claim for me, and for me to come as quickly as possible, but it was pretty late in June before I could leave to go to Alder, and when I got there some one had taken possession of my claim, according to miners' rules, and those were if the owner was not there to represent his claim it could not be held only so many days; consequently I went to work for Bill Sweeny for $14 per day. After working for Sweeny for several weeks, I decided to go back to the bar and do more prospecting. Early in the summer of 1863, I found twenty-five cents to the pan on a bar where the city of Helena is now. I filled the hole up again and built a fire on the fresh dirt to conceal the place, with the intention of going back; that was an old trick which was practiced by the prospectors. As I was interested with John Peeterson in the ditch and the mines on the bar (American bar), and as it was necessary for us to have more sluice boxes, one day I went to cut logs to make lumber. I was on the side of a mountain, when a log rolled and caught my leg between it and a stump. It was some time before I could release myself, and when I did so I found that my leg was broken, and that is why I am lame now. There was no doctor to be had. I squeezed the broken place together the best I could and wrapped it up in some bandages I made out of a pair of overalls I had. That winter (1863–4) I stopped in a little cabin. I hired a man named Talbot, who was a Baptist preacher, to cook and stay with me; I paid him twenty dollars a week for his services and companionship. All this time my leg was troubling me terribly. Knowing Father Ravalli, in whose honor Ravalli county is named (he is now dead, and peace be to his memory, for he was a good man), and hearing that he was at the Mission, near where the

Ulm station on the Montana Central railroad is located, I decided to go and see him, for I knew that he was a good physician. I gave a man named Merrill all my interest in the mines to take me as far as Malcolm Clarke's place at the head of Prickly Pear canyon; from there a man named Morgan, from Fort Benton, took me to the Mission, a distance of fifty-five miles, and he charged me two hundred and fifty dollars, which was all the money I had. Father Ravalli was not at the Mission, but Father Jurada was, he also being a good surgeon. He told me that he could break the leg over again, but it would be shorter. He operated on my leg, and by the summer of 1865 I was able to work.

In 1867 I located the ranch where I am now, and have been ever since. It is like a dream to me when I think of the old trails I traveled over, forty years ago, and, on the other hand, it is a revelation to listen to the rumbling of the heavy trains that pass to and fro on the Montana Central railroad only a few miles from my door; while, looking in another direction, I see clouds of smoke arising and hear the whistle of the locomotives of the Great Falls and Canada railroad, and looking in still another direction I see the city of Great Falls and the towering smokestacks of its great smelters. Where once were the lone trails I helped to blaze through a wilderness inhabited only by wild beasts and savage men, I now see a flourishing city, and the country around me dotted with fine homes and prosperous towns.

While looking back, my imaginary view is tinged with sadness as I realize that the old days are gone forever; nevertheless my declining years are made contented and happy by the knowledge that I have done all that I could to convert this one-time wilderness into an empire, I now lay down the rifle of the pioneer and the pick and shovel of the prospector to pass the remainder of my days in the peace and content that comes from the consciousness of having done my best to help develop this western country that it might become the abiding place of an intelligent and prosperous people. And now, in the sunset of life, as I realize that before many years I shall strike the trail that leads "over the great divide," I rejoice that I can leave to my children a name honored by being enrolled on the scroll of Montana's pioneers."

Now Mr. Brown is past seventy-five years of age and lives with his family on a farm. Sun river is his post office. He is a well-preserved man for his age and has a remarkably good memory. What I have written here is but a fraction of that which he told me that evening of what the West was forty-two years ago. The only way to get a true early history of a country is to get such a narrative from its pioneers, and surely John D. Brown should be counted as one of the early historians of the state of Montana.

ROBERT VAUGHN.

JANUARY 4, 1900

A Pioneer Minister.

As the following was written for this book by "Brother Van," it needs no introduction. The writer tells of the first services that he held in Montana—when he fought the Nez Perces as well as sin and the whole host of hell. He said:

"We reached Fort Benton by the steamer "Far West" on Sabbath morning, June 30, 1872, at 7 a.m. It was in the midst of a heavy rain. In making inquiries, we were told that we could have the court house in which to hold service. However, on examination, we found it to have a roof composed of native soil, in which there were some places where the water came through in great quantities. We were then told that a room had been prepared in which Father Van Gorp was to hold service that morning. In asking him for the use of the same room in the evening, he replied most courteously that he would use it in the morning, then we were welcome to use it as often as we might desire, so our first service in Montana was held that evening.

"There was a large congregation, composed of the business men, freighters and river men. There was only one lady in the congregation—Mrs. George Baker—now of St. Louis.

"Here I first met, and they were my first acquaintances in Montana, W. G. Conrad and C. E. Conrad, young men then full of business and energy. They, with others, gave us a most hearty welcome. The greater part of the freight for Montana then came by the Missouri river, and freighting was a great business from Fort Benton to other points in the territory.

"Leaving Fort Benton, after a journey of fifty-two miles over bleak prairie without habitation, except one lonely stage station, I came to Sun river valley. The first settler I met there was Mr. Robert Vaughn, a much respected and honored citizen. He was one of the earliest settlers of this great valley,

REV. W. W. "BROTHER VAN" VAN ORSDEL.
Courtesy Montana Historical Society, Helena

which, at that time, was a part of Choteau county. I was indeed a stranger in a strange land, but I can never forget the hearty welcome accorded me by him. Though a bachelor, he knew how to give a welcome and make home pleasant to the young itinerant who had but very little money and whose best mode of travel was to go afoot.

"At that time there roamed over those prairies great herds of buffaloes, antelopes and deer. The Indians were hostile, and great risks had to be taken to protect life and property. It is said that more of the early settlers were killed in what was then Choteau county, than in any other part of the state.

"The first religious service held at Sun River was conducted in the house of Mr. Charles Bull, who kindly threw open his door and invited the neighbors in. As we sang the old hymns and preached the gospel, there were many eyes dimmed with tears as recollections of the old home and the old home church came to memory. Without any solicitation on the part of the preacher, the people took up a very liberal offering and presented the same to him.

"It was at this time a visit was made to the Blackfeet and Piegan agency on the Teton river, and near where is now located the town of Choteau. Major Jesse Armitage was agent, and Mr. B. W. Sanders teacher. A hearty welcome was given and a very interesting service was held at that time with the employes and Indians.

"I made my first visit to Butte in May, 1874. All but ten of the population of Butte attended the service; the congregation numbered about forty. Rev. Hugh Duncan (now of sainted memory), one of the first pioneer preachers, who came to Alder gulch in 1863, was then pastor of that large circuit, and met me there. Mr. and Mrs. Reese Wampler entertained the preachers. A striking contrast between past and present—then about fifty, now about that many thousand.

"In 1876 the population of the territory was very much decreased, the Black Hills and Leadville excitements, then at their height, drew away many of the miners; others went East to see friends and attend the Centennial, which was held that year. In June of the same year the Custer massacre took place on the Little Big Horn.

"Those who remember attending Fourth of July celebrations that year can well call to mind the sorrow that overshadowed the homes of the Montana frontiersmen, for the war cloud commenced to gather over all the small and isolated settlements in this then new territory.

"Early in the summer of 1877, after some hard fought battles in Idaho, Chief Joseph and Looking Glass, with their band of Nez Perces Indians came over the mountains on the Lo Lo trail passing up the Bitter Root valley, and were encamped for a few days on the Big Hole river, when General Gibbon, with his soldiers from Fort Shaw and some citizen volunteers from the Bitter Root, met them in battle on the Big Hole, August 9th.

"On the next Sabbath we were at Bannock, where we held service that evening. Some of the men and nearly all of the women from the surrounding country were there for safety and others came in that night. One young man was wounded in the arm; others had escaped almost miraculously. That night fifteen of us volunteered to go out to Horse Prairie. Melvin Trask was selected as captain, and before sunrise we were on the move. We had information that some men were killed and others severely wounded at the ranches of Montague, Winters and Mr. Hamilton's. Mrs. Winters was in town. She said she was going with us; we said no, and persuaded her to remain, but when we were about twelve miles out she overtook us. She was a woman of fine form, her long, black hair hanging down her back, mounted on a very fine horse, and a revolver buckled on, and she knew how and was not afraid to use it.

"When we arrived at the ranch, about sixteen miles from Bannock, it was plain to be seen that there had been trouble there. One of their fine cows was shot in front of the house, feather and straw ticks cut open and their contents emptied in the front yard. I was selected to go with Mrs. Winters into the house. Just as we went into the kitchen there lay a man who had been shot four times. On first sight he had the appearance of her husband. Some thought at this juncture she would faint, but she said she could stand it as well as any of us; that she loved her husband and her home, and the sooner she knewx the facts in the case the more reconciled she would be. From there we passed into another room where we found the dead form of Mr. Montague, the partner of Mr. Winters. Everything in the house was upset and broken. The question then came as to where her husband was, and that was the particular object of the search just then. A short distance from the house we found the body of Mr. Smith, pierced with five bullets. He left a widow and eight children. In another direction from the house was the body of Mr. Farnsworth, who was killed just before our arrival. We patched up the harness with some leather and ropes and hitched to a light wagon that had been left near the ranch, and started to Bannock with the four bodies, where they were all buried the next day, two of them by the Masonic order, of which they were worthy members.

"During the time that we were at the ranch, just across the creek (which was heavily skirted with willows and brush), there was a war party of Indians, from thirty to forty in number, yet they hesitated to cross and meet us, for our party had now increased to eighteen men, well armed. Mr. Winters had a very narrow escape from the Indians, having reached Bannock just before our party came in, much to the relief of Mrs. Winters. At the next ranch—Mr. Hamilton's—he, with some others, also made narrow escapes. Mr. Cooper was killed close to his house. The next day General O. O. Howard and his command came into the prairie and camped at Mr. Martin Barrett's ranch. W.A. Clark was captain of the Butte company of volunteers. He, with his company did good service for Montana at this perilous time.

"I first met the Rev. T. C. Ilif and the Rev. Mr. Riggin at Sheridan in August, 1873, at the funeral services of Charles Bateman, the only son of R. C. Bateman, who, at that time, lived in Sheridan. They, in company with Revs. J. A. Van Anda and Hugh Duncan, had just come by private conveyance from conference, which was held at Salt Lake City. The appointments that year were: J. A. Van Anda, presiding elder; W. C. Shippin, Helena; T. C. Ilif, Bozeman; Hugh Duncan, Missoula and Deer Lodge; Virginia City and Bannock, F. A. Riggin and the writer.

"At that first meeting we had a typical old-fashioned quarterly conference. The first conference of the Methodist church held in Montana was a district conference held in Helena in February, 1874. Two of the preachers attending this meeting came 150 miles on horseback.

"Some of the popular airs that were used at that time were: 'Oh, the Prospect; It Is so Inviting;' another: 'The Gospel Train Is Coming, I Hear It Just At Hand.'

"There were no railroads in Montana at that time. The nearest was at Ogden, Utah. Many of the people were anxious to see a railroad, and that made this hymn particularly popular."

At that time "Brother Van" was Rev. W. W. Van Orsdel of Pennsylvania, a young man full of faith and heroism. As soon as he landed in the 'then' 'Wild and Woolly West,' without hesitation he began his faithful mission by preaching his first sermon at Fort Benton, and this was the first protestant sermon in that town. He was now a stranger in a strange country, but he felt, 'truly the Lord is in this.' And, as he journeyed southward to the older settlements, through rude mining camps and among rough frontiersmen, the people everywhere gave him a cordial welcome, and every place he went, he was prompt in attending to his "Master's business."

In 1890 he was appointed presiding elder of the new Great Falls district; in 1892 superintendent of the North Montana Mission; and "now" (1898) he is presiding elder of the Western district, Montana conference, with headquarters at Helena.

ROBERT VAUGHN.

JAN. 4, 1898.

An Old Letter.

Those who settled in a new country, and located in a new settlement, will agree with me, as a rule, that every one was ready to assist another when in his power to do so; no class nor any of the faction element existed; all were happy and attended to their own affairs. Whenever a dance or a church social was given, all were invited to attend, and, invariably, their presence was a proof of their acceptance.

The early settlements in Montana were of this character, and the small settlement in the valley of the Sun river was no exception. I remember when the Benton Record and the River Press, both published at Fort Benton, made their first appearance. Every family and bachelor in the settlement subscribed for those papers. Your humble servant, who then lived in the extreme outskirts of the settlement, was a correspondent for those journals.

When writing about matters of interest I was always careful to get the facts and sign my name to the article written.

But for the amusement of myself and the people of the little settlement (who were one and all my friends), sometimes a story of the following nature would appear in one or the other of those papers, with a fictitious name attached to it. At the request of an old settler, who has one of those stories referred to in his scrap-book, I here give a copy of the same. It was written in the cold winter of 1880, when the snow was very deep and many cattle starving:

Being a stranger in the valley and anxious to become acquainted with the people, I saddled my horse to go to the crossing. It was one day last month, and, not being accustomed to Montana winters, I soon discovered that I was not wrapped sufficiently to stand such polar storms. Coming to a house where lived a German family, I asked if I could borrow a scarf or something to cover my ears; with the heart of a liberal soul the German told me to come in, and handed me a shawl.

"Rather cold day," said I.

"Fery cold; it is durty-dree pelow zero, and I have no beer to give a stranger; des am awful country," said he.

I made a new start, feeling very comfortable, and determined to speak to every one I met, and I did not expect to meet many but strangers, for Mr. H. and family were the only ones I knew in the neighborhood. As I was passing the next house, near the road there was a man repairing a gate, with a fur cap pulled over his ears.

"Good morning," said I, and he nodded. Stopping my horse, I asked:

"Do you think that it is going to storm?"

"Hey," said the man at the gate.

"Do you think this cold weather is going to last much longer?"

"What you say?" asked he.

I was getting discouraged, but as a last resort I asked in a loud tone:

"Do you think I had better go?"

"I go tomorrow," he answered.

Giving my horse the spur, I caught up with an old freighter; he said that he was making regular trips between Sun River and Fort Benton. I remarked that it was rather cold weather for freighting.

"Oh, this is nothing," he exclaimed; "in '63 I wintered on Snake river, and when I unyoked the cattle I had to drive a wedge between the two oxen to get them apart, and at the camp fire I had a long stick holding my coffeepot in the flames to boil, and it turned cold so sudden that I had to let go of the stick and rub my nose, being afraid I was going to freeze it. I ran in the wagon and went to bed without any supper, and when I got up the next morning the smoke stood like a trunk of an old dead tree, and the coffeepot was still in the flames, frozen stiff to the ground; breathing the cold blast that very night it froze all my teeth, and as I was getting up that morning they dropped out of my mouth like corn from a patent corn sheller."

When he told of freezing his teeth I believed him, for he had not a tooth in his head. I thought I would not say a word to anyone about cold weather again, and I gave my horse the rein.

Arriving near a large white house to the left of the road, I noticed smoke coming from the chimney, as if there was a good fire. Tying my horse to the fence, I went to the door and knocked; a man opened it, and asked me to come in and get warm. He went out to split some wood, and, while rubbing my hands before the red hot stove, I noticed milk pans, churn, etc., and this convinced me that it was a milk ranch. Soon he came in with some dry wood, and his wife came in from the pantry.

"Can I get a glass of milk to drink," I asked him.

"I don't know, ask the old woman," said he.

"Yes," said she, "of course you can."

While drinking it, I asked him again:

"Do you think we are going to have another snow storm?"

"Well, I really don't know. Ask the old woman, she can tell."

"I think we are going to get one right away," said she.

"Are you going to the debate tonight?"

"Well, I really don't know. Ask the old woman, she can tell you."

"I don't think we shall," said she.

Again I asked: "How many of your cattle have died this winter?"

"Well, I really don't know. Ask the old woman, she knows."

"About half of what we had," she replied.

Just then a troop of boys came running into the room "Are these your boys?" said I.

"Don't know. Ask the old woman, she knows."

I did not wait to hear her reply. I said I wanted to be at the crossing before the Benton coach arrived and I put on my hat and walked out. Half a mile further I met two school girls, a big and a bigger one, and they looked as if they were very cold. I said very politely: "Young ladies, I will lend you this shawl, and you can return it to Mr. Steell's store whenever convenient."

"Humph!" replied the biggest girl, "I wouldn't be found dead in the woods with that shawl on."

"I wouldn't either," said I, and I went on. Soon I was at Mr. H.'s house, which is near the road, and as I had an invitation from the hotelkeeper to attend a ball of the 22d, I thought I would call and ask Miss Annie to go to the ball with me. I met the old gentleman at the corner of the house.

"Good evening, Mr. H.," said I.

"Good evening, Mr. S.," said he.

"Is Miss Annie at home?"

"Yes, I believe she is, sir."

"Is she engaged?"

"Is it engaged, ye say, sir? Faith, an' I can't tell ye, sir, but she kissed Mr. Maguire last evening as if she had not seen the loikes ov him, an' it's engaged I believed they are, sir."

Just then there was a man going by on the road, and I said that I wanted to speak to him, and I ran through the gate, but I did not want to speak to anyone at that moment.

I came on, and at the bridge I noticed a sign, "Whoop Up." I could not imagine what it meant. Thinking it was a menagerie, I entered. A man with a bloody nose met me at the door, and another stood in the opposite corner with a black eye, and both were panting as if exhausted.

"Who owns this place," I asked the man with the bloody nose.

"A man in Fort Benton owns it, but if you want to know who runs it, just wait a few minutes until we have one more round to decide the question."

But I left in about as much of a hurry as ever. I crossed the bridge, tied my horse to the hitching post back of the store, and went up the street. It was growing dark and I was getting discouraged. Passing a saloon, I heard some loud voices. One man was saying that modern spiritualism was a humbug, while another argued that it was the greatest wonder of the age. At one end of the counter there was cheese, crackers, herring, etc. Seeing all the fellows helping themselves, I came to the conclusion that it was a free lunch. I commenced eating, and kept on until I almost made out my supper, when the barkeeper walked up to me, saying:

"See here, stranger; those eating here are expected to take a drink."

"I eat for my health; I always take a drink after I eat," I said.

A while afterwards, as the barkeeper leaned on the counter, I said: "Now I will take a drink."

"What will you have, sir," said he.

"Water," said I.

I saw him reach for something, and as I passed through the door—bang came a chair at my heels. I ran for my horse (a beautiful chestnut, with long mane and tail), but alas! he was not to be found. Where I had hitched mine there was a bob-tailed horse, surrounded by a band of starving cattle. I hurried to the other side of the store, looking for my nag, expecting every minute to see the barkeeper after me with a shotgun. I jumped over two or three poor cows. The second time I came in front of the bob-tailed horse, and, to my surprise, discovered that it was mine. The starving cattle had eaten his tail, and as I came upon my venerable steed they were chewing the saddle, of which nothing was left but the tree and a few buckles. I mounted the remains and left the town.

STRANGER.

SUN RIVER, MONT., FEB. 18, 1880.

The River Press has been published ever since, and is one of the brightest newspapers in the state; its subscription list is now a thousand fold larger than it was then. Great changes have taken place in the Sun river valley since "Stranger" made that trip. A few have left for other parts; many are still on the old camping ground that was then almost a barren desert, but now highly cultivated and decorated with trees and shrubs as beautiful as many of the eastern homes. The old freighter, the man at the gate, the good mother at the milk ranch and one of the school girls, and my old friend, Mr. H., have left what was then a new settlement, and have crossed the great divide and settled in the "New Jerusalem," where all good people go and live forever.

ROBERT VAUGHN.

MAY 20, 1899.

Warren C. Gillette's Early Experiences in Montana.

"Graig, Montana, April 16, 1900.

"Robert Vaughn, Esq., Great Falls, Montana.

"Dear Sir: Your kind letter asking me to give you some account of what I saw and did in the early days of Montana is at hand. I accede to your request with no little diffidence, but trust it will answer your purpose.

"I was living in New York City in the spring of 1862, when I received a letter from James King of Galena, Illinois, stating that a number of our friends had gone to Salmon river mines, Washington territory, by steamboat from St. Louis to Fort Benton, and thence overland to the diggings. He asked me if I would be willing to join him and go by the next boat, which would leave about the 1st of July. I immediately replied that I would be glad to go, and would meet him in St. Louis in time to make arrangements for the trip.

On my arrival in St. Louis, we proceeded to buy a span of mules, wagon and provisions enough to last us a year. We did not get away until about the 12th of July. Joseph La Barge was the captain until we arrived at St. Joseph, where we met the boat Emile, returning from Fort Benton, where his brother, John La Barge, took his place. We learned from the passengers who came from up the river that mines had been discovered near Cottonwood, which is now called Deer Lodge, in this state, and on account of this news we added to our stock more miners' supplies. At Sioux City, La Barge, Harkness & Co., who owned our boat, the 'Shreveport' (and the Emile), had purchased horses to be taken on the boat, to be used in freighting goods to their destination, should they be unable to reach that point by water. These horses were to be loaded at Yankton, that was several miles up the river. Captain La Barge kindly gave me permission to put my mules with them and to help drive the animals from Sioux City to that place.

In making this trip we crossed the Vermillion river, and I was then deeply impressed with its beauty and the great fertility of its valley. At Yankton we put the stock on board the steamer. The man who helped me to drive the horses was a French half-breed by the name of Juneau, a thorough frontiersman. At Fort Pierre we tied up for several hours. Major Vaughn was one of the passengers. He was formerly an Indian agent under President Buchanan, and had with him his Indian wife and child. Her relatives lived in the vicinity of Fort Pierre. It appears that the major had purchased at St. Joseph for his wife an elegant silk gown, brocaded with satin figures. She went on shore for a visit with her relatives, and with them went on a berrying expedition attired in this gown. When she returned this garment was a sight to behold, and the major, using language more forcible than polite, declared that hereafter she should be clad only in the regulation Indian blanket.

"It being rather late in the season of navigation, we made slow progress, with frequent delays on sand bars and frequent stops for wood, at which times passengers readily assisted the roustabouts in gathering and loading; nevertheless, I remember that we enjoyed the trip. A day or two before we reached the mouth of the Yellowstone, we came upon an immense herd of buffalo. They approached the river from our right in one vast army, reaching as far as we could see, and going out on the other side after swimming across. Our boat pressed through this living mass, which quickly closed behind us. The passengers shot down into this huddling herd until the river was red with blood. Three were secured and landed on board by the crew. We had some Indians on board, who, when the buffaloes were being dressed for the boat's use, procuring the offal, emptied the grass from the first stomach and ate the warm, raw tripe with evident relish.

"Nothing of more than ordinary interest occurred until after we passed Fort Union, near the mouth of the Yellowstone river, for up to this time we had seen only friendly Indians, but now the captain said we were in the Sioux country, and a stricter watch was kept when we tied to the bank at night. One morning, before we had left the bank, we were aroused by the cry of Indians. They were seen in a bend in the river a couple of miles below. The captain had a barricade of boxes made upon the shore and sent a runner up the river to a camp of friendly Indians for assistance. The Sioux made signals by flashing the sunlight from their little mirrors from the opposite cliffs. When the friendly Indians came, they were mounted on slick ponies; the men had on their war paint and war bonnets, and after a harangue from the chiefs dashed off to where the hostile Indians had been seen. It was a fine sight, and looked much like war, but in two or three hours they returned without any scalps, after driving the Sioux into the hills. In recognition of their valor, the captain gave them a great feast, consisting of hard bread, coffee and sugar, with buffalo meat ad libitum.

"We were unable to proceed above this place but a few miles, for the water seemed to lessen every day. Finally the captain gave orders to pull ashore where there was an old stockade fort, and we were put ashore. Here the cargo was discharged and moved to the abandoned stockade. As soon as the captain ascertained that we could proceed no further by water, he dispatched an Indian runner to Fort Benton with an order for teams to help transport the Shreveport's cargo and passengers. Some of the passengers returned with him, having had enough of upper Missouri life. We met many Mackinaw boats coming down from Fort Benton, carrying from three to five men each. These men had come from the Pacific coast, and they told us of the rich diggings there, and also of the prospecting on the Prickly Pear (now American bar, in Montana), which made us anxious to get along; so, after remaining at the old stockade about a week, we got Mr. Picotte, in whose charge the captain had left the passengers and cargo, to take what teams we had and move on up the river, and not wait for the outfit from Fort Benton. One time after several days' travel we made a camp near the mouth of Milk river, in a very level country, and nearby there was the largest aggregation of Indian lodges I had ever seen. There were several thousand Indians of different tribes. I remember the names of three only— Crows, Gros Ventres and Assiniboines. I have forgotten what the object of this great council was. Femmisee (Sitting Woman), who was the head chief of the Gros Ventres, was there. He was very friendly to us. Here we had our first actual trouble. Some Indians came into our camp and tried to take our guns away from us and acted in an ugly manner. It appeared that the Indians were divided as to whether we should be permitted to go any further through their country or not. The chief, Femmisee, said that we could go through, but was opposed by the younger Indians. That evening our party took a vote as to whether we should move on the next day or turn back. A majority voting to return, in the morning we headed for the old stockade, but after we had gone only a short distance several warriors rode up to our leading team and with drawn guns and arrows strung compelled us to turn again in the direction of Fort Benton.

"Mr. Picotte informed us afterwards that the Indians also had a council, and it had been decided that we were to go through, and that Chief Femmisee, in enforcing his authority, had shot and wounded one of the opposition. Mr. Picotte made many presents to the head men, and from this time on we had no more trouble, though we met many Indians. There were fifteen white men in our party and several half-breeds.

We took turns standing guard at night, making two watches—
one from dark till midnight, the other from midnight till morning. After several days' of travel, we met the company's teams
from Fort Benton on their way to the stockade; they were in
charge of Robert Lemon. We reached Fort Benton without
other important incident and made our headquarters at what
was then styled Fort La Barge; an aggregation of log houses situated about three fourths of a mile above the old Fort Benton,
which was occupied by the American Fur Company and about
a quarter of a mile above Fort Campbell, whose only occupants were Malcolm Clark and family. A day or two after our
arrival we awoke one morning to the sound of alarm, and saw
a war party of Indians circling about in the bluffs to the west.
At Fort La Barge all was excitement, a cannon was brought and
preparations for defense quickly made. This post was unforti-
fied, while Fort Campbell and Fort Benton had walls of adobe
with bastions and heavy gates. Clark sent up for someone to
come to Fort Campbell to help him to hold the fort, and I was
deputized for that duty; I got my gun and marched down. The
heavy gate was opened and Mr. Clark welcomed me to his little garrison. The Indians, for most of the day, could be seen
among the bluffs, but finally a parley was secured, presents
were given and the war was over. Christopher L. Payne, who
was one of our party and had some goods to go over the
mountains, bought some ponies and broke them to harness
and we waited a few days for him, as we wished to go together. During this time we heard that good diggings had been
found on the Big Prickly Pear, and we left for that point, following the Capt. J. L. Fisk trail, whose expedition had preceded us about a month. Near the last of October we arrived at
where is now located Montana City, or East Helena. Here we
found several families who had come through with the Fisk
expedition, among whom was E. M. Dunphy. We made

arrangements with Dunphy to go to Benton with four wagons with oxen for our goods and bring them to the Prickly Pear camp where we expected to winter. I preceded him on horseback, and, on reaching Fort Benton, learned that no tidings of Lemon's train had been received. I kept on down the river and fortunately met him below the mouth of the Marias river after one day's travel from Fort Benton. Mr. Lemon reported that after leaving Milk river he encountered a party of Indians who demanded whisky and were very troublesome, cutting his harness and making threats of murdering the whole outfit. To escape them he took the heroic measure of rolling out a barrel of whisky and setting it on end; he knocked in the head and they were soon all dead drunk. While they were in this condition he pulled out his train, and, pushing on night and day, he saw them no more.

"Dunphy's wagon being loaded we started back, leading behind one of the wagons a little black mare. This mare had been purchased of a half breed at the Fort by Mr. Tingley (the father of R. S. and Clark Tingley), and he wanted me to take her to the camp on the Prickly Pear. Reaching Sun river, we found four lodges of Blackfeet. Here was stationed a government farmer who was teaching the Blackfeet Indians how to cultivate the soil. His name was Vail, and he had an interpreter who informed me that the chief of the Blackfeet camp said that the mare which I was leading belonged to his squaw and he wanted me to give her up. I told him it was not my mare; that it had been intrusted to me, and I could not do it. The Indian said that so far as he was concerned he did not care, but that it was a pet of his wife's; that she was crying and nothing but the mare would console her. I finally settled the matter by his giving me another horse, and I turned over the animal and one plug of tobacco. In the meantime the wagons had gone on and I followed an hour or two later on horseback, leading the new horse. About twelve miles beyond Sun river, as I was riding slowly up a rocky hill, I heard a sound and, looking back, I saw an Indian on horseback within twenty feet of me and he was warning me of some danger; so I hurried on, and overtaking the wagons, I informed the men of the incident, and when we went into camp, which was opposite the Bird Tail mountain, we deemed it wise to place the wagons in a square, and, putting the horses inside, we slept on our guns that night, but had no trouble. The next night we camped on the Dearborn river. The days since leaving Fort Benton had been beautiful, and when we retired to our blankets that evening the weather was mild, but in the morning we awoke to find ourselves covered with a foot of snow and the Dearborn river frozen over. We laid there two days and nights, and on the third day traveled to Wolf Creek, about seventeen miles, when we found that the snow had all disappeared. The next day we passed over the hill in Prickly Pear canyon, where there was the grave of a young man named Lyon, who had accidentally shot himself but a few weeks before. He was buried where he died and a rough headboard gave an account of his death. This point was called then and is still known as Lyon's Hill. The third day from Wolf Creek at Three-Mile creek, which is three miles south of Silver City, we met Mr. King, accompanied by 'Gold Tom.' It appears that the camp on the Prickly Pear had been broken up and nearly all had moved out to go to Gold Creek and Bannock; so Mr. King had come to tell us to keep our wagons moving and to go over the Mullan Pass. About the last of November we rolled into Deer Lodge. Here we stored our goods in one end of a building owned by A. Fall. In the meantime we purchased an unfinished building owned by C. A. Broadwater, who was living there then. It was there I first saw Kohn Kohrs. He had come to Cottonwood to buy some cattle of John Grant to be butchered in Bannock. For want of funds he was unable to buy more than three head, while now his herds are counted by thousands. Also Captain Mick Wall came up from Gold Creek on his way to the states. He had with him Thomas Levatta, a mountaineer whom he had hired as a guide, and was going by the way of Bannock and Salt Lake. Mr. King was induced to join him and I was left to sell our goods and send the dust down the river the coming spring. As trade was dull in Cottonwood, I hired Dunphy to haul my goods to Bannock and put me up a cabin. It took about a week to make the trip, going over the mountains and down the Big Hole river. The weather was clear, but cold, with no snow except upon the divide. We reached Bannock about the twentieth of December. At Bannock I saw a rustling mining camp, with many saloons and gambling houses. Goods commanded astonishing prices.

I here met the Minnesota contingent, some mining, others keeping boarding houses, and all seeming to prosper. It took but a short time to dispose of the major part of the goods at a sound profit in gold dust. Knowing that I could obtain goods at Fort Benton, which I could pack over the mountains, and sell at Bannock at a good profit, I left my place in charge of Warren Whitcher and started about the middle of February, 1863, on horseback, with James Gourley, for Fort Benton. The distance from Bannock to Fort Benton is about three hundred miles, and we made the trip in eight days. Major Dawson was the manager of the American Fur Company at Fort Benton and Matthew Carroll and George Steell were his head men and did the trading. This company had a large herd of horses which were kept up the Missouri river about fifty miles. They bought many of these horses very cheap, for when a man got ready to go down the river it was the company's price or nothing. I bought fifteen of these horses at from thirty to forty dollars each, and enough of such goods as were in demand in Bannock to load them A good horse would carry easily two hundred pounds. I hired a cook, for his board and passage, and returned to Bannock without accident. Tobacco, for which I paid $2.50 per pound, sold for $10 and $12. Seven by nine window glass brought one dollar per pane; other articles in proportion. The venture having proved so profitable I was soon on my way back to Fort Benton. Henry Plummer gave me a letter for Miss O'Brien, who was the sister of the wife of I. A. Vail, the government farmer who lived at the crossing of the Sun river, so that when the pack train reached the river my men camped across from his house, and I went over to deliver the letter, and on invitation I remained all night at the farm. In the morning one of my men came over and told me that all of the horses had been stolen, which proved to be true. And Mr. Vail had only one horse left. It was a sore-backed sorrel that had been left in the corral over night, which I bought for thirty dollars, and started for Fort Benton, sixty miles away, to buy more horses in order to move my packs. After traveling twelve miles I left the river and took a trail up the hill, now known as Frozen Hill, and in a little hollow, I took off the saddle and picketed the horse that had been all night without food. I laid down, intending to rest about an hour. As I was very tired I went to sleep. I could not tell how long I had slept when an Indian aroused me, and, as I looked back down the road, I saw quite a large party of Indians coming up the trail. I hurried to my horse, quickly put on the saddle and rode on. The Indians left the trail on the top of the hill and bore off to the northwest to my great relief. I did not get into Benton until after daylight. There they told me that, from my description, the Indians I met were Little Dog, a Blackfoot chief, and his band, and that Little Dog was a friend to the white men. I told Major Dawson my trouble and that I wanted to buy some horses; he gave me a good horse to ride and sent me with "Buffalo Bill," whose name was William Keyser, to the horse herd. We forded the Missouri river where the city of Great Falls is now located, then went over the hill to where Mr. Paris Gibson's stock farm is situated, and found the horses there in charge of the herders. After the round up of the band I selected the horses I wanted and drove them up to where my packs were, crossing the Missouri where we forded it the day before. My men had recovered some of the stolen horses that had given out and were abandoned. The Indians who stole the horses were Shoshones or Snakes and had followed me from Bannock. They had killed one man near Square Butte who was employed by Mr. Vail as a hunter, and his widow, a Blackfoot squaw, had cut off one of her fingers as an evidence of sorrow and was bewailing his death in loud cries, sitting with other women on the side of a hill. Taking another start, I got to Fort Benton, bought more goods, and returned to Bannock. While I was in Bannock this time occurred the shooting of Jack Cleveland by Henry Plummer. He was shot in a saloon which was opposite my place. I heard the shots, and going to the door I saw Plummer come out of the place with a pistol in his hand and walk with a friend down the street. I immediately went across to the saloon and saw Cleveland lying on the floor with a bullet hole in his cheek and surrounded by a string of men. He would raise himself on his elbow and mutter some words and then fall back. Some one in the crowd asked him if he had any friends. He said, 'Old Jack has no friends,' when one of the crowd replied: 'Yes, you have; you bet your life.' He was shortly removed to a butcher shop, which was near by, and he lingered for a day or so and died. Plummer was tried and acquitted, as it was proven that Cleveland had said that 'Plummer was his meat.' There were frequent rumors of robberies by road agents, and among trusted friends men would be pointed out as belonging to such organizations, and that Henry Plummer was their leader. James Gourley once informed me that he had good reason to know that I was once followed, when on a trip to Fort Benton to buy goods, by three of Plummer's band who intended to rob me in the Sun river country, but that they were delayed on account of losing their horses and did not reach that place until I was well on my way to Benton.

"The weather during the whole winter and spring had been wonderfully fine, with only one or two snow storms. On my last trip to Benton that spring I carried considerable dust and some mail; letters coming from the states by the way of Walla Walla often costing from one to two dollars each. When Oliver's express was started, letters from Salt Lake cost one dollar each and newspapers fifty cents. The gold dust I carried was not all my own. I put the purses (buckskin) in an old carpet bag which was put on top of the pack on the back of one of the pack horses and securely lashed it. We proceeded along without any trouble until one morning at a camp on Willow Creek, near what is now known as Mitchell's Station, the horse carrying the dust became fractious and tried to buck off his pack. The dust being so heavy, burst through the lining of the carpet bag and scattered the sacks of gold. After some little search we found all the purses, and, taking care that such an occurrence should not happen again, I finally landed the treasure safely in the American Fur Company's safe. Owing to the light snows in the mountains the Missouri river was low and the steamer Shreveport, which carried the goods that Mr. King had purchased in the East, did not reach Fort Benton, and had to unload her freight at Cow Island, where she arrived about the last of June, 1863. Captain Nick Wall, of I. I. Roe & Co. of St. Louis, also had merchandise on this boat. Cow Island was inaccessible to wagons on account of the high bluffs without the construction of a road. So after waiting some time for La Barge to get the freight up to Benton we made a contract with Wall to haul his goods to Virginia City in Alder Gulch (a newly discovered mining camp) for thirty cents per pound. We did not get this freight through to its destination until the middle of November, hauling our own goods at the same time. This proved to be a wonderful camp. The times were good. It was only a question of how much you should ask for what you had to sell, for gold dust was plentiful. The next spring, 1864, I opened a new road to go to Fort Benton by the way of the Jefferson river, White Tail Deer, Boulder and Big Prickly Pear. Heretofore wagons had to cross the main divide twice. C. A. Broadwater was the wagon master, I had about twenty-five teams and hired a hunter who kept the train supplied with game, which was principally antelope and deer. It took about a month to make a passable road for freight teams. In the fall of that year, 1864, gold was discovered in Last Chance gulch, and the goods which we shipped the next spring, 1865, were taken to Helena and Last Chance gulch. We put up a store house here, and the coming spring, 1866, we bought of Malcolm Clark and Edward A. Lewis their charter for a toll road through the Little Prickly Pear canyon. This road was finished in time for the travel from Fort Benton that season. Owing to the high price of labor and the rocky character of the canyon this road cost about forty thousand dollars, but as tolls were high also, it took only about two years to get it back. The charter of this road expired in 1875, and it now belongs to Lewis and Clark county. In the summer of 1865 I sold to Mr. Copeland for I. I. Roe & Co. two freight trains of twenty-four wagons each and two hundred head of oxen. That year Copeland had much freight put off near the mouth of Milk river on account of low water. This was the commencement of the Diamond R. Freight Company. Cattle in those days varied much in price. Then ox teams brought freight all the way from Leavenworth, Kan., and St. Joseph, Mo., and the cattle lean, and with tender feet, would be often sold for thirty or forty dollars per yoke. A few months of rest and feeding on the native grasses, and they would treble in value. As far as possible merchants held their dust until the spring of the year and sent it down the river in preference to having it go by stage coach by way of Salt Lake. I remember (I think it was in 1865) of leaving Helena with $8,000 in dust to take to Fort Benton. I carried it in canteens on the horn of my saddle. When I got to the Dearborn crossing, I found among others camped there for the noon, Malcolm Clark. He was traveling with a light spring wagon and he kindly consented to carry my canteens and lighten my load as the gold alone weighed over forty pounds. He said he wanted to give his horses rest and would not start till late in the afternoon. I saddled up and went on and had gone about eighteen miles when I saw some person ahead coming toward me, driving a packed mule. He was going as fast as possible, whipping the mule continually. When we met I saw it was a man by the name of Coppick, whom I had known in Virginia City. He was much excited and told me that a runner (Joseph Kipp) had come to Sun River in the night, and that he had been sent from Fort Benton to warn all travelers that there had been an uprising of the Indians, and that they had killed ten men on the Marias river and were murdering all the white people they could find. Coppick said he would rather take chances with the road agents than the Indians, and that he would go back to the states by the way of Salt Lake. I tried to persuade him to turn and go on to Sun river with me, that it was only twelve miles away, and as there were several outfits camped there, would stand the Indians off. He said he had on his mule about thirty thousand dollars in dust, and he believed it would be safer to go the other way. I went on to the crossing of Sun river, but kept a sharp lookout for the redskins all the while. I found there quite a large

party of freighters who by arranging their wagons, were prepared for any surprise the Indians might make. During the
night who should come into camp but Coppick. It appears
that Mr. Clark had persuaded him to put his gold into his
wagon, and that, as they would travel at night, they could get
through safely. We lay at this place all the next day and at
night started for Fort Benton, getting there in the morning. We
found that the story was true; that Barris, Angevine and eight
others, who had been camped at the mouth of the Marias,
were waylaid and all killed.

"Up river freights that had been from ten to eighteen cents
per pound came down in a few years to three, and wagon
freights from Benton to Helena from six cents to one cent.
Business conditions changed as gold and greenbacks were approaching an equality in value, and goods purchased in the
East were sometimes sold at a loss. I virtually went out of merchandise in 1869.

"When I commenced this narrative I did not think it
would be so long, and to draw it to a close, I will skip the years
until 1877, in which year I first engaged in sheep raising with
Gov. B. F. Potts and D. H. Weston as partners. This was the
year of the Nez Perces war, in which Chief Joseph was captured by General Miles in the Bear Paw mountains. We located on the Dearborn river, about three miles above the present
bridge, in August, 1877. The following year, as the shearing
time approached, I was going up to one of the sheep camps
with some supplies tied behind me on the saddle for the
herder. When I was about four miles from the home camp I
saw two horsemen coming over a hill. At first I thought they
were cowboys, but as they came nearer I could see the red
blankets; then I knew they were Indians. As they approached
one rode opposite me and said, 'How,' to which I replied,
'How.' The other stopped his horse about forty or fifty feet

away and dismounted, coming towards me. I thought maybe he wanted tobacco or matches. The Indian who remained on his horse had his gun across the saddle in front of him, the other had laid his gun down, and as soon as he came to the side of my horse he put his hand under my right foot and I landed on the other side of my horse. I had no coat on, therefore they could see I was not armed. He then took off my saddle, which was a new one, and put it on his horse. As I stood holding my horse by the bridle he came up to me and suddenly grabbed my watch chain with his right hand, jerking the watch from the vest pocket, but the chain hung to its fastening at the buttonhole. As the watch was of great value, being a Jurgensen, as a stop watch for timing horses, and the chain of heavy gold, I would not let it go, so I grasped his wrist with my left hand making him let go and shoved him back. He then drew his gun, a short Henry rifle and threw in a cartridge with the lever and aimed it at me; by that time I had concluded that I did not want the watch, and as I made motions to give it up, he lowered the muzzle of his gun and received the watch and chain. He then mounted his horse and rode away to the south, carrying the watch and chain in his hand. When this Indian drew his gun the one on the horse spoke something quickly which sounded to me as if he had said, 'Don't shoot.' The one that robbed me was a tall and fine-looking man, twenty-five years old, I should judge, his face was painted and he wore brass rings in his hair. The other was older, shorter and not so good looking. I took the old saddle, put it on my horse with the provision that had not been disturbed and went on to the camp. I found that these Indians had been there before me and had taken a gun, some cartridges and food. I learned afterwards that they were a part of Chief Joseph's band who had escaped from General Miles and had been in the British possessions all winter and were at that time trying to get back across the mountains to their old home. A few days after two of my neighbors were killed on the Dearborn river by this same tribe, Cottle and Wareham. They are buried at the Dearborn Crossing, where Carson also reposes who was previously killed by Indians.

"I had considerable trouble to keep herders in those days, and I then decided that the growing of sheep was a great industry in Montana, only for the Indians.

"Warren C. Gillette."

Mr. W. C. Gillette is a native of the State of New York, having been born there in 1831. He has always been an active and useful citizen. He was a member of the Montana Territorial Legislature three terms—once in the council—and was a member of the Constitutional convention in 1889. Mr. Gillette now resides in the Dearborn valley, in Lewis and Clark county, where he owns one of the largest and best stock ranches in Montana. He has a large herd of cattle and several thousand sheep. He is considered to be one of the wealthiest men in the state and one of the most honorable in his dealings with his fellow men.

Robert Vaughn.
May 21, 1900.

A Meal in the Indian Camp.

One of the Diamond R. Company's men had been down about the falls of the Missouri river looking for some oxen that had strayed away. He came up the valley to my house. He told me that there were six Indian tepees a little ways above the mouth of Sun river and that there were five horses that he thought belonged to me not far from the tepees. He gave a description of them and I could see that they were my horses. I mounted my saddle pony, which I always had at home, and went to the place where the horses had been seen, but I could not find them. I went to the Indian camp (now Sun River Park belonging to the city of Great Falls). A fine old Indian came and met me. I told him that I was looking for horses, describing them and making my brand, the letter V, with my finger in the dust on the ground. He said that he had seen them and that they had galloped away over the hill, at the same time making signs and pointing his hand in the direction the horses had gone. I thanked him, and when we got to the camp he called on a young Indian to come and take my horses to good grass. He took me to his own tepee and brought from his wardrobe a very fine buffalo robe, spread it upon the ground and asked me to sit on the robe. I accepted the invitation. Then he filled his pipe with dried red willow bark (kin-ni-ki-nic) and after lighting and smoking it, long enough to get the pipe going in full blast, he handed it to me. Although I never indulged in smoking a weed of any kind, at this time, to please the old fellow, I passed the pipe around with him half a dozen times, and, of course, I had to take a whiff every time he did; after that I asked to be excused, telling him that my heart was good and that I knew his heart was good also. In the meantime he had told his wife to give me some victuals (much-a-muck). She took about one dozen grains of coffee and put it in

"INDIAN CAMP #2"—PAINTING BY CHARLES M. RUSSELL.
Courtesy Montana Historical Society, Helena, Mackay Collection

a piece of buckskin and pounded it between two stones and made me some coffee; she brought it to me in a tin cup, and also some dried antelope meat. No one could be treated with more respect by an Indian than I was by them. Bringing the best robe, and presenting the pipe of peace, as this Indian did, is one of the most courteous acts an Indian can do for a man. When I told him that I was going to leave and go over the hill to get the horses, he ordered the young Indian to bring my horse. I gave the old fellow fifty cents in silver and he was much pleased, and I am sure I was, for I was treated royally. I found the horses on the other side of the hill where the Indian told me they had gone. This was in the summer of 1873.

ROBERT VAUGHN.

JAN. 21, 1898.

The First Settlement of
What Is Now Montana.

No doubt it will be of interest to many, especially us Montanans, to know the history of the first settlement of this state and which was made in the western portion in 1841. Knowing that Hon. Frank H. Woody of Missoula is one of the old pioneers and among the oldest residents of the city of Missoula, I wrote asking him to give me a brief history of western Montana. In reply he sent me a carefully prepared paper written by himself some two years since, giving a very complete early history of that part of this state, also a letter containing valuable information on the same subject and giving me permission to make use of so much of his writings as I desired. No one is better qualified to give such a sketch than Judge Woody, for he has been a resident of what is now Montana for over forty-four years. The following are extracts from Judge Woody's letters:

"All that portion of the state of Montana bounded on the north by the British possessions, on the east by the main range of the Rocky mountains, on the south and southwest by the Bitter Root mountains, and on the west by the one hundred and sixteenth degree of longitude, at one time constituted a portion of the vast domain of the great Northwest, known as Oregon Territory. When and by what means the government of the United States obtained possession of the great Territory of Oregon are facts not generally known. Oregon was for a great number of years claimed by the United States and Great Britain, and was held in joint occupation by citizens of both nations. Great Britain claimed by the right of discovery, and the United States by the right of discovery and by virtue of the French cession of the Territory of Louisiana of April 3, 1803, and the treaty of limits with Spain of Feb. 22, 1829, and also by right of actal occupation of soil for a great number of years. The 'Oregon Question' engrossed the attention of congress and came near result-ing in a war between the United States and Great Britain, but the matter was amicably adjusted by the treaty of June 15, 1846, by which the forty-ninth parallel of latitude was estab-lished as a boundary line between the two nations, and the United States became the sole and undisputed owner of all that portion of Oregon lying south of that line.

"Oregon was organized as a territory by act of congress, passed in August, 1848, and included within its limits all that por-tion of Montana lying on the west side of the Rocky mountains.

"By act of congress approved March 2, 1853, the Territory of Oregon was divided, and this portion of it became a part of Washington Territory. The first legislature of Washington Ter-ritory created the county of Clarke, named in honor of Cap-tain Clarke, of the Lewis and Clarke expedition. Clarke coun-ty extended from a point on the Columbia river, below Fort Vancouver, to the summit of the Rocky mountains, a distance of some six hundred miles. This portion of the present State of Montana was then a portion of Clarke county, and was then for the first time included within the limits of a county.

"Clarke county was afterwards divided, and the county of Skamania created, and we became a portion of the last named county. The legislature then divided Skamania and created Walla Walla county, and then we became a portion of Walla Walla county, with our county seat located on the land claim of Lloyd Brooks, on the Walla Walla river, in the present State of Washington. Walla Walla county was afterwards divided and we became part of Spokane county, with the county seat located at Fort Colville. We remained a part of Spokane coun-ty until December 14, 1860, when the legislature of Washing-ton Territory divided the county of Spokane and created the county of Missoula, with the county seat at or near the trad-ing post of Wordens & Co., Hell's Gate Ronde.

"The county of Missoula, as first established, embraced all those portions of the present counties of Missoula and Deer Lodge, lying on the west side of the main range of the Rocky mountains. Missoula county remained a portion of Washington Territory until Idaho Territory was organized on the 3d of March, 1863, when it became a portion of that territory.

"The first legislature of Idaho created Missoula county, and located the county seat at Wordensville. On the 26th day of May, 1864, congress created Montana Territory, and the first legislature, which met at Bannock, created, on the 2d day of February, 1865, the county of Missoula, and located the county seat at Hell's Gate. From the foregoing it will be seen that Missoula county has at different times comprised a portion of four territories and five counties.

"Probably the first white men who visited this portion of Montana were Lewis and Clarke, who with their party, sometime during the summer of 1805, entered the Bitter Root valley from the south, through a pass known at the present time as the Big Hole mountain, a small valley near the head of Bitter Root river, where the party of Lewis and Clarke first met and gave the name of Flatheads to the tribe of Indians now known by that name.

"A number of years since the writer was well acquainted with Moise, the second chief of the Flatheads, who was a boy at the time Lewis and Clarke passed through the Bitter Root valley and well remembered the event and many circumstances connected therewith, the party being the first white men ever seen by these Indians. Moise was a warm and devoted friend of the whites from the time of his first meeting with them up to the time of his death, which occurred about 1887.

"Western Montana has been occupied from time immemorial by three different tribes of Indians, to-wit: The Salish—called by Lewis and Clarke the Flatheads, and by which name they are generally known—the Kelespelmns, now exclusively known by the French name of Pend d'Oreilles, and the Kootenais. These tribes speak dialects slightly different, and most probably constituted at a remote date one tribe or nation. They have a tradition that came from the far north, but this tradition is exceedingly vague and indefinite.

"From the time of Lewis and Clarke's expedition up to about the year 1835 to 1836, we have no definite knowledge of what transpired in this portion of Montana. At a very early date a number of Canadian voyagers and Iroquois Indians from Canada visited this country, and sometime between 1820 and 1835 the employes of the Hudson's Bay company visited it for the purpose of trading with the Indians and extending the power of dominion of that gigantic company, but these early adventurers left us no available data from which to write their travels and adventures.

"About the year 1835 to 1836 the Flathead Indians, who inhabited the Bitter Root valley, had gathered some little knowledge of the Christian religion from the Canadian voyagers and Iroquois Indians, who visited the country for the purpose of trapping and trading for furs. The Flatheads were anxious to gain further knowledge and sent to St. Louis, Missouri, for a priest, or as they called him a 'Black Gown.' Three different parties of Indians were sent in as many different years. Of the first party sent but little that is definite is known, except that none reached St. Louis. The second party, on their downward trip, were all killed by Indians—probably Blackfeet—near Fort Hall. The third party started in the spring of 1839, and in the summer of that year two of the party reached St. Louis. Of the two who successfully accomplished the journey, one was named Ignace Iroquois and he died at or near the St. Ignatius Mission, in Missoula county, sometime during the winter of 1875–76. The other was the father of a Flathead named Francoise Saxa of Bitter Root valley. The superior of the Jesuit establishment at St. Louis promised to send them a priest in the following spring. Ignace remained in St. Louis all winter and came up with the father in the spring. The other Indian came back the same fall to tell the news. In the spring of 1840 Father De Smet and Ignace came across the plains and found a camp of Flatheads and Nez Perces near the Three Tetons, near the eastern line of the present state of Idaho. The father baptized a few Indians and came with the Flatheads to the Gallatin valley, near the place where Gallatin City now stands, and, finding that he could do little without aid, returned to St. Louis for assistance. In the spring of 1841 Father De Smet returned, coming by the way of Fort Hall. He brought with him two other fathers—Point and Mengarine—and several lay brothers, among whom were Brothers W. Classens and Joseph Specht, who are eminently entitled to the appellation of 'oldest inhabitants,' having been residents here for more than a third of a century. The party brought with them wagons and carts, horses, mules and oxen, and came by the way of the Deer Lodge valley and down the Hell's Gate canyon. These were the first wagons and oxen brought to Montana. In the fall of that year the first settlement was made in the Bitter Root valley by the establishment of St. Mary's mission on the tract of land upon which Fort Owen is now situated. During the fall and winter of the same year dwelling houses, shops and a chapel were built, and nearly all the Flatheads and some Nez Perces and Pend d'Oreilles were baptized.

"Probably the first farming attempted in our state was in the spring of 1842, by the fathers at the mission. This year they raised their first crop of wheat and potatoes. The same year the first cows were brought from the Hudson's Bay company's post at Fort Colville on the Columbia river. About this time or a little later the fathers erected a saw and grist mills— the burrs for the latter being brought from Belgium.

Those same mill stones, which are fifteen inches in diameter, with other relics of this early settlement, are now in the archives of the museum at St. Ignatius mission.

"After establishing the St. Mary's mission, Father De Smet returned to St. Louis, and thence to Europe, but returned to the Bitter Root valley in 1844, making his third trip, and bringing with him a number of fathers and lay brothers. Among the number was the well known and highly esteemed, the late Father Ravalli. St. Mary's mission was kept up until November, 1850, when the improvements were sold by Father Joset to Major John Owen. The bill of sale—now in possession of the writer—bears date St. Mary's mission, Flathead county, November 5, 1850, and is without doubt, the first written conveyance ever executed within the limits of Montana.

"In 1847 the Hudson's Bay company established a trading post on Crow creek, on the northern portion of the present Flathead reservation, and the place is still known as Hudson's Bay post. Angus McDonald, Esq., who came to the mountains as early as 1838 or 1839, was probably the first officer placed in charge of the new post.

"In 1849 Major Owen started from St. Joseph, Missouri, as sutler for a regiment of United States troops known as the Mounted Rifles, destined for Oregon. The troops came as far as Snake river, when winter caught them, and they built winter quarters on the bank of that river about six miles above Fort Hall, where they spent the winter. The camp was called Cantonment Loring and the place was long known by that name. Major Owen remained at Cantonment Loring until the troops resumed their march in the spring of 1850, when he relinquished his sutlership, and spent the summer on the emigrant road, trading with the emigrants bound for California and Oregon. In the fall of 1850 he came to the Bitter Root valley, and, having bought the improvements of the Catholic fathers, erected a trading post at that point and christened it Fort Owen, a name which it still continues to bear. The fort was constructed of a stockade of logs placed in an upright position with one end planted in the ground. The stockade was necessary to protect the inmates and their property from the incursions of the numerous war parties of the Blackfeet Indians that continued to make raids into the valley up to 1855. It was the custom to drive the horses into the stockade each night during the spring, summer and fall of each year to prevent them from being stolen by the Blackfeet, and even this precaution did not always save them. One night a party of Blackfeet came to the fort, and, with knives and sticks, dug up some of the logs forming the stockade and drove away all of the horses belonging to the fort.

"In the fall of 1852, while hauling hay, a young man named John F. Dobson, from Buffalo Grove, Illinois, was killed and scalped by the Blackfeet in sight of the fort. The writer of this article has in his possession a diary kept by Dobson from the day that he left Illinois, in the spring of 1852, up to the day he was killed. The last entry that he made in it was on the day that he was killed, and is as follows: 'Sept. 14, 1852. I have been fixing ox yokes and hay rigging. Helped haul one load of hay. Weather fair.' The next entry is in the handwriting of Major Owen—apparently made the next day, and in these words: 'Sept. 15. The poor fellow was killed and scalped by the Blackfeet in sight of the fort.' These facts are only cited to show with what trials, dangers and privations the early settlers had to contend with in those days.

"In March, 1853, the Territory of Washington was organized, and Isaac I. Stevens appointed governor of the same. He was also interested in an expedition fitted out from St. Paul, Minnesota, to make the first survey to determine the practicability of a route for a Northern Pacific railroad. This expedition arrived, in what is now Missoula county, in the fall of 1853, bringing with it a number of men who afterwards became citizens of Montana, among whom were Captain C. P. Higgins of Missoula and Thomas Adams and F. H. Burr, who were for a long time residents of Missoula and Deer Lodge.

"In the fall of 1853 Lieutenant John Mullan, a member of the expedition, was directed to establish winter quarters in the Bitter Root valley and make certain observations during the winter. In the fall of 1855 Neil McArthur, an old Hudson bay trader, having retired from the company's service, came to the Bitter Root valley, accompanied by L. R. Maillet and Henry Brooks. McArthur brought with him a band of horses and cattle and located and occupied the buildings at Cantonment Stevens, having during the summer of 1855 concluded a treaty with the Flatheads, Blackfeet, Crows and other mountain tribes of Indians. The Blackfeet had, in a great measure, ceased making raids into the Bitter Root valley and lives and property were comparatively safe.

"The treaty between the United States and the Confederated Flathead nation, consisting of the Flatheads, Pend d'Oreilles and Kootenai tribes, was concluded in a council held in July, 1855, in a large pine grove on the river about eight miles below the present town of Missoula and opposite to the farm of John S. Caldwell. The place was for a number of years known as Council Grove.

"In 1854 the first white woman came to the country now constituting Missoula county, and she was probably the first white woman who honored our state with her presence. In the next year a Mrs. J. Brown came from the East, and, while crossing the Rocky mountains, gave birth to a male child, now grown to manhood and a citizen of a neighboring state. She, with her baby and two little girls, rode alternately a stout, hardy Manitobian steer and a Canadian pony. She visited the Hudson's Bay post in the northern part of our country and remained several days, and then proceeded the same season to Washington Territory. This was probably the first white child born within the limits of our present state.

"In the fall of 1856 several parties who had been spending the summer trading on the 'Road' relinquished that business and came to the Bitter Root valley and took up their residence, among whom were T. W. Harris, Joseph Lompre and William Rogers. During the winter of 1856–57 the population of the Bitter Root valley was larger than it again was until the fall of 1860.

"Up to that time no settlement had been made in the Hell's Gate Ronde. Soon after arrival of Major Pattee he contracted with Major Owen and commenced the erection of a grist and sawmill at Fort Owen. In the latter part of December, 1856, McArthur, having determined upon erecting a trading post in the Hell's Gate Ronde, dispatched Jackson, Holt, Madison, 'Pork' and the writer to Council Grove to get out the necessary timbers to erect the buildings the next summer. Our quarters consisted of an Indian lodge and we fared sumptuously on bread and beef, with coffee without sugar about once a week. The snow fell deep during that winter and the weather was quite cold, but we lost but little time and by spring McArthur paid us off for our winter's work, each man receiving a Cayuse horse in full of all demands. With the coming of spring there was a general breaking up of winter quarters and not many men were left in the country. James Holt and the writer remained in the employ of McArthur, broke about eight acres of land and sowed it to wheat and also planted a garden. This was the first attempt made at farming in the Hell's Gate Ronde. The potatoes, carrots, beets turnips and onions grew well, but the wheat, while in the milk, was completely killed by a heavy frost on the night of the 14th of August, 1857. McArthur was absent during the entire summer and fall, having gone to Colville and thence to the Suswap mines in British

Columbia. In those days we did not have our daily papers and telegraphic dispatches containing the latest news from all parts of the globe, but thought ourselves fortunate if we got one or two Oregon papers in six months; Eastern papers we never saw. The following will show our isolated condition: The presidential election was held in November, 1856, but we knew nothing of the result until about the middle of April, 1857, when Abram Finley arrived from Olympia with a government express for the Indian department, bringing two or three Oregon papers, from which we learned that Buchanan had been elected and inaugurated president.

"Few events of historical interest occurred from the fall of 1857 to the fall of 1859. During the spring and summer of 1858 an Indian war in the Spokane and Lower Nez Perces country cut off all communication with the west and placed the settlers of this county in a dangerous situation. Congress having made a large appropriation to build a military wagon road from Fort Walla Walla to Fort Benton, placed Lieutenant John Mullan in charge of the work. He organized his expedition at the Dalles, Oregon, in the spring of 1858, but was forced to disband it on account of the Indian hostilities. He again organized in the spring of 1859 and constructed the road over the Coeur d'Alene mountains as far as Cantonment Jordan on the St. Regis Borgia, where he went into winter quarters, sending his stock to the Bitter Root valley. During the winter the greater portion of the heavy grades between Frenchtown and the mouth of Cedar creek was constructed. In the spring of 1860 he resumed his march and took his expedition through to Fort Benton, doing but little work, however, between Hell's Gate and Fort Benton.

"In June, 1860, Frank L. Worden and C. P. Higgins, under the firm name of Worden & Co., started from Walla Walla with a stock of general merchandise for the purpose of trading at the Indian agency, but, upon their arrival at Hell's Gate, they determined to locate at that point and accordingly built a small log house and opened business. This was the first building erected at that place and formed the nucleus of a small village that was known far and wide as Hell's Gate. During this year four hundred United States troops under the command of Major Blake passed over the Mullan road from Fort Benton to Fort Walla Walla and Colville. During the fall of this year a number of settlers came into the county and new farms were taken up at Frenchtown, Hell's Gate and in the Bitter Root valley, and during the winter of 1860–61 a considerable number of men wintered in the different settlements.

"On the 14th day of December, 1860, the bill creating Missoula county was passed by the legislative assembly of Washington Territory. The county extended from the 115th degree of longitude east to the summit of the Rocky mountains and from the 46th degree to the 49th degree of latitude, which included all that portion of Deer Lodge county lying west of the Rocky mountains.

"In the spring of 1861 Lieutenant Mullan organized another party and started for Fort Benton to finish up the road he had nearly opened the year before. His expedition was accompanied by an escort of one hundred men under the command of Lieutenant Marsh. The expedition came as far as the crossing of the Big Blackfoot river where they erected winter quarters and named them Cantonment Wright, in honor of Colonel, afterwards General, Wright who quelled the Indian war of 1858 so effectively. During that winter the heavy grades in the Hell's Gate canyon were constructed.

"On the 5th day of March, 1862, the first marriage of two white persons in Missoula county was solemnized at Hell's Gate; that of George P. White to Mrs. Josephine Mineinger. The ceremony was performed by Henry Brooks, justice of the peace, and who was afterwards known as 'Bishop Brooks.' This was probably the first marriage of white persons within the limits of the country that is now Montana.

"The first lawsuit ever commenced in Missoula county, or in fact in Montana, was commenced and tried at Hell's Gate, in the month of March, 1862, before Henry Brooks, justice of the peace. The proceedings were under the laws of Washington Territory. A Frenchman called 'Tin Cup Joe'—other name forgotten—accused Baron O'Keefe with beating one of his horses with a fork handle and then pushing him into a hole, thereby causing his death, and claimed damages in the sum of forty dollars and sued O'Keefe to recover that amount. The place of trial was in Bolte's saloon. Jury of six was impaneled and sworn to try the case. W. B. S. Higgins, A. S. Blake and Bart Henderson were of the jury. As the trial progressed the proceedings became less harmonious until it ultimately culminated in a bit of unpleasantness, the friends of the respective parties lent a hand and it was far from being a select or private affair. While the unpleasantness was in progress the court and the jury had fled for dear life, and when harmony was restored they were nowhere to be found. After considerable search the court and jury were captured and the trial proceeded. The case was finally given to the jury, and after a brief time they came into court and rendered a verdict for the plaintiff for forty dollars damages. The costs swelled the judgment to about ninety dollars. This was probably the most hotly contested case ever tried in the state. The defendant endeavored to take an appeal to the district court, but as that court was held at Colville, three hundred miles distant, he concluded to settle the judgment, which he did. Poor Bishop Brooks was, in 1865, killed in Uncle Ben's gulch near Blackfoot City, shot through a glass in a door by whom or for what cause was never known.

"On the 3d day of March, 1863, Idaho Territory was organized and this county became a part of that Territory and an election was held in the fall of that year for members of the legislature. The writer has no knowledge that any county officers were appointed by the governor of Idaho for this county, and from the fact that Montana was organized on the 26th of May, 1864, he is of the opinion that none were appointed. In the fall of 1864, under the proclamation of Governor Edgerton, an election was held for delegates to congress and members of the legislature. September 27, 1867, the first district court convened in Missoula county, Hon. L. P. Williston presiding. The first churches established in Montana were in Missoula county, the first being at the old Catholic mission established in the Bitter Root valley, and the next that of St. Ignatius mission. Prior to 1865 there was scarcely a protestant minister within the Territory of Montana. Bishop Tuttle of the Episcopal church visited Missoula in 1870, and the services held by him were the first by any protestant minister in the town of Missoula. In 1872 Rev. T. C. Iliff of the Methodist Episcopal church organized a congregation in Missoula. The first Presbyterian church was organized in Missoula in 1876.

"The first train over the Northern Pacific railroad reached Missoula August 7, 1883, and the last spike connecting the east and west divisions of the road was driven at a point between Garrison and Gold Creek by Henry Villard, president of the road, on September 8, 1883."

Judge Woody came to what is now Montana in October, 1856, when the western portion of the state of Montana was a part of Washington Territory. He has resided in the country ever since, and nearly all of this time in Missoula county, thus giving him a residence in Montana of over forty-four years. During all this time he has, without moving, been an inhabitant of three territories and one state. The western portion of Montana was, in 1856, Washington Territory, then became

Idaho Territory, Montana Territory and finally the state of Montana.

Judge Woody was born in Chatham county, North Carolina, on December 10, 1833, and on his paternal side was of Quaker descent, and on his maternal side of good old revolutionary stock. His early life was that of a farmer with very limited educational advantages. At the age of eighteen he entered New Garden Boarding school (now Guilford college), a Quaker institution of learning near Greensboro, North Carolina. After remaining at this institution one year, he taught school in the eastern portion of the state for six months. He then, in the summer of 1853, attended another Quaker school in Indiana, after which he taught school in that state until April, 1855, when he removed to Kansas. Not being satisfied with the country, and with a desire to see more of the West, he joined a merchant wagon train bound for Great Salt Lake, and remained with the train until it reached a point west of Fort Laramie. He then joined an emigrant party bound for Shoalwater bay, in the Territory of Washington, and remained with it until it reached Independence Rock, a once noted point on the Sweetwater river, near the South Pass, in the state of Wyoming. At this point he became sick and was forced to remain several days and eventually fell in with a party of Mormons bound for Salt Lake and went with them, reaching there August, 1855.

He remained in Utah until the fall of 1856, when he joined a party of traders coming to the "Flathead country" (now Missoula and Ravalli counties), to trade with the Indians, and about the middle of October arrived on the Hell Gate river, near where the town of Missoula now stands.

From that time until February, 1866, he followed different pursuits, engaging in freighting, mining and merchandising, and, on the last date named was, by the board of county commissioners, appointed county clerk and recorder of Missoula county, which office he held continuously by re-election until the fall of 1880, when he refused to again become a candidate. During a portion of this time he also filled the office of probate judge, which office had been consolidated with that of county clerk and recorder. For eight years of this time he also served as deputy clerk of the second judicial district court of the county of Missoula. While acting in the latter capacity, he began the study of law and was admitted to the bar in January, 1877. He soon built up an extensive clientage and took the rank as one of the leading lawyers of western Montana. In 1869 he was elected a member of the legislative council from the counties of Missoula and Deer Lodge.

He once edited a weekly newspaper, and at a period when editors labored under difficulties and disadvantages of which the present generation can scarcely conceive. Then mails were but weekly and later on tri-weekly, and often in the winter it was from eight to twelve days between deliveries, therefore an Eastern or California paper was seldom to be obtained so that the old-time editors had great difficulty in making their editorial columns or securing clippings for the general news page. But, after all, the infrequent arrival of the mails was in favor of the Montana editor, for in those days few of the general readers of the territorial papers ever read an Eastern or a Pacific coast paper, consequently everything printed in their home paper was news to them, and the editor, who was supposed to be the writer, was praised as a smart fellow, when, in fact, it was often copied from other papers.

At the annual meeting of the Montana Press Association at Anaconda last fall, Judge Woody was present and was called upon to give his experiences as an editor. The judge arose, and, in a humorous way, said:

"I remember well when we received the news of the death

of Napoleon III., in 1873. I wanted to write an editorial about him and give a short sketch of his career, but there was not a work of reference in town. Fortunately the San Francisco Chronicle, which was received, contained an account of his death and also an elaborate editorial on his life and achievements, and from this I constructed an editorial which would have astonished the editor who wrote the one for the Chronicle.

"These pilferings were hardly legitimate, but were excusable under the plea of 'military necessity.' In the early days the editors of many of our weekly papers were not only editors, but 'local,' and often proprietors, and they were required to furnish not only the copy, but the means to keep the paper running, which was not always easy to do when we shipped our paper by express from Helena to Missoula at twelve and one-half cents per pound, cash down, before we could get it out of the express office. Talk about 'steamer day!' No one ever rustled on steamer day as we were compelled to on the day when the express arrived with our week's supply of paper. We never failed to get our paper out of the express office, but it sometimes made us sweat blood to do it. In those days there was never a circus in the vicinity. There were no shows of any kind, and complimentary tickets to such entertainments were never seen by the editorial 'staff.'

"In those days, while we did not get any complimentaries, and but little wedding cake and wine, we received our regular supply of threatened lickings, and the kickers of those days were more robust, muscular and dangerous than the kickers of the present time. Most of them wore six-shooters, which had a decidedly ugly look. It was not always safe to write what we deemed a complimentary personal, and on more than one occasion I raised a storm by printing what I deemed an innocent local. I wrote a harmless item—as I thought—concerning some school mams who were coming to Missoula to spend their vacation and incidentally mentioned that a bachelor of the town, hearing of the intended visit of these school mams, had caused a new picket fence to be constructed around his bachelor quarters in order to protect himself from invasion. Now I thought this was exceedingly clever, but just here I made a mistake. The bachelor friend was highly indignant and did not speak to me for more than a month, and when I received the next number of the New Northwest, of Deer Lodge, it contained a letter from one of the aforesaid school mams, in which she walked all over me with spikes in her shoes. This was a good opening, and in our next issue I returned to the fray a little, just vigorously enough to get the lady to go another bout. She came back sharper than ever in the next issued of the New Northwest, and thus it went until Captain Mills, the editor, shut her off, and that ended the fight.

"About this time there was quite a sensation in New York city concerning the 'Little Church Around the Corner.' At the time of which I write, Dr. T. C. Iliff, now of Salt Lake City, was stationed in Missoula as a Methodist minister, and was quite a young man. He had in the summer of 1872 erected a church in Missoula now known as the Methodist church, and during the winter of 1872–73 he, with some other preachers, were holding a protracted meeting in the church. They had quite a revival. One day, during the time the meeting was in progress, I wrote a short local notice of it, in which I referred to the revival in the little church around the corner, and said something to the effect that Brother Iliff had brought into the fold 'Tapioca' and some other tough cases, and that, having succeeded so well with them, there was hope for 'Yeast Powder Bill' and some others in town.

"Be it known that there were then in town two rather hard cases, known by these titles. 'Tapioca' joined the church and became a bright and shining light—for a short time. Well,

Brother Iliff and my other Methodist friends took great umbrage at my little item and appointed a committee, headed by Brother Iliff, to wait on me and demand some kind of a retraction, all of which they did not get.

"However, the storm soon blew over and Brother Iliff and I have ever since been the warmest kind of friends. Such were a few of the amenities of early journalism in the Wild and Woolly West."

Frank H. Woody is now, and has been since his election in 1892, the district judge for the Fourth judicial district of Montana, which comprises Missoula and Ravalli counties.

Thus, in brief, is the history of the first settlement in the state of Montana, and also a short biography of one of her first pioneers.

ROBERT VAUGHN.
DEC. 18, 1899.

Montana Then and Now.

Montana! The name carries with it the "legend of the aborigines" who called it "Tay-a-be-shock-up," or "Country of the Mountain," a name appropriate and expressive that its beautiful significance will ever suggest a synonym as permanent as "The everlasting hills."

It was created a territory by act of congress approved May 26, 1864, and admitted as a state into the Union February 22d, 1889. As now constituted, Montana covers all that vast region lying between the 45th and 49th parallels of north latitude, and the 104th and 116th meridians of west longitude, extending 550 miles from east to west, and nearly 300 north to south, a total of about 150,000 square miles, or nearly 100,000,000 acres. We can more fully appreciate the meaning of these figures when we remember that the six New England states and the great state of New York would not cover this area, that Minnesota and Iowa could be turned over upon it and a margin left for Connecticut to rest upon, or that England and Wales, Ireland and Scotland combined do not near equal it in size.

In another letter I have spoken of Montana as an infant, and well I may for she was "then" only a few days old, her population was only a few hundred gold seekers, her wealth was undeveloped, except for a limited number of gold placer claims; "then" it was thought fit for nothing else. Her civil courts were but those of the miners' courts that were held in the open air or in some miner's log cabin. No one can give a description of what Montana was "then" better than Judge Wade in Joaquin Miller's "History of Montana." He said: "history tells the story of race movements and migrations and the planting of laws and institutions in new countries, but there is nothing in the history of the migration of races more interesting or remarkable than the story of the march and journey of the masses of men, women and families from the states over plains and mountains to the gold fields of the Pacific slope—a march more perilous than that of Xenophon and the ten thousand and the establishment of law and order in a vast and desolate region, and such law as would secure individual rights and promote and protect the mighty industries and enterprises which arise therein.

"These hardy pioneers, these builders of states yet to be, more venturesome than Columbus or Marco Polo, found themselves in a new world, full of resources and surrounded by new and strange conditions. They were beyond the reach of law. They were effectually beyond the protection or control of the government of the United States. These mineral lands had not been declared open to exploration or purchase. There was no means of acquiring title. These immigrants, miners and prospectors were trespassers upon the public domain, and as between themselves actual possession was the only evidence of ownership.

"They organized miners' courts, preserved order, protected life and property, and adjudicated rights, and commenced the conquest and reclamation of a vast unexplored country that has since then added so much to the wealth and power of the United States.

"Montana had a history before it had a name; it enacted laws and established courts before it had a legislature or judges; it planted a state before it was born a territory. The period from the discovery of gold in 1862 to the organization of the territory in May, 1864, was an era of government and control by the inherent force and majesty of American citizenship, unaided by executive, legislative or judicial departments, and as to mines, mining and water rights, this era continued until July, 1866, and May, 1872, when congress opened the mineral lands to exploration and purchase, and validated the miners' rules and regulations theretofore existing. The first courts in what is now Montana were miners' courts, presided over by judges elected by the miners of the districts to enforce miners' rules and regulations by and for themselves. Besides providing for themselves a system of mining law, the people acting together were compelled to exercise their original criminal jurisdiction, which corresponds to the right of self defense in the individual."

At this time new gold discoveries were constantly made, and a rush would follow, or "stampede," as it is called in a mining country. This attracting all classes, and among them the very lowest element, until criminals and outlaws from other places flooded the country and were getting so bold that the well disposed people were compelled to get together and organize for self-defense. At this time comes the work of the vigilance committee, which will always be a thrilling chapter in the history of this great state.

The following was written by one of those that were here "then:" "In the wake of every gold 'stampede' follow a horde of thieves, robbers, desperadoes, criminals of the worst class and refugees from justice. Too idle and thriftless themselves to take up the pick, shovel and pan, they prey upon the honest miners and despoil them of their hard-won treasure. And Montana, during the gold excitement of 1862–3, was no exception to the rule. Among the later arrivals were some desperadoes and outlaws from the mines west of the mountains. In this gang were Henry Plummer, afterwards the sheriff, Charley Reeves, George Ives, Moore and Skinner, who, as soon as they got 'the lay of the country,' commenced their nefarious operations. These ruffians served as a nucleus around which the desperate and the dishonest gathered, and quickly organized themselves into a band, with captain, lieutenant, secretary, road agents, and 'outsiders.' They became the terror of the country. When the stampede in Alder gulch occurred in

HANGING OF JOSEPH WILSON AND ARTHUR L. COMPTON (OLD HANGING TREE).
Courtesy Montana Historical Society, Helena

June, 1863, and the discovery was made of the rich placer diggings there, many of the dangerous classes were attracted
thither. Between Bannock and Virginia City a correspondence
in cipher was constantly kept up. To such a system were
things reduced that horses, men and coaches were marked in
some manner to designate them as fit objects for plunder. The
headquarters of the marauders was at Rattlesnake ranch, in
the upper Beaverhead country, and a favorite resort was
Dempsey's Cottonwood ranch. The plan of operations of the
road agents was to lie in wait at some secluded spot on the
road for a coach, a party, or a single individual, of whom information was given by their confederates, and when near
enough, would spring from their cover with shotguns with the
command, 'Halt! Throw up your hands!' And while a part of
the gang kept their victims covered others would 'go through'
their effects. A failure to comply with the order or any hesi-
tancy in obeying it, was sure to cause the death of the person
so disobeying; and, indeed, if there was probability that any
information which a victim might communicate would result
in danger to themselves, he was shot, on the principle that
'dead men tell no tales.'

"By the discoveries of the bodies of the victims, the con-
fessions of the murderers before execution and other information, it was found that one hundred and two people had within a few months certainly been killed by these miscreants in
various places, and it was believed that many more had shared
the same fate. The whole country became terrorized, and, although the few ranchmen and dwellers in the mining camps
knew the road agents, they dared not expose them for fear
their lives would pay the penalty. Some action on the part of
the honest portion of the community to check these wholesale
murders and robberies and bring their perpetrators to justice
became imperatively necessary. But what was to be done? It

was four hundred miles to the nearest man who was authorized to administer an oath. Clearly no relief could be had from the law. The conclusion that something should be done was hastened by the murder and robbery of Lloyd Magruder and his party, the sum stolen being over fourteen thousand dollars. They were murdered by a number of road agents whom they had unknowingly hired to drive their teams. Magruder was well known and very popular throughout the whole region. This culminating outrage of the desperadoes led to the formation of the vigilance committee late in the year 1863. Five men in Virginia City and one in Nevada City took the initiative in the matter. Two days had not elapsed before their efforts were united, and when once a beginning had been made the ramifications of the league of protection and order extended in a week or two all over the territory. From the 21st of December, 1863, to the 14th of January, 1864, twenty-four of the desperadoes, including the leaders, Henry Plummer and George Ives, were captured and hanged at various places. Every one confessed, or there was testimony to show, that he had murdered one or more men. This vigorous action of the Vigilantes brought to an end the terrible deeds of blood and rapine of the road agents in Montana, and criminals of all classes and grades fled for their lives."

Again Judge Wade says: "Life, liberty and property were without any protection. The situation was desperate and unparalleled. It was crime against society, criminals against honest men, murder and robbery against life and property. The people, few in numbers and scattered over a wide extent of country, were compelled to organize and confederate together for self-preservation. They acted with deliberation. The supreme hour had come. They were to test their right to live. Their calmness was not that of despair or cowardice, but of self-respect, manhood, American citizenship. They did nothing in the nature of mob violence or lynch law. Remembering the forms of law in their distant homes, where judge and jury tried men for crime, they organized citizens' courts with the miners' judge to preside, formed juries who listened to the evidence, had attorneys to prosecute and defend, and not until the testimony had excluded every doubt was a verdict of guilty returned; and when returned, without undue delay, uninfluenced by petty technicalities, maudlin sympathy, or unholy passion it was, in an orderly manner, carried into execution. There is nothing in history like these trials. They were open and public; they were attended by the well disposed people and the desperadoes alike, all being armed and on the alert, some looking for the arrival of confederates and preparing to rescue the prisoners, and others, with their lives in their hands, ready to prevent the attempt. It required supreme courage for a lawyer to prosecute, or for a witness to testify against, a prisoner at these trials."

"Now" Montana has its courts of civil and criminal jurisdiction equal to any state in the Union, and the sturdy stroke of the miner followed by that of the mechanic, farmer, stockman and manufacturer has brought out her hidden treasures, until today Montana is the wealthiest state in the Union in proportion to its population. The total value of the product of her mines and ranges for the year 1897 amounted to $69,139,675, or about $324 per capita of her population, which is about 210,000.

To carry on the vast commerce given rise by this great wealth, Montana has in operation 2,928 miles of railroad, equipped equal to any railway system in the world.

The yearly lumber product is estimated to be worth $1,500,000. The coal product, at an average valuation of $2.60 per ton, is counted at $8,000,000. Nearly all of the lumber and coal are consumed at home.

The towns and mining camps that were "then" propagating crimes and greed, and filling the air with blasphemy, "now" have well selected libraries and are lavish in their expenditures to secure the best class of educational and beneficent institutions. Forty years ago there were but two places of worship in what is now Montana, and they were at St. Mary's and St. Ignatius' missions, where Fathers Giorda and Hoecken were teaching Christianity to the red men of the forest. The four religious denominations—Methodists, Presbyterians, Catholics and Episcopalians—have in Montana "now" over two hundred churches, and other denominations will add seventy-five more to the number. There are social and benevolent organizations, and nearly every secret society known is represented with well-equipped lodges. "Now" Montana has 709 public schools, 55,473 pupils, and 1,186 teachers, and it has its normal school and school of mines, state university and agricultural college. It has 488 postoffices, eighty weekly and fifteen daily newspapers, besides ten semi-weekly and monthly journals.

An Eastern writer tells of the libraries in some of the cities of the West and expressed his astonishment at the intellectual character of the people. The facts are, as far as reading is concerned, that the people of the West are a long ways ahead of those of the East. The brightest, most energetic young men and women of the East make up the leading element of the West. There are more college-educated men in the Western cities than in cities of the same size in the East. People in the West are generally more progressive than in the East. Few towns of the size of this (and none of its age) in the East have the electric lights, the miles of electric railroads, the telephone exchange, the churches, the public library, the elegant opera house, the fine public school buildings, the beautiful parks and, in fact, all the modern improvements which this city has. As to her resources, no one but nature herself can lay claim to placing them where they are. The many precipices, where the mighty Missouri plunges over one and then another with a force of several hundred thousand horse-power, the mountains of various minerals that are near by, the extensive coal fields that are at her doors, the thousands of acres of rich pasture and farming land that surround her. All these have been placed there by Him who created all things; camping ground for the advanced civilization of the West. The great water power at the falls of the Missouri is "now" largely employed in operating reduction works and smelters that reduce ore of the Rocky mountains to the amount of two thousand tons every twenty-four hours and here is operated one of the largest electric refining plants on the continent, where all kinds of metals are separated and refined. All this industrial growth has taken place during the last ten years. This is only a small portion of the development that has taken place in this state during the same length of time. It is not Montana alone that has experienced these changes during the last thirty-six years. The "Then and Now" has revolutionized things in many other sections of the West as greatly as it has in this state. For "then" there was no Southern Pacific railway, no Union nor Central Pacific, no Great Northern or Northern Pacific, neither a Canadian Pacific, nor any transcontinental railway in existence. "Now" it is safe to say that 30,000 miles of railway have been built west of the Missouri river since "then." And "now" great cities have sprung up on the sites that were "then" occupied by Indians and wild game. Verily, great have been the changes wrought in the mighty West by "Then and Now."

ROBERT VAUGHN.

DEC. 2, 1899.

A Sample of the Pioneers of Montana.

Of all the instances in this book giving illustrations of the "then and now," not one is more striking than the following sketch of a once humble Norwegian boy, who, in 1854, landed in the United States with barely enough money to pay his first night's lodging, but who is now one of the millionaires of Montana. The young Norwegian referred to is A. M. Holter, one of Montana's first pioneers, and who now resides in Helena, the capital of the state. A sketch of the frontier life of such a man is a chapter well worth reading. It shows what a man with push, pluck and energy can accomplish.

The first place at which Mr. Holter resided after coming to the United States was Freeport, Iowa, and he remained in that state until 1859, making Osage his headquarters. In the spring of 1860 he joined the rush of gold-seekers to Colorado, then called Pike's Peak. By this time he had joined his brother Martin. After arriving in Colorado, the brothers went to mining and farming; in these pursuits they made some money, but nothing big. In the fall of 1863, in company with his partner, E. Evensen, A. M. Holter left Denver, Colo., bound for Alder gulch, bringing with them a small sawmill. It took them about thirty days to make the trip. After much difficulty, they arrived in Alder gulch. To give an account of this arrival, I cannot do better than to give the following which appeared in the Helena Independent Sept. 7, 1899, after an interview with Mr. Holter concerning his early days in Montana. He said:

"The fact is that we—my partner and I—didn't get there until Dec. 1, 1863, and we selected a location on Ramshorn gulch. We managed to get our outfit as far as the summit between Bevin and Ramshorn gulches with teams, where we found deep snow and more snow falling. It kept on snowing; I remember seventeen days in succession that it snowed every

ANTON M. HOLTER.
Courtesy Montana Historical Society, Helena

day. We camped there under some spruce trees, with no other shelter, and the wind blowing all the time. There we made a hand sled to handle the machinery and built a brush road a distance of a mile and a half to get the machinery we had down to the creek, where our water power was to be had. We finally got the stuff down there and had a cabin up without doors or windows and moved into it on Christmas day. The snow was then four feet deep and it was still snowing. In fact, we had snow all winter, although I do not remember that it ever got much deeper than that around us.

"I didn't know a thing about the sawmill business, and my partner, who had represented himself to be a millwright, proved that he didn't know much about it either. We unpacked our machinery and began to put it together and found that some of the parts that were necessary for its use were missing. The feeding apparatus was gone, among other things. We set to work and invented a new movement, which, by the way, was afterwards patented—by other parties.

"In the first place, we had to have blacksmithing done, and we had no tools, so we set out to make some. We had a broadax and we drove it into a block of wood and used it for an anvil. We had a sledge, and made a pair of bellows out of some wood and our rubber coats. There was a nail hammer with the outfit, and with it and the sledge, and the anvil and a forge we got together, we managed to make the other tools we absolutely needed. We made our own charcoal, and finally got that part of the preliminary work done.

"We had no lathe to turn the shafting, and we finally rigged a contrivance in the cabin wall to thrust one end into. We fixed up a wheel for the other end and made a belt out of rawhide to turn the thing by hand until we got the shafting turned. The lathe was even more primitive than the blacksmith shop, but we got the work done after a fashion, although it was a slow process.

"After that we whipsawed some lumber, made our water wheel, fitted up the mill, and got out several thousand feet of lumber before spring set in. That was my first winter's work in Montana, and it was a hard one, too; part of it was all the more trying because I had my face cut up in a little unpleasantness with the road agents about that time.

"We had no belting, and we made some of rawhide, but there was no way of keeping it dry, for we had a water mill. We heard of eighty feet of six-inch belting at Bannock. I went over and tried to buy it. The man that owned it had no use for it and said so, but he wouldn't set a price and I made him several offers, finally telling him that I would give him $600, all the money I had with me. He wouldn't sell even then, and I had to go back without it, and we made a shift to use a canvas belt that we made ourselves. It was a poor affair, but we got along somehow.

"Lumber brought high prices, though, and we made some money after all our trouble. We got $140 a thousand for sluice lumber, and $125 for common lumber. The sluice lumber was finished on the edges and the other wasn't. The second year we started a yard at Nevada City, and I remember that the demand was so great that whenever we expected a wagon in there would be a crowd of men waiting for it, who wouldn't let me get to it at all. As soon as the binding was taken off the load, they would make a rush for the wagon and every man would take off what he could carry. The demand was so keen that they felt justified in taking it by force, and I wouldn't even have a chance to keep an account of what was taken. As far as I know, however, it was always correctly accounted for and I do not believe that there was ever a stick that went out that way that I didn't get my pay for."

The reader will notice that Mr. Holter spoke of having "a little unpleasantness with the road agents." The story of that occurrence is now fresh in my memory. It was this way:

Mr. Holter was on a return trip from Virginia City, Dec. 11, 1863, when he came very near being killed by highwaymen, who were then terrorizing the country with their violence. George Ives, the leader of a gang of desperadoes, and some of his companions, had met Holter on the way near the mouth of Big Hole, and had evidently been keeping track of him, thinking that he might sell some goods which he had in Virginia City and that on his return he would have some money. Mr. Holter had marketed some articles in Virginia City, but, as it happened, he did not draw the money for them. This time he was returning with the two yoke of oxen without the wagon, and at the point of the road where the trail over the hill strikes the gulch, just below Nevada City, Ives and his companion, Erwin, passed him, and, as they went by, one spoke to the other, addressing him as George. They went on ahead and took the lower road by Laurin's place, but Holter with his oxen took the upper road. When near the crossing of Brown's gulch, Ives and Erwin, finding that Holter had taken the upper road, galloped their horses and met him. They began business at once; Ives drew and leveled his revolver on Holter, standing about four feet from him, and ordered him to pass over his money. Holter said that he did not have any, but Ives said that he knew better, and made him turn all his pockets inside out. Holter passed over his empty purse; Ives examined it and threw it away; and he gave him his pocketbook, in which there were some papers and a small amount of postal currency. Ives was angry at not getting money, as he evidently expected. He ordered Holter to leave the road and follow their trail. Holter remarked that as they had the drop on him he supposed he would have to obey. Just then he turned and spoke to his cattle, turning instantly again only to see Ives deliberately aiming at his head. The bullet entered Holter's hat just above the band and grazed his scalp, cutting the hair as smoothly as with a razor and taking the skin off part of his brow. For a moment Mr. Holter was stunned, and would have fallen had it not been for the fact that he was near the oxen and threw his arm over the neck of one of them and staggered against the animal. On recovering his senses, his first impulse was to pick up a new ax and a handle that had dropped from under his arm. Ives at this instant, seeing that his first shot had not killed, raised his gun and deliberately aimed again at Holter's heart, but the gun snapped. Seeing a possibility of escaping, Holter jumped in front of the cattle and got on the other side of them before Ives could fire again. The off oxen suddenly started up and crowded the others onto the mounted desperadoes, diverting their attention and making them move back. During this commotion, Holter at once thought of some beaver dams in the creek a few yards away and broke for them. The road agents, seeing some men with a team coming up the road, went off in another direction as unconcerned as if nothing had happened. Holter then made his way to a cabin on the lower road, where "One-Eyed Reilly" and his associates lived. Here he tried to borrow a rifle or get them to go back with him, but they refused him any assistance whatever. From their answers and conduct, Mr. Holter became satisfied that they were confederates or silent partners with the road agents. As it was then growing dark, Holter went back to where he had left the oxen. After having unyoked them, he recovered his hat and went up the gulch and stayed over night with Stuart, Malcolm Morrow and Charles Olsen, who were then mining there. It turned out that the reason Ives' pistol only snapped the time he tried to shoot Holter the second time was that at Lauren's Ives, being already pretty full and being refused any more liquor, he had amused himself by shooting at the decanters and had but one shot left.

After getting back to camp, thinking and talking to his partner about the matter, Mr. Holter made up his mind deliberately that it was his duty above all things to arm himself and hunt up Ives and kill him or perish in the attempt. His partner did all he could to persuade him to give up the idea, but at last said that he would go with him. After outfitting themselves, they both started out to hunt Ives, when at the very first place they stopped they were told that Ives had been hanged. The news made Holter feel very badly, not because Ives was hanged, but because he was not present to assist with the job.

The first quartz mill Mr. Holter said that he saw in the territory was on the Monitor lode in Bevin's gulch, and not far from his sawmill. The stamps were made of wood with iron bands around the bottom to keep them from splitting, and spikes were driven thickly into the wooden stamp to receive the blow when striking the ore.

The next year Holter and his partner started lumber yards at Virginia City and Nevada City in Alder gulch, and the same summer Holter, with two other men by the name of Cornelius and Olsen, built some water works in Virginia City. This was rather a hard undertaking, for everything had to be invented anew from the ordinary way of building water works. The piping and hydrants had to be made of logs, and there was no way to procure a manufacturer's auger with which to bore the logs. As high as $150 apiece was paid for three augers made by a blacksmith for the purpose. Mr. Evensen, his partner in the sawmill, had gone back to Denver to get more machinery and a planing mill. He purchased a freight outfit, consisting of oxen and wagons, and secured a second-hand planing mill, but was unable to get any machinery, so he loaded up with provisions and started back. On his return he was snowed in on Snake river, where he lost most of his outfit. What remained of the goods was brought on pack animals into Virginia City in the spring of 1865 at 10 cents per pound freight. But good prices were obtained for these remnants, however. Ten-penny nails were sold at Virginia City for $150 per keg, in gold dust. These were again retailed at $2 per pound. Some flour had arrived in Virginia City, and the price had dropped from $150 per sack of ninety pounds to $60. Holter reshipped what flour he had to Helena, where it was disposed of at $100 per sack.

That winter he bought a second-hand portable steam engine and boiler, and had managed to make a sawmill and move it onto Ten Mile creek, about eight miles west of Helena. To this was added the planing mill his partner had bought in Denver, Colo., and which was the first one of the kind in Montana. Soon afterwards the firm opened a lumber yard in Helena, at a point which is now the corner of Main and Wall streets. While the price of lumber at Virginia City had been $125 per thousand for common and $140 per thousand for sluice or flume lumber, the price at Helena was only $100 per thousand for common lumber. In the latter part of June, 1864, Mr. Holter bought out Mr. Evensen and took in his brother Martin as a partner, and the firm became known as A. M. Holter & Bro., and the demand for lumber was increasing very fast.

In the autumn of 1866 Mr. Holter went East by the Overland stage. The price for transportation to Omaha was then $350 in gold dust, or $700 in currency. While nearly a month on the road to Chicago, he said that after deducting stop-overs it took him but seventeen days and nights actual travel. It was the quickest trip on record up to that date.

While East he purchased a new steam sawmill; also machinery for a door and sash factory, and appliances for a distillery and an assortment of general merchandise, which he shipped by the way of St. Louis and Fort Benton, but as some of these purchases did not reach St. Louis in time to go on the first boat it was nearly two years before they reached Fort Benton. Freight from St. Louis to Fort Benton was then 12 cents per pound, and from Benton to Helena 10 cents per pound.

Holter had spent most of the winter in Chicago, and, when ready to return, was married to Miss Loberg on the 6th of April, 1867. Their wedding trip, as Mr. Holter tells it, was an enjoyable one, the bride journeying to Montana by way of St. Louis and the Missouri river route to Fort Benton, then by stage to Helena, while the groom came by the way of Salina, Kan., then by the Overland stage over the Smoky Hill route, by the way of Denver and Salt Lake, with sixteen other passengers. Each passenger was furnished by the stage company with rifle and ammunition, for the Indians east of Denver were then on the warpath. Fortunately, the Indians did not make an attack, but great inconveniences were met by the burning of stage stations and the killing and stealing of the stock by the Indians. Mr. Holter said that at one place all hands lay three days and nights in a haystack, for there was not stock to draw the coach, and at one time the same mules had to be driven three drives, aggregating seventy-five miles, on account of the burning of the stations and the killing of the stock. He said that one of the stations was on fire and the roof falling in as they passed it, but he finally reached Helena after "staging" it twenty-five days and nights.

He said that at Salt Lake City he was informed that the steamer Gallatin, on which his wife was a passenger, had been captured by the Indians, and, at different points along the Missouri river, she, in turn, was told that all the overland stages on the road to Montana had been captured by the Indians. This unpleasant news caused considerable uneasiness on both sides at the time. But this remarkable wedding trip ended by Mr. and Mrs. Holter's having a happy meeting in Helena.

On his return to Helena, Mr. Holter erected a building on Main street, where the Pittsburg block now stands and, after the arrival of the goods in the fall of 1867, he opened a general merchandise store. The sawmill, also the sash and door factory and the distillery, were completed during 1868 and 1869. The sash and door factory and the distillery were the first of these industries erected in Montana.

In 1869 Mr. Holter sustained a loss of about $40,000 by fire; the sawmill and planing mill were burned in March, and a month later the first big fire occurred in Helena, in which he sustained a loss.

The Rumley mine was discovered in 1871, in which Holter purchased an interest, and started negotiations with Frederick Utch of Cologne, Germany, for his right in the United States for the then existing patent on the Utch concentrating jig. He had one of these shipped to Montana, but it took a long time to get it here, as it was shipped by way of the Union Pacific railroad, which was then being built; consequently it laid a year at Rawlins, Wyo., but finally arrived, and was set up on the Legal Tender mine, east of Helena. Along in the early 70s he erected the first concentrator in the Rocky mountains on the Rumley mine. The mechanics were inexperienced, and it soon became evident that the machinery was not of sufficient strength, and the venture was a failure, with the exception that it showed what could be done in the way of concentration by properly erected machinery, and Montana is today the foremost in concentrating ore by this process.

In the spring of 1877 he purchased a part of the Parrot mines, which proved to be one of the best investments he ever made. In 1880 this property was organized into the Parrot Silver and Copper Company.

In 1879, on account of ill health, Mr. Holter took a trip to Europe, sending most of the time in Norway and Sweden, and returned to Montana in about eight months.

In 1878 Holter & Bro. built a sawmill on Stickney creek and started a lumber yard at the mouth of Sun river, with George Wood in charge, where Great Falls now stands, and erected a planing mill at that city in 1855.

In 1880 Mr. Holter and others purchased the Elkhorn mine at Ketchum, Idaho. In 1881 he became interested in the Maginnis, the Kit Carson, the Stuart, the Silver Bell, Peacock in Idaho and in the Elkhorn mine in Montana. In 1882 he became identified with the Helena Mining and Reduction Company, which was afterwards changed to the Helena and Livingstone Mining and Reduction Company, which established the East Helena plant in 1888. In 1884 the same company erected the first street railway in Helena and also organized a gas company in the same city.

In 1886 he, with others, organized the Helena Concentrating Company. This company afterwards erected the first concentrator in Idaho, at Wardner. This, however, has been replaced by a larger and more modern plant. In 1886 this company purchased an interest in the Helena and Victor Mining Company, and erected a concentrating plant at Victor. The same year Mr. Holter and others organized the Livingston Coal and Coke Company, and opened the mines and built a washing plant at Cokedale in Park county.

In 1887 the Holter Lumber company and the A. M. Holter Hardware Company were incorporated, of each of which companies Mr. Holter is president. In 1888 Mr. Holter and others purchased the properties at Wardner, Idaho, now known as the Helena Frisco, and constructed there a large concentrator, which was destroyed by the riot at Frisco in 1892, but has been rebuilt. In 1890 he and others organized the Cascade Land Company.

In 1892, in company with his family, he took another trip to Europe, being absent about five months. Again, in 1892 and 1893, Holter and his partners did a large amount of development work in the Trail creek district, now known as Rossland, B.C.

In 1891 the same parties purchased the Blue Canyon coal mines, and commenced building the Bellingham Bay & Eastern railway. In 1892 they organized the Coeur d'Alene Hardware Company at Wallace, Idaho. Mr. Holter was one of the promoters that erected a Peck Montana concentrating plant at Corbin in 1891, and another at East Helena in 1898. This process promises to revolutionize concentration. In 1898 they organized the Sand Point Lumber Company, at Sand Point, Idaho.

Going back a little, Holter and others organized the Montana Lumber and Manufacturing Company, in 1888. This company met with a heavy loss in 1895 by the burning of its sash and door factory at Helena. The next year they bought a half interest in the Capital Lumber Company, and the two companies were, in 1898, sold to the Washoe Copper Company.

I am personally acquainted with A. M. Holter, and have been since he located his mill on Ten-Mile creek. Then I kept a butcher shop in Nelson gulch and furnished him meat for his men.

Mr. Holter is a Republican in politics and the first of that party who was elected to office in the city of Helena. He has held several offices, always with credit to himself and satisfaction to his constituents.

In 1868 he was elected a school trustee and served three terms. He was elected to the territorial legislature in 1878, and in 1880 was elected a member of the city council of Helena and was honored with the presidency of that body. He was elected a member of the house of representatives of the state of Montana in 1888. He has also held the office of president of the Helena board of trade. He was president of the Pioneer Society of Montana, and delivered a very able address at the annual meeting of the society in 1890.

Mr. Holter's success in life is due to his own efforts. He has carved out a liberal competency for himself and family from the rugged forces of nature, and the struggle has left the impress of vigorous resolution and tenacity of purpose upon his character. His judgment has been called into requisition on many occasions of public importance, and he has always been foremost in every effort for the advancement of the public weal. He is a man of quiet and unassuming demeanor, recognizing his old-time friends wherever he meets them—whether poor or rich, it makes no difference to him. As a far-seeing man of business affairs, he stands almost without a peer.

Mr. Holter was born June 29, 1831, at Moss, on the eastern shore of Christiana Fjord, Norway. He came to the United States in 1854. His wife was a native of Modum, Norway. They have five sons and one daughter.

And "now" A. M. Holter dwells in one of the finest mansions in the state and is surrounded by one of the most cultured families in the city of Helena.

I could name scores of others that came to the territory in the early days, who endured all kinds of perils and hardship, besides being in danger of being killed by Indians or highwaymen, and who never flinched from "putting their shoulder to the wheel" from that time to this. Always engaged in enterprises that were of benefit to the people as well as to themselves and the general progress of the country.

It is because of my familiarity with the subject of this sketch that I selected Mr. Holter as an example to give the people of today an idea of the work of the pioneers in the early days of this state.

ROBERT VAUGHN.
OCTOBER 25, 1899

The Indian.

Before going any further I will endeavor to give a brief sketch of the Indians and their behavior in Montana from the time I came into the country in 1864 to the present time.

The Indian is a born warrior. When an infant pappoose, his first toy is a bow and arrow. About twenty-five years ago I was in a Piegan camp just after they had killed an Indian of the Crow tribe, who had been stealing some of their horses. After mutilating the body beyond description, the pappooses had the hands that were cut off at the wrist; they were having great play over them, romping and throwing the dead Indian's hands at each other. By such means they cultivated the savage, warlike disposition in the young Indian minds from the beginning. Until lately, if they could not have the whites to fight, they would be at war with some other tribe. They always had their war paint prepared and their hatchets sharpened, so they could go on the warpath whenever the evil spirit moved them. They were naturally treacherous, savage and cruel to those they were not at peace with, be it the whites or their own race, it made no difference. I do not know of any better testimony to show the Indian in his element than the illustration given by Ross Cox, an English gentleman, who, in 1813, came to what is now called Montana, by the way of Columbia. He was at the head of a fur trading company, and was a man of responsibility. He says: "We spent a comparatively happy Christmas, and by the side of a blazing fire in a warm room forgot the sufferings we endured in our dreary progress through the woods. There was, however, in the midst of our festivities a great drawback to the pleasure we should otherwise have enjoyed. I allude to the unfortunate Blackfeet who had been captured by the Flatheads. Having been informed that they were about putting one of their prisoners to death, I went to their camp to witness the spectacle. The man was tied to a tree, after which they heated an old barrel of a gun until it became red hot, with which they burned him on the legs, thighs, neck, cheek and stomach. They then commenced cutting the flesh from about the nails which they pulled out, and next separated the fingers from the hand, joint by joint. During the performance of these cruelties, the wretched captive never winced, and instead of suing for mercy he added fresh stimulus to their barbarous ingenuity by the most irritating reproaches, part of which our interpreter translated as follows: 'My heart is strong; you do not hurt me; you can't hurt me; you are fools; you do not know how to torture; try it again; I don't feel any pain yet; we torture your relations a great deal better, because we make them cry out loud like little children; you are not brave; you have small hearts, and you are always afraid to fight.'

"Then, addressing one in particular, he said: 'It was by my arrow you lost your eye,' upon which the Flathead darted at him and with a knife scooped out one of his eyes, at the same time cutting the bridge of his nose almost in two. This did not stop him; with the remaining eye he looked sternly at another and said: 'I killed your brother and scalped your old fool of a father.' The warrior to whom this was addressed instantly sprung at him and separated the scalp from his head. He was then about plunging a knife in his heart, until he was told by the chief to desist. The raw skull, bloody socket and mutilated nose now presented a horrible appearance, but by no means changed his tone of defiance.

"'It was I,' said he to the chief, 'that made your wife a prisoner last fall; we put out her eyes; we tore out her tongue; we treated her like a dog. Forty of our young warriors'—the chief became incensed the moment his wife's name was mentioned; he seized his gun, and, before the last sentence was ended, a ball from it passed through the brave fellow's heart, terminating his frightful sufferings. Shocking, however, as this dreadful exhibition was, it was far exceeded by the atrocious cruelties practiced on the female prisoners. We remonstrated against the exercise of such horrible cruelties. They replied by saying the Blackfeet treated their prisoners in the same manner; that it was the course adopted by all red warriors, and that they could not think of giving up the gratification of their revenge to the foolish and womanish feelings of white men.

"Shortly after this we observed a young female led forth, apparently not more than fourteen or fifteen years of age, surrounded by some old women, who were conducting her to one end of the village, whither they were followed by a number of young men. Having learned the infamous intention of her conquerors, and feeling interested for the unfortunate victim, we renewed our remonstrance, but received nearly the same answer as before. Finding them still inflexible, and wishing to adopt every means in our power consistent with safety, in the cause of humanity, we ordered our interpreter to acquaint them that, highly as we valued their friendship and much as we esteemed their furs, we would quit their country forever unless they discontinued their unmanly and disgraceful cruelties to their prisoners. This had the desired effect, and the miserable captive was led back to her sorrowing group of friends. Our interference was nearly rendered ineffectual by the furious old priestesses who had been conducting her to the sacrifice. They told the young warriors they were cowards, fools, and had not the hearts of fleas, and called on them in the names of their mothers, sisters and wives to follow the steps of their forefathers and have their revenge on the dogs of Blackfeet. They began to waver, but we affected not to understand what the old women had been saying. We told them that this act of self-denial on their part was peculiarly grateful to the white men, and by it they would secure our permanent residence among them, and in return for their furs we would furnish them with guns and ammunition sufficient to repel the attacks of their old enemies, and preserve their relations from being made prisoners. This decided the doubtful and the chief promised faithfully that no more tortures should be inflicted on the prisoners, which I believe was rigidly adhered to, at least during the winter of 1813."

Those tribes Mr. Cox speaks of are still in existence in Montana, and "now" the most civilized in the state. It is a marvel what civilization has accomplished since "then." Some of the young Indians that attended the Cascade county fair last fall at this place, with the excellent exhibit from the Fort Shaw Indian school (of which a reference will be made in another letter), belong to the same tribes.

We will go back to but thirty-one years ago, and see what the Indians were then. I will not attempt to follow their warpath, for it is too long; besides, we would be continually delayed by arriving at the innumerable bloody spots where one or more of the brave pioneers fell at the hands of the redskins. To give an account of all these unmarked graves would make volumes. The story of the massacre at Fort Phil Kearney saddened the hearts of every frontiersman, but aroused their feelings and made them more desperate against the Indians than ever when they learned that eighty-one people were killed; not one escaped the scalping knife in the hands of the redskins.

About that time Fort Buford was attacked by the Indians, but they were repulsed. The savages returned with a strong reinforcement, renewed the attack, and, after losing over three hundred of their number, succeeded in capturing the post and putting to death Colonel Rankin and his entire command. Colonel Rankin shot his wife himself rather than have her suffer the cruelty of the savages.

Also the Blackfeet, in the northern part of the territory, disregarded all treaties that they had heretofore agreed upon, and began their murderous depredations by killing freighters, prospectors and immigrants who were then coming into the country in great numbers.

Thomas Francis Meagher, who had been a general in the Civil War, was secretary of Montana, and, at this time, was governor pro tempore in the absence of Governor Sidney Edgerton. General Meagher called for six hundred volunteer cavalry. There was not time to lose; it would take too long to have communication from Washington, for it was 1,700 miles to the nearest railway station, and about as many miles of red tape to go through. So everybody rallied; some gave money, others horses and saddles; the most difficulty was to equip the men, it was no trouble to get volunteers. When there were two in a cabin together, one joined the volunteers while the other one stayed at home and divided the profits, be it working for wages or otherwise. General Meagher was in command of the volunteers, and while in the service was drowned in the Missouri river at Fort Benton by falling off the steamer G.A. Thompson. His body was never found, although every effort was made to find the remains.

It was at Fredericksburg, I think, that General Meagher and his gallant Irish brigade made the daring charge. Leading his men he said: "Come on boys, let us have more dead Irishmen nearer the mouth of them cannon than anybody else." The death of the general was a great loss to the territory, for all such men were in demand in Montana then.

A proclamation was issued by Governor Smith, dated July 3, 1867. The proclamation is thus given:

"Helena, M.T., July 3, 1867.—Whereas, it has pleased Almighty God to take from us by accident our esteemed friend, Secretary (late acting governor) Thomas Francis Meagher, who was drowned at Fort Benton on the night of the 1st inst., by falling from the steamer G.A. Thompson;

"Now, therefore, I, Green Clay Smith, governor of the Territory of Montana, do direct that the headquarters of the military, which were established under his directions and authority in the various districts of the territory, be draped in mourning for thirty days.

"I further request that the offices of the federal officers of the territory be likewise draped in mourning for the same length of time.

"It is but due to the memory of our deceased friend and fellow officer that we should hold him in fond remembrance.

"He was a man of high social qualities, great urbanity, a high order of intellect, a brave soldier, a true gentleman and an honor to his territory and government."

The year 1867 Fort Shaw was established by the Thirteenth Infantry, with Colonel Andrews in command. This checked the Indians for a while; but it was only for a short time before they were back to their old tricks, murdering people and stealing their stock. In 1869 the following indictment which was drawn by W. F. Wheeler, the United States Marshal of the Territory of Montana, will show to what desperate resorts the people were driven to. As this instrument of writing was drawn by an officer of the government and signed by twelve citizens under oath we must accept it as a truthful statement of the conditions existing then:

"The Grand Jury of the United States for the Third Judicial District of Montana, have examined a number of witnesses, and from the evidence presented to them find that the people of this district have suffered within the last few months great loss of life and property from predatory bands of Indians. We have been furnished the names of nine or ten citizens who have been murdered in cold blood by them. Over three hundred head of stock have been stolen within two months past, and we believe that within six months fully one thousand horses have been stolen, and a number of valuable citizens sacrificed, whose names we could not learn. The Piegans, Bloods and Blackfeet, who all talk in the same language and constitute the Blackfeet nation, have moved their women and children north of Montana, and in that country have procured ammunition and improved arms. This is a declaration of war on the whites of Montana, and some measure should be taken to meet the emergency. The civil authorities have not the means, and the people are not able to bear the expense of pursuing and punishing these robbers and murderers, who destroy our property and lives, and come and go like the wind. Ours is a contest between civilization and barbarism, and we must risk our lives and sacrifice our hard-earned property to defend them, unless the general government gives us the means of defense. To this we are entitled, as we have left homes of comfort in the East to plant civilization in the wilderness. It is in evidence that the 'Pend d'Oreilles,' who make periodical journeys from their homes to the valleys of the Judith and Yellowstone on hunting expeditions, and through some of the settled portions of our territory, are guilty of horse-stealing if not of murder. Their passage through our settled valleys should be prohibited by the authorities. The River Crows murdered two white men near Fort Benton about the 20th of July last and took their horses to their camp.

"In none of these cases of murder and theft have the Indians been pursued and punished. Our population is necessarily scattered along the valleys, or isolated in mining camps and gulches, and hence is exposed to sudden attacks from the Indians. We make this statement, which is substantiated by truthful evidence, and respectfully request that it may be sent to such officers of the general government as are entrusted with the care of the Indians, and our protection by military force, trusting that they take the necessary steps to give us full protection, or, if the means in their hands are not adequate, that they will represent our exposed and dangerous position to the heads of the government at Washington, who have authority to punish or prevent Indian outrages.

"Grand Jury Rooms, Helena, M.T., Oct. 9, 1869.
"Signed: G. W. Tubbs, foreman; D. W. Buck, A. A. Green, James P. Mabbett, John H. Curtis, Moses Morris, Benjamin Stickney, Jr., E. S. Mansfield, William Simms, D. M. Gillette, E. L. Baker, Felix Poznainsky, L. Behm, W. F. Richardson, Hugh Glenn."

It was the winter following that Colonel Baker destroyed the Piegan camp on the Marias river, an account of which I have already given. To the different tribes, peace commissioners were sent by the government to have council with the Indians. They were wise men from the East. They meant well, but they did not know their business. The first thing they did was to listen to the Indians telling their cunning stories, and the conclusion they came to was that the poor red man had been imposed upon and a kind of treaty was made by giving the Indians nearly everything they asked for. From this time on the Indians were getting "heap rich." As General Sheridan once said: "If a white man steals we put him in prison; if an Indian steals we give him a blanket; if a white man kills we hang him; if an Indian kills we give him a horse to put the blanket on." And what he said was true. For between the Indian commissioners and the traders it was not very long before nearly every Indian had a gun, plenty of ammunition and new blankets. Again, in 1876, the Indians became so arrogant that they defied the United States government, and the great Sioux war commenced. And a year later Chief Joseph, with his desperate band of Nez Perces, passed through the country terrorizing the small settlements and causing death and destruction as he went.

ROBERT VAUGHN.

The Sioux War.

In this series of letters I will give a brief history of the war in Montana between the United States troops and the Indians from 1876 to the death of Sitting Bull in 1890. Several battles were fought in the Rosebud and Big Horn country, and near where myself and comrades camped over night twelve years before the Sioux war commenced. It was no wonder that McKnight, our guide, wanted "five hundred good, resolute, determined men" to go with him in 1864, and through this same nest of savages, as we did them. Here where the never-forgotten battles, where the gallant General Custer, with his five companies of cavalry were killed, not one was left to tell how it happened. By the way the dead lay on the field it was evident that they fought bravely. And now the government has erected on this bloody spot a substantial monument in memory of Custer and his brave men. Not wishing to trust altogether to my own memory—to give the facts and as briefly as possible—I will give a few extracts from Joaquin Miller's "History of Montana," including official reports, together with what I know and have learned from eye witnesses:

The Indians that were on the warpath had been reported as numbering about twenty thousand. Sitting Bull could not be persuaded to stay on the reservation, neither could he see what right the government had to interfere, for he claimed that that country belonged to him and his people, and that he had the right to go wherever he pleased and to do as he pleased, and his men were continually robbing and killing white people; their murders and robberies were so frequent that at last the government took extreme measures and put a stop to their depredations. Sitting Bull had his forces on the tributaries of the Big Horn river, in what is now Custer county, Mont. General Crook was coming from Fort Fetterman, Wyo., leaving March 1, 1876, with a force of seven hundred men and officers, sixty wagons and four hundred pack mules. It was not long before he was skirmishing with the Indians, and the Sioux war commenced. On March 17th, near the mouth of Little Powder river, a desperate battle occurred lasting five hours, in which an Indian village was destroyed with much supplies and munitions of war. Crook's losses were four men killed and many wounded. One hundred and twenty-five tepees were burned and several Indians killed. Part of his letter to the Secretary of War touching on this matter is as follows:

"Fort Reno, March 22d.

"General Reynolds, with part of the command, was pushed forward on a trail leading to the village of Crazy Horse, near the mouth of Little Powder river. This he attacked and destroyed on the 17th inst., finding it a perfect magazine of ammunition, war material and general supplies. I am satisfied that if Sitting Bull is on this side of the Yellowstone he is camping at the mouth of Powder river.

"GEORGE CROOK.

"BRIGADIER GENERAL."

After this battle Crook returned to Fort Fetterman and remained there until May. Then he came back, and on June 15th he was near to the place where he had his battle in March. By this time Terry and Custer had come from Fort Lincoln, Dakota, and General Gibbon was on his way from Fort Shaw, Montana. The total forces were three thousand men and officers. It can be seen that the best part of the United States army, in charge of four as good generals as ever wore uniforms, were now heading for Sitting Bull's camps on the Rosebud and Big Horn rivers. What settlers there were in Montana then were few and far between. There was no railroad nearer than

Corinne, Utah. Some apprehension was felt that the soldiers might cause the Indians to scatter, and that small settlements on the borders would be in danger of being massacred; consequently they all armed and fortified themselves the best they could in case such should happen. At this time in the Sun river valley there were about thirty settlers, including several families. Besides the Sioux war east of us, the Piegans and Blackfeet were north of us; they, too, were acting very ugly by stealing stock and not infrequently killing some one.

In addition to the perils and dangers that were already confronting the settlers of Northern Montana, many of the chiefs of the northern tribes and of the Sioux were meeting in council at Cypress mountain, just north of us. The council was called by the Sioux with the object in view of inducing the Blackfeet, Bloods and Piegans to declare war against the whites. But fortunately the chief, Little Plume, refused to sign the proclamation, thus causing the breaking up of the council, and probably saving the lives of many settlers.

During this critical time, the Sun river settlers organized a protective association for protection to ourselves and property, for nearly all the soldiers that were at Fort Shaw had gone to fight the Sioux in the eastern part of the territory. Two men were detailed to go on the outskirts of the settlement once every day, and if hostile Indians were seen, they were to go through the settlement as fast as their horses could carry them, at the same time firing their guns for a signal; the women and children were to be taken to the village at the Crossing.

Again on the 17th of June General Crook had a desperate battle with Sitting Bull on the tributary of the Rosebud and whipped the Indians badly. After the battle he went back to his base of supplies, for he needed more rations and ammunition in order to follow up the enemy. Near this battle ground and but one week later is where Custer fell. Terry, Custer and

Gibbon, at the time of this battle, were about eighty miles down the Rosebud. Not knowing of Crook's battle, they had a consultation and were determined to advance up the Rosebud at once. Sitting Bull, with all his force, was directly between them and Crook.

As bearing on the movements of the forces, here appear extracts from Major Reno's reports: "As we approached a deserted village in which was standing one tepee, about 11 a.m., Custer motioned me to cross to him, which I did, and moved nearer to his column, until about 12:30 a.m., when Lieutenant Cook, adjutant, came to me and said the village was only two miles ahead and moving away; for me to move forward at as rapid a gait as I thought prudent and to charge afterwards and that the whole outfit would support me; I think those were his exact words. I at once took a fast trot and moved down about two miles, when I came to a ford of the river. I crossed immediately and halted about ten minutes or less to gather the battalion, sending word to Custer that I had everything in front of me, and that they were strong. Deployed and with the Ree scouts on my left we charged down the valley, driving the Indians with great ease for about two and a half miles. I, however, soon saw that I was being drawn into some trap, as they certainly would fight harder, and especially as we were nearing their village which was still standing; besides I could not see Custer or any other support and at the same time the very earth seemed to grow Indians and they were running towards me in swarms and from all directions. I saw I must defend myself and give up the attack mounted. This I did, taking possession of a point of woods, and which furnished near its edge a shelter for the horses; dismounted and fought them on foot, making headway through the woods. I soon found myself in the near vicinity of the village, saw that I was fighting odds of nearly five to one, and that my only hope was to get out of the wood, where I would soon have been surrounded, and gain some higher ground. I accomplished this by mounting and charging the Indians between me and the bluffs, on the opposite side of the river. In this charge First Lieutenant Donald McIntosh, Second Lieutenant Ben H. Hodgson, Seventh Cavalry, and A. A. Surg and J. M. De Wolf were killed. I succeeded in reaching the top of the bluff; with a loss of three officers and twenty-nine enlisted men killed and seven wounded. Almost at the same time I reached the top, mounted men were seen running towards me, and it proved to be Colonel Benteen's battalion, Companies H, D and K; we joined forces and in a short time the pack train came up. As senior, my command was then Companies A, B, C, D, H, G, K and M, about three hundred and eighty men, and the following officers: Captains Benteen, Weir, French and McDougall; First Lieutenants Godfrey, Mathey and Gibson; Second Lieutenants Edgerly, Wallace, Varnum and Hare; A. A. Surg, Porter. First Lieutenant De Rudio was in the dismounted fight in the woods, but having some trouble with his horse, did not join the command in the charge out, and, hiding himself in the woods, joined the command after nightfall of the 26th.

"Still hearing nothing of Custer, and with this reinforcement I moved down the river in the direction of the village, keeping on the bluffs. We had heard firing in that direction, and knew that it could only be Custer. I moved to the summit of the highest bluff, but seeing and hearing nothing, sent Captain Weir with his company to open communication with the other command. He soon sent back word by Lieutenant Hare that he could go no further and that the Indians were getting around him; at this time he was keeping up a heavy fire from the skirmish line. I at once turned everything back to the first position I had taken on the bluff, and which seemed to me the best. I dismounted the men, had the mules and horses of the pack train driven together in a depression, put the men on the crests of the hills making the depression, and had hardly done so when I was furiously attacked; this was about 6 p.m.; we held our ground, with the loss of eighteen enlisted men killed and forty-six wounded, until the attack ceased about 9 p.m."

Here is Major Reno's report, or so much of it as applies to the approaching battle:

"Headquarters, Seventh Cavalry,
"Camp on Yellowstone River, July 5, 1876
"Captain E. W. Smith, A.D.C. and A.A.A.G.:

"The command of the regiment having devolved upon me as the senior surviving officer from the battle of June 25th and 26th, between the Seventh Cavalry and Sitting Bull's band of hostile Sioux on the Little Big Horn river, I have the honor to submit the following report of its operations from the time of leaving the main column until the command was united in the vicinity of the Indian village. The regiment left the camp at the mouth of the Rosebud river, after passing in review before the department commander, under command of Brevet Major General G. A. Custer, lieutenant colonel, on the afternoon of the 22d of June, and marched up the Rosebud twelve miles and encamped; 23d, marched up the Rosebud, passing many old Indian camps, and following a very large lodge pole trail, but not fresh, making thirty-three miles; 24th, the march was continued up the Rosebud, the trail and signs freshening with every mile until we had made twenty-eight miles, and we then encamped and waited for information from the scouts. At 9:25 p.m. Custer called the officers together and informed us that beyond a doubt the village was in the valley of the Little Big Horn, and that to reach it, it was necessary to cross the divide between Rosebud and Little Big Horn; and it would be impossible to do so in the daytime without exposing our

GEN. GEORGE A. CUSTER, U.S.A.
Courtesy Montana Historical Society, Helena

march to the Indians; that we would prepare to move at 11 p.m. This was done, the line of march turning from the Rosebud to the right, up one of its branches, which headed near the summit of the divide.

"About 2 a.m. of the 25th the scouts told him he could not cross the divide before daylight. We then made coffee and rested for three hours, at the expiration of which time the march was resumed, the divide crossed, and about 8 a.m. the command was in the valley of one of the branches of the Little Big Horn. By this time Indians had been seen, and it was certain that we could not surprise them, and it was determined to move at once to the attack. Previous to this no division of the regiment had been made since the order was issued, on the Yellowstone, annulling wing and battalion organizations. General Custer informed me he would assign commands on the march. I was ordered by Lieutenant W. W. Cook, adjutant, to assume command of Companies M, A and G; Captain Benteen, of Companies H, D and K; Custer retaining C, E, F, I and L under his immediate command, and Company B, Captain McDougall, in rear of pack train. I assumed command of the companies assigned to me, and without any definite orders moved forward with the rest of the column and well to its left. I saw Benteen moving further to the left, and as they passed, he told me he had orders to move well to the left, and sweep everything before him."

It is plain that Custer laid his plans to win the fight, and at once. From the position in which the dead were found it is also clear that, having found themselves entirely outnumbered and beyond the reach of help, they took position as best they could in a sort of triangle on the rough, hot hill side, and there died in battle. Custer's brother, Colonel Tom Custer, held one corner of the triangle, and down nearest the river his brother-in-law, Calhoun, another, while the general held the higher ground, so as to see and direct the battle to the end. The men fell almost in line. The officers, Calhoun and Crittenden, fell in their places, as if on parade.

Two years afterwards Robert E. Strahorne, a particular friend of mine, who was all through the campaign with General Crook, sent me the following statement in regard to this Indian war:

"I was, during the trying days of 1876–77, the representative of an Eastern journal and attached to the expeditions which Brigadier General George Crook led against the hostile Sioux and Cheyennes, then commanded by Crazy Horse, Sitting Bull, Dull Knife and Little Wolf.

"In this campaign we were obliged to go without clothing or bedding, save such as we carried on our backs, and without food, except the scantiest allowance possible of bacon and coffee. In this one point, Crook is without a rival in the regular army; he subjects himself to just the same discomfort and hardships as his men have to endure and cuts loose from his wagon train for weeks and months at a time. His wagons are never allowed to become receptacles of luxuries and toothsome delicacies for himself and officers; they carry only grain, ammunition and the necessary articles of daily food.

"At the engagement on the Rosebud, Montana, June 17, 1876, Crazy Horse and Sitting Bull 'bounced' Crook with a force of painted and feathered red devils numbering well up in the thousands. Poor Custer met his fate at the hands of these same warriors only a week later. Crook's forces were not much, if any, superior to Custer's whole command, but he was fortunate in keeping them undivided. He withstood the attack with great skill and courage, although for a while things certainly looked very blue. On this day, a little company of Montana miners, who had been out in the Black Hills prospecting and had joined Crook while on their way back to Montana, did splendid work with their Sharp's sporting rifles. Crook and Terry, those grand soldiers, after poor Custer's command had been wiped out, united their forces on the Yellowstone. How Terry then took for his share the task of cleaning out any hostiles to be found north of the Yellowstone, while Crook, like a bull-dog, hung to the trail which led to the south; how he followed it without bedding, without shelter, without food other than horse meat and berries found in captured villages, and in spite of the pitiless rain which beat down upon us (for I was one of those who camped on the trail), day after day, during the entire march from the mouth of Powder river to the Black Hills.

"I could write a book about our trials and tribulations on those marches, and sometime in the future the half-formed fancy of the present moment may take shape. One thing I wish to impress upon the minds of present and future Montanians, and that is the fact that the campaigns of General Crook and brother officers and men in 1876 and 1877 had the positive result of opening to their permanent occupation and use those vast and beautiful regions drained by the Yellowstone, Big Horn, Rosebud, Tongue, Powder, Musselshell and Judith rivers—regions which up that time had swarmed with the most powerful, vindictive and treacherous tribes of savages America has produced. I went into those campaigns knowing little of the regular army, and indeed somewhat prejudiced against it; I came out satisfied that the mass of its officers and men, the 'youngsters' especially, were brave, intelligent, patriotic, ambitious and courteous—men of whom any country should be proud.

"Closing this reminiscence of an arduous season of toil and danger, I am glad to say that among the lieutenants with whom I faced the red foe, and for whom I formed a great attachment, was the witty, bright and brave Schwatka, whose successes as an Arctic explorer have since made him world famous; Bourke, who besides being an officer of exceptional gallantry and good judgment, has devoted himself, with great patience, to the collection of memoranda upon the manners and customs of the aborigines; Carpenter, noted as an entomologist, and dozens of other officers—Eagan, Charles King, Schuyler, Allison, Chase, Lemley, McKinney (since killed), Delaney, Randall, Sibley, Nickerson, Henry, as brave and intelligent as any men can be—in the army or out of it.

"As Sherman's army had an important element following and surrounding it—'the bummers'—so this hard-worked force that Crook commanded had attached to it a force of correspondents whom I compare, and in all kindness, to the 'bummers' whom Sherman led to the sea. They were an exceptionally fine lot of men. There was Jack Finerty of the Chicago Times. I have always had a notion that he stepped out from some place in Lever's novels; he was brave to rashness, and devoted to the interests of his great journal. Joe Wason, of the Alta California and the New York Tribune, always on the skirmish line after 'pints.' His red head shone like the danger signal of a freight train, but in spite of his red head he was one of the best fellows I ever knew. T. C. MacMillan of the Chicago Inter Ocean, and J. J. Roche of the New York Herald, both physically weak, but intellectually strong, and so on through the list. Readers of the Boston Advertiser, New York Herald and Tribune, Alta California, Philadelphia Press, Washington Star, Denver News, Omaha Republican and Herald, Cheyenne Sun, and other papers represented at various times during that campaign of seventeen months' duration, never imagined while they were reading our letters at their comfortable breakfast table, and growling at the dashed correspondents because they 'didn't make 'em more full,' that the 'dashed correspondent,' dressed in rags, soaked through with rain, and almost crazed with want of food and rest, was writing his letters on a cottonwood chip or a piece of flat stone, and often at the risk of his life from a stray bullet."

There is now in this state one witness of the Custer battles, who is perhaps the only one living. He is William Jackson, an intelligent and well educated half-breed, who now lives at the Blackfeet reservation sixty-five miles from here.

After a long life as government scout, he has turned his attention to farming and cattle raising, and in this pursuit he has been quite successful. He was in this city a few days ago on his way from Helena, where he had been as a witness in a trial which was held in the United States court. A correspondent of the Anaconda Standard, at this place, had an important interview with Mr. Jackson, which is as follows. He says: "Mitch Bouille, William Cross and myself were acting as guides and scouts for the Custer-Terry expedition against the Sioux and Cheyennes who were under the leadership of the wily old Sitting Bull. The battle, as you know, took place on June 25, 1876. On the morning of that day the troopers had made an early start and we, the scouts, had to report we met the command crossing the divide between the Rosebud and Little Big Horn rivers, General Custer rode at the head of his command, the Seventh Cavalry, and Captains French and Benteen and Major Reno were in command of other divisions.

"We had discovered the hostiles camped near the Little Big Horn and about seven miles straight ahead of the soldiers. We so reported to General Custer, and he, calling a halt, summoned the officers under him for a council. The troops were shut out from view on the part of the hostiles by a ridge of land, and it was at the base of this that the council of war was held. It lasted but a few minutes, and Custer's desire for an immediate engagement carried the day. The soldiers were divided into three battalions. Major Reno with the three companies and all of the scouts was to advance rapidly and from a commanding ridge make a charge upon the upper end of the Sioux camp, first gaining a patch of timber about six hundred yards from the enemy. In the meantime General Custer, with five companies, would deploy around the edge of the ridge where they were now halted and attack the lower end of the village and cut off all retreat on the part of the Sioux. Captain Benteen, with four companies, would take up a position on the east band of the Little Big Horn, overlooking the village and protecting the pack train and baggage.

"As the officers left the council they quickly gave orders to the men, and in an instant all were busy inspecting and loading their pistols and carbines, filling their ammunition belts, tightening saddles and looking to every detail preparatory to the fight. Soon the bugle sounded, 'Prepare to mount; mount, forward!' Custer and his men went to the right, Reno to the left, toward the ford of the Little Big Horn. The horses went forward at a sharp trot, and in the moment of waiting on the bank of the stream I looked back and saw Custer with his five companies charging upon the village, Custer fully fifty yards in the lead. That was the last time I ever looked upon that heroic soldier alive or his gallant men. We were soon busy in making the ford, which was somewhat difficult, and then we advanced up the ridge, taking the position assigned us at the council. Up to that time there had been no incident of interest. The troops were dismounted and the horses left in the care of every fourth soldier. Everything was ready for the fight to begin and the wait was not long.

"The hostiles had discovered us at once and took the initiative by making a vicious charge up the hill. Their main body gained a vantage ground behind an elevation sufficient to protect them and just in front of our position. As they charged they drove in our skirmish line, which took a position just inside the timber. The fight was furious for a time, the Indians outnumbering Reno's command at least ten to one. A second charge from the hostiles drove us still higher up the ridge, at least one mile further from the village, and it was in our retreat that we first heard the sounds of firing in the lower end of the village where Custer was engaged. It could not have been very heavy, as he met but few hostiles at the first of the engagement, but it was sufficient to draw the attention of the Indians away from us and turn it upon the unfortunates who were attacking them in the rear. This was between 3 and 4 o'clock in the afternoon and from that time the fighting in the lower end of the Indian camp was hot and heavy. The sound of firing increased steadily until it became a roar, and then it died gradually away until there was only the scattered reports of single shots. All this took place in the space of two hours, and when the June sun set behind the Little Big Horn mountains the Custer command had been entirely wiped out.

"Of course we did not know this at the time, but wondered how the fight had gone. Soon we suspected that something was wrong, for the Indians again turned their attention to Reno, and from that time there was no opportunity to think of anything save what we saw going on about us, and in which we were vitally interested, for the onslaughts of the painted warriors became desperate. Inflamed by their success in killing the Custer command, they now determined to sweep away the rest of their enemies, and time and again they charged up the hill to capture Reno. Only the strength of our position prevented our meeting a fate like that of Custer, and it was after dark before the hostiles gave up their attempt to dislodge and slaughter us. My personal interest in the fray was strong. I had been in the skirmish line, and when we were driven back by the hostiles we retreated slowly, protecting the withdrawal of the main body of Reno's command. In doing this fourteen of us were cut off from the command and had to take to the brush and hide. Before we could conceal ourselves ten of the fourteen had been killed, leaving only Lieutenant Deridio, F. F. Gerard, Tom O'Neal and myself.

"Fortunately we were not discovered, and at midnight, after all danger of the enemy was past, we slipped from our covert and made ready to join our command. We stripped the blankets from the bodies of dead Indians, which were plentifully strewn through the timber, and wrapping these about us we filed Indian fashion up the bank of the stream. We did not know just where Reno was camped and our first desire was to get outside of the 'dead circle,' or picket line, of the Sioux. We advanced cautiously and making as little noise as possible, but in spite of that we suddenly ran into a body of fifteen Sioux pickets. To hesitate was to be suspected, and suspicion on their part just then meant death to us. We had partly passed the party when one of them demanded who we were. I could speak Sioux as well as my own tongue, and without delay replied 'Us.'

" 'Where are you going?' was the next question, and my answer to this was, 'for our horses.' This satisfied the interrogators, and we had escaped the first danger.

"We had succeeded in crossing the stream and following the trail along the bank, faint in the dim moonlight, when we came to an opening in the dense cottonwoods, and there we ran into a camp of several hundred Indians. Gerard immediately took them to be our men and belonging to Reno's command. He shouted: "Don't shoot, boys; we are friends.' The startled Indians cried out: 'Lay non; wa-see-cha ah-he-pe ah-lo!' (It is the enemy; the evil bad snows are upon us!) At this I dropped my blanket and ran, getting into the brush and away from the trail. Some one followed me closely, and I made up my mind that if he ever caught me there would be a fight to death between us. I could actually feel the knive thrust between my ribs in my highly excited imagination, and when I reached the river bank I turned to face my pursuer. Then I found that it was none other than Gerard, who had chosen the same path as myself. We waited a minute or two and listened. Then we heard four shots, and we were sure that our companions were lost.

"We waited no longer but plunged into the stream and gained the opposite bank, following it as far as we dared. Dawn was breaking and through the day we lay hidden in the willows, watching the battle which followed between the Indians and Reno's command. As the sun arose we could see the Indians circling about the camp and occupying every adjacent hill. A scattering fire was maintained until 9 o'clock, when the Indians made a savage assault upon the east side of Reno's position. The soldiers appeared to be very cool and poured in a murderous fire, which forced the hostiles to fall back with heavy loss. An hour later they made a second desperate charge, and so fierce was this that they actually fought with the soldiers over the breastworks, hand to hand. But again the discipline of the soldiers was more than a match for the fanatical frenzy of the Sioux, and they were driven back the second time. The soldiers had lost but few in this conflict, while their savage foes were strewn all over the side of the hill. From that time until noon there was only firing at long range. Then came a third charge, easily repulsed. From that time until 4 o'clock in the afternoon each side rested on its arms. About that hour, sheltered by a hill and no more than one thousand yards distant from the soldiers, the Indians held a council of war. In a few minutes there were evidences of departure in the Indian village, and it was then that the strength of the foe appeared. They could be seen by the lodges, loading the ponies with packs and with travois, and when the baggage train was finally completed, hurrying off to the north under a strong escort of warriors, making for the Big Horn mountains. At sunset all of them had disappeared and we dared venture out from our hiding place.

"Approaching Reno's position cautiously, for fear of being shot by the sentinels in the darkness, we were fortunate in getting inside the lines in time to meet Major Reno himself with members of his staff. To them I related what we had seen and heard, including the story of the loss of our companions, but before I had finished a challenge was heard, and into the camp came an orderly with Deridio and O'Neal. We were overjoyed, but there was little time for congratulations. Mounted on the best horse remaining in the command—for the long range fighting had killed many of those in the troop—I was sent with dispatches to Generals Custer and Terry.

"Three miles down the Little Big Horn I came upon the battlefield and it was a most grievous sight. Scattered or heaped up on the plain were the bodies of 237 men, every one save that of Custer mutilated in the most horrible manner known to the Indian mind. Not one had a vestage of clothing upon it; all had been stripped off and carried away by the exulting fiends. In Custer's body there were the marks of two bullet wounds, and undoubtedly I was the first man to look upon the terrible sight. It was too much for me and I turned and rode swiftly away down the river, shortly afterward meeting General Terry and his soldiers. To him I gave my dispatches and was immediately sent back to Major Reno with instructions to bury the dead. This was completed about 1 o'clock in the afternoon of the 27th. The wounded in Reno's command were taken to the mouth of the Big Horn river, and thence conveyed down the Yellowstone on the steamer Far West to Bismarck. The next day we gathered up large quantities of pemmican and other provisions and camp utensils left by the Sioux in their hurried flight, and burned them. Although I was but a youth when this occurred, it made an impression upon my mind that I shall never forget, and the details of those horrible two or three days are as fresh now as they were at the time of occurrence. Five years ago I went over 'The Custer Battlefield,' where the soldiers are buried, with Mrs. Eustis, whose son Jack, then a recent graduate from West Point, had been one of the victims under Custer. She had cherished a hope of recovering his bones, but although we had with us a number of Sioux and Cheyennes who had taken part in the fight, and each tried his best to recall all of the fearful scene, we were unable to help her, and she was obliged to return to her Eastern home with frustrated hopes. The incident, however, called up in mind all of the gruesome details of the battlefield as I saw it on that memorable morning, and I shall never care to repeat the experience."

General Terry, in his official report dated Camp on Little Big Horn, June 27, 1876, noticed the direction where Custer and his men had fallen, and submitted for the information of the war department the following important explanation:

"At the mouth of the Rosebud I informed General Custer that I should take the supply steamer Far West up the Yellowstone to ferry General Gibbon's column over the river; that I should personally accompany, that column, and that it would in all probability reach the mouth of the Little Big Horn on the 26th inst. The steamer reached General Gibbon's troops, near the mouth of the Big Horn, early on the 24th, and at 4 o'clock in the afternoon all his men and animals were across the Yellowstone. At 5 o'clock the column, consisting of five companies of the Seventh Infantry, four companies of the Seventh Cavalry, and a battery of three gatling guns, marched out to and across Tullock's creek, starting soon after 5 o'clock on the morning of the 25th. The infantry made a march of twenty-two miles over the most difficult country I have ever seen. In

order that scouts might be sent into the valley of the Little Big
Horn, the cavalry with the battery was then pushed on thirteen or fourteen miles further, reaching camp at midnight. The
scouts were sent out at 4:30 on the morning of the 26th. The
scouts discovered three Indians, who were at first supposed to
be Sioux, but when overtaken they proved to be Crows, who
had been with General Custer. They brought the first intelligence of the battle. Their story was not credited. It was supposed that some fighting, perhaps severe fighting, had taken
place, but it was not believed that disaster could have overtaken so large a force as twelve companies of cavalry. The infantry, which had broken camp very early, soon came up and
the whole column entered and moved up the valley of the Little Big Horn. During the afternoon efforts were made to send
scouts to what was supposed to be General Custer's position,
and to obtain information of the condition of affairs, but those
who were sent out were driven back by parties of Indians,
who, in increasing numbers, were seen hovering on General
Gibbon's front. At twenty minutes before 9 o'clock in the
evening the infantry had marched between twenty-five and
thirty miles; the men were very weary and daylight was
falling; the column was, therefore, halted for the night at a
point about eleven miles in a straight line above the mouth of
the stream. Next morning the movement was resumed, and
after a march of nine miles Major Reno's intrenched position
was reached. The withdrawal of the Indians from around
Reno's command, and from the valley, was undoubtedly
caused by the appearance of General Gibbon's troops. Major
Reno and Captain Benteen, both of whom are officers of great
experience, accustomed to see large masses of mounted men,
estimated the number of Indians engaged at not less than
twenty-five hundred. Other officers think that the number
was greater than this. The village in the valley was about three

miles in length and about a mile in width. Besides the lodges proper, a great number of temporary brushwood shelters were found in it, indicating that many men, besides its proper inhabitants, had gathered together there."

William Sellow, who now lives in Teton county, Montana, also one of the scouts who served under General Custer, contributes the following to the Dupuyer Acantha, July 15, 1899:

"Quite often, especially of recent years, I have seen articles in papers and magazines relating to the actions and motives of General Custer that led up to the massacre of his historic band. Most of these do grievous wrong to the bravest and best officer the United States government ever sent out to fight Indians on the frontier. Books, too, go so far as to call him a suicide and murderer for going at the head of his men into the battle of Little Big Horn on June 25, 1876.

"At that time I was in Custer's employ as a civilian scout, and had known him for a long time. I knew his ways of attacking Indians, and knew his unbounded confidence in his men. I had known him to win Indian fights against greater odds than his last one. For instance, at Wichita, he routed them with a force that numbered ten to one. Had he, in his last fight been supported as he could and should have been, he would have won the day, and then the Sitting Bull war would have ended and not have lasted until it cost much money and many lives. Not until the buffalo were killed and other game became scarce were the Indians satisfied to accept government rations and spend their honeymoon at home. An Indian's heart is never good until he is hungry and cold.

"Custer has been accused by would-be historians of going contrary to orders in his last campaign, and to refute these charges I write to follow him as far, or farther, than anyone else is truthfully capable of doing. That he did not go contrary to orders in his last movements the captain acting as General

Terry's adjutant at the time, if he is alive, will gladly, doubtless, testify. Unfortunately, I have forgotten his name. He will remember the greater part of the orders.

"After we, the scouts, delivered to Custer his last orders, I know he had no opportunity to receive any more, and as I recount the events as nearly as I can remember them at this length of time, it will be seen that I am correct.

"General Terry started myself and another scout to overtake and join Custer. After leaving the supply train and headquarters on about June 22, 1876, we reached the camp that night and delivered our message. The reader will see that in those stirring times when a scout was given a message it was in duplicate, one for the perusal of the scout and one for the receiver. These precautions were taken for fear one or both might be lost en route. In the first case the open one could be delivered, and in the second the scout might deliver the message from memory. I have yet in my possession the extra copy of this message, but unfortunately, it is so old and pocket-worn as to be only partially decipherable. From this aided by memory, I give the message:

" 'The brigadier general commanding desires that you proceed up the Rosebud in pursuit of the Indians, whose trail was discovered by Major Reno's scouts a few days ago. Of course, it is impossible for me to give definite instructions with regard to this movement, and were it not impossible to do so, the department commander places too much confidence in your zeal, energy and ability to wish to impose upon you orders that would conflict with your own judgment and which might hamper your actions when nearly in contact with the enemy. I will, however, indicate to you his ideas of what your movements should be and he desires you to conform to them unless your own judgment should give you sufficient reasons for departing from them. He thinks you should proceed up the Rosebud until you ascertain definitely the direction in which the trail above spoken of leads. Should it be found that it turns toward the Little Big Horn he thinks you should still proceed southward as far as the headwaters of Tongue river and then toward the Rosebud and the Little Big Horn, keeping scouts out constantly to your left, so as to prevent the possibility of the escape of the Indians to the south or southeast by passing around your left flank. The column of Colonel Gibbons is now in motion for the mouth of the Big Horn. As soon as it reaches that point it will cross the Yellowstone and move up as far at least as the forks of the Big Horn and the Little Big Horn. Of course, its future will be controlled by circumstances as they exist. But it is hoped that the Indians, if upon the Little Big Horn, may be so nearly enclosed by the two columns that their escape will be impossible.

" 'The department commander desires that, on your way up the Rosebud, you should have your scouts thoroughly examine the upper part of Tullock's fork, and that you should endeavor to send scouts through to Colonel Gibbon's command with the result of your examination. The lower part of this will be examined by Colonel Gibbon's scouts.

" 'The supply steamer will be pushed up the Big Horn as far as the forks of the Big and Little Big Horn, if the river is found navigable that far.

" 'The department commander, who will accompany the column of Colonel Gibbons, desires you to report to him there no later than the expiration of the time for which your troops are rationed, unless in the meantime you receive further orders.'

"After sleeping about two hours that same night we got fresh horses and Custer started us with instructions to go to the east of Tullock's fork and to follow it down to its mouth at Tullock's creek and to keep a sharp lookout for any signs of Indians, and to report to him again that night if possible. This we did, seeing nothing but the trail of a small war party going toward the Big Horn.

"We had been rolled up in our blankets but a few hours when Charlie Reynolds and a half-breed Sioux scout, Bill Cross, came in with a report which caused Custer to send for us again. After getting fresh horses we were given a dispatch to carry to Colonel Gibbon's command. We reached the river, which we crossed by the aid of our horses' tails with our clothes tied so as to keep them as dry as possible. We reached the command that day. The next morning I was sent back to the supply train, which was still at Powder river, and my companion was sent to join Benteen's command. He was with the latter during his engagement with the Indians, and he gives Colonel Benteen great credit for bravery. The colonel, he says, when the men behind the breastworks ran short of ammunition, with his own hands carried it and threw it over to them, being all the time exposed to the deadly fire of the enemy.

"In twenty-four hours I reached the supply train and was afforded another opportunity to fill up and get some sleep. On the 26th we met a Sioux scout, Bloody Knife, coming in badly scared and he seemed to think that Custer had been killed, although he had not seen him. Another scout, George Mulligan, and myself had been sent out to find Custer.

"We had not gone far when we met Bill Cross and eight Ree Indian scouts. They had a few Sioux ponies which they said they had captured. They told us that Custer and his command were killed, but they did not seem to know much about it. They could not tell us just where the fight took place, hence we took little stock in their story. We learned afterward, however, that when Custer made the charge they gathered up the Sioux horses that had strayed out on the hills, and pulled out for a more healthy climate. Scout Reynolds had the same privilege, but chose to go into the battle, and was afterward found in the same deadly circle with General Custer with many empty shells around them as evidence of a desperate fight.

"Reynolds well knew of Custer's ability to deal with the Indians against fearful odds, for he had previously fought with him. He also knew the odds he had to face that day, as we spoke of it when we last met and he proved by his actions that he could not have been aware of any wrong-doing, on the part of the general when he, of his own free will, followed him that day.

"After leaving Cross and the Ree scouts we met Curley, the Crow Indian scout, who was with Custer at the beginning of the fight. The pock-marked villain and liar, Rain-in-the-Face, says Curley is a liar, that he was not there, but I know for a fact that Rain-in-the-Face had never met Curley, nor to the best of my knowledge has he ever seen him since. I have heard Rain talk and he will never get into the happy hunting grounds if veracity is to be his passport.

"When we met Curley he was so badly scared that I doubt if he would have known himself. He had a Sioux medicine or war pony in full paint and feathers, a Sioux blanket and part of a war bonnet that he wore in his escape, and which he got from a dead Sioux medicine man who was killed near him in the first attack. The blanket had some blood on it. His own horse was killed and he appropriated the medicine man's property, and instead of trying to run the gauntlet he moved along with the enemy, trusting to his disguise to deceive them. When he saw an opportunity he dropped out of his bad company and escaped. When I last saw him with Custer he had his Crow clothes on and had his own pony, and he had no other chance to get the outfit. Had he been a white man he would have not had any chance of escape even with that rig. He does not claim to have tried to fight, but only to escape, and his first account of the affair is no doubt the correct one, as anyone acquainted with the Indians and their mode of fighting will admit its feasibility.

RAIN-IN-THE-FACE (WAR CHIEF).
Courtesy Montana Historical Society, Helena

"I understand that there was an ex-soldier at the World's Fair in Chicago, who posed as a soldier in the Seventh cavalry, who escaped from the fatal field. He was an imposter, for none but Curley left the ground alive. He may have dreamed it and believes in dreams.

"When the Seventh cavalry rode away from Fort Lincoln with the White Horse company, the band belonging to it played one of Custer's favorites, 'The Girl I Left Behind Me.' Ever after that, when I heard the familiar tune on the plains, my mind was carried back to the parting scene at the fort, and in the foreground of memory's picture stands, with tear-dimmed eyes, a sad, brave woman. Well might her heart nigh break, for she knew, as no one else did, that her brave husband was going on an expedition fraught with untold, hidden dangers, and not upon a summer outing.

"Crazy Horse and Goose, each with a band of Cheyennes, fought against Custer. In fact, the former was looked upon as the head war chief, Sitting Bull being more of a medicine man and prophet. The prevalent belief is that Sitting Bull was the worst Indian and head war chief. This is a mistake. There were several worse than he and more treacherous, but as most of them are dead and good Indians, I will not take trouble to name them or to recount their good (?) deeds. Gall was the head man among those who fought Reno and Benteen, and would have got away with them only for the personal bravery of the latter.

"When General Terry left the field and General Miles took command all Terry's and Custer's scouts who were alive went to work for the new commander, except George Mulligan and Jimmy-from-Cork. But there were only five of us left—Bob and Bill Jackson, Vick Smith, Cody, and myself. However, Miles re-enforced us with several others.

"Scout Billy Jackson was with Custer on the morning of

"BUFFALO BILL"—WILLIAM F. CODY.
Courtesy Montana Historical Society, Helena

the 25th, but left before the engagement to join Reno, and knew nothing of the terrible conflict until the next day. On the 27th they came to the battlefield, and Jackson, with four other scouts, identified the remains of General Custer and Scout Reynolds. His report of the battlefield my be vouched for, as he was ever known as a brave, cool, clear-headed and truthful scout, whom General Miles said he could always depend upon. He, too, maintains that Custer did not go contrary to orders."

Custer had divided his force into three parts. Benteen had orders to sweep everything before him to the left, and Reno was to drive right at the enemy. But it seems that neither he nor any other officer who was in this campaign had an idea that the Indian forces were as strong as they proved to be. There were at least eight Indian warriors to one soldier; neither did he know that they were so well supplied with arms and ammunition. Here is where Custer was deceived, or likely he would have kept his men together and won the battle.

On the arrival of General Gibbon the dead were buried and the wounded men of Reno's and Benteen's commands were given attention. After Gibbon and his men returned to Fort Shaw, I had an interview with the general and with many of the soldiers who were on the battlefield and assisted in burying the dead. They said that all the men, except Custer, were horribly mutilated and divested of all their clothing.

Again we return to Sitting Bull. Soon after the death of Custer, Sheridan, who was at the head of the war department, called out troops and fought him the balance of the season almost continuously, but the great chief always avoided open battle. In October General Miles drove him across the Missouri river, killing some Indians, capturing two thousand men, women and children, and destroying many of their supplies. The warriors who remained were scattered and discouraged; skulked back into the mountains, while Sitting Bull, with his followers crossed the line into the British possessions. In the meantime Generals Crook and Terry fought and defeated Chief Crazy Horse on the Rosebud towards the close of the year.

To give an idea of the vastness of the country where the hostile Indians had established their camps, I will give the approximate area, which was 125 by 200 miles, or 25,000 square miles. The Yellowstone river is about 350 miles long, 200 of which was included in this area. The length of Powder is 150 miles; the Tongue river the same, the Rosebud 125, the Big Horn about of similar length. With all of the tributaries of these rivers, and with the hills and mountain passes, the Indians were familiar; in this respect they had the advantage over the military. To go into details of those campaigns, extending over this great territory—the fearful severity—the long marching for months at a time through an untrodden wilderness, and sometimes a scarcity of food, clothing and bedding—the many battles that were fought, to which I have made no reference; burying the dead and taking care of the wounded—to tell all this would make a book in itself. But one thing I well insert here: That monument in Custer county, which marks the graves of those who have given their lives for this mountain land, and are peacefully sleeping at the base of it, will be kept erect by the Montanians as long as those everlasting peaks which overlook this sacred spot from the mountain tops near by shall remain.

Robert Vaughn.
July 24, 1899.

SITS DOWN SPOTTED (CARRIES HIS FOOD) A CROW SCOUT IN WINTER CLOTHES.
Courtesy Montana Historical Society, Helena

General Sherman's Letters

The following letters were written by General Sherman, then general of the United States Army, to Secretary McCrary, describing his tour through the valley of the Yellowstone soon after the Sioux war. They were published at the time in some newspaper, the clippings of which I have had in my possession ever since.

Thinking that there are no other records of these interesting letters, I give them place in this book, for they are a valuable addition to the history of Eastern Montana, or what was then termed "the Sioux country," and of that eventful time when the military had taken possession after Sitting Bull and his followers had been driven across the border into Canada.

Letter I.

"Cantonment on Tongue river, M.T., July 17, 1877.
"To Hon. Geo. W. McCrary:

"My Dear Sir: Before leaving Washington I promised to write you from time to time of matters of public and private interest.

"As originally appointed, I left St. Louis the evening of July 4, accompanied by my son; reached Chicago on the 5th and St. Paul the 6th. Here I was joined by my aides, Colonels Poe and Bacon; also by Gen. Terry and his aide, Captain Smith, and quartermaster of his department, General Card. Leaving St. Paul by rail the morning of the 7th, we reached Bismarck the evening of the 8th. There were three steamers there, two of which, the Rosebud and the Ashland, were loading for the Yellowstone, and we selected the former because she was smaller and safer, and better adapted to the strong current of the river. During the day of the 9th we crossed over by ferry to Fort Abraham Lincoln, and inspected the post. It is composed

GEN. WILLIAM T. SHERMAN.
Courtesy Montana Historical Society, Helena

of two distinct posts—a small infantry post, perched on a high hill overlooking the country and valley of the river, and a larger cavalry post on the river bank below, raised about twenty feet above the bottoms, which are usually overflowed by the spring freshets. There is but a small garrison there, because the Seventh Cavalry, its regular garrison, is detached to this point, and is now out on a scout.

"The Rosebud was boarded by 4 p.m. on the 9th, dropped down from Bismarck three miles to Fort Lincoln, to take us on board, and began the ascent of the Missouri, which was full, with a strong current. It was about as large and of the same character as at Sioux City. In three days we reached Fort Buford, on the north bank, just below the mouth of the Yellowstone. We stopped there over the night of the 12th, making as much of an inspection as the mosquitoes would allow, and at daybreak on the 13th resumed the trip, entering the Yellowstone, which for a hundred miles seemed almost as large as the Missouri, with numerous islands and a wide valley. This valley contracted after about a hundred miles, and the river changed its character somewhat, being lined on either side with fantastic hills, known as 'bad lands,' making short bends with a powerful current, against which we made slow headway, but in four days we reached this post, on the south bank of the Yellowstone, just above the mouth of Tongue river. The troops, mostly the Fifth Infantry, occupy the huts made last winter, but a new post is in process of construction, about a mile higher, and half a mile back from the Yellowstone, the ground being higher and less in danger of an overflow.

"General Miles is in command here—has about three hundred Indian prisoners—says none of the boats on the river this year have been molested—that all the hostiles which swarmed hereabouts last year are gone, the greater part to the agencies, while Sitting Bull has taken refuge across the border in Canada, about 250 miles north. When the new post is finished, which will be before winter, the troops will be comfortably quartered, and the Indians cannot return. Already a class of frontiersmen are making ranches and settlements hereabouts, and in a few years we can make the route to Montana by way of the Yellowstone as safe as the Platte and Arkansas, thus forcing the hostile Indians to break up into small and harmless parties. For some years hence we will have to keep a pretty strong garrison here, because, besides defending this point, detachments must go out to protect other threatened points, and to follow any small parties engaged in depredations. In other words, the forts along this line will not only have to defend themselves, but be able to send out strong detachments.

"There is a great deal of valuable country along the line of the Northern Pacific railroad. That road, from Duluth to Bismarck, although a financial failure, has been and will continue to be of advantage to the country at large. As far as Bismarck it is done, and well done. The next link, from Bismarck to the mouth of Powder river, is very important. It will be a distance of 250 miles, but will cut off 300 miles of the Missouri river and 150 of the Yellowstone, leaving the Yellowstone from Powder river to the mouth of the Big Horn for navigation.

"The valleys of the upper Yellowstone afford lands capable of cultivation in wheat, corn, oats, barley, and all garden vegetables, with an unlimited range for cattle, horses and sheep, etc. I do not know a single enterprise in which the United States has more interest than in the extension of the Northern Pacific railroad from its present terminus at Bismarck to the mouth of Powder river on the Yellowstone. After that is done we can safely leave to time the extension of the road to the head of navigation on the Columbia river. After a couple of months I can speak with more confidence on that point. I now regard the Sioux Indian problem as a war question as solved by the operation of General Miles last winter, and by the establishment of the two new posts this summer. Boats can come and go now where a year ago none would venture except with strong guards. Woodyards are being established to facilitate navigation, and the great mass of the hostile Indians have been forced to go to the Agencies for food and protection, or have fled across the border into British territory. I have driven all about this post, looked into the barracks, which are as yet mere huts of cottonwood posts, with dirt floors and dirt roofs, but will soon be replaced by good frame barracks and quarters. The stores of all kinds on hand are abundant and good, so that no apprehension is felt on account of the enemy or severity of the winter. Six small companies of infantry are here, two more are on the way, and four are mounted on captured ponies and are out on a scout. The Seventh Cavalry are also near here, scouting to the north, but discover no marks of an enemy.

"As winter approaches, part of the cavalry will doubtless be sent back to Fort Lincoln for economy of maintenance. Tomorrow night we resume our trip up the Yellowstone and Big Horn to the other new post building, at the forks of the Big and Little Horn. There I expect to meet General Sheridan. * * * I beg you not to construe this as official, as I have been constantly interrupted, and must close, as the steamer is ready to go. With great respect, etc.,

"*W.T. SHERMAN,* GENERAL."

Letter II.

"On the Steamer Rosebud, Big Horn River, July 25, 1877.

"My Dear Sir: We left the cantonment at the mouth of the Tongue river on the evening of July 18, and reached the mouth of the Big Horn in three days, then entering the Big Horn, we steamed hard for three days against a powerful current, and reached the new post at the forks of the Little and Big Horn, yesterday morning early. Many boats had preceded us, all, or nearly all, discharging part of their freight on the west bank, from which hauling is comparatively easy. Our boat, which was built especially for the navigation of this and similar streams, had to land four miles below the post one-third of her cargo. The difficulty was not the want of water, but by reason of the strong current, which in the bends must be about eight miles an hour.

"We found at the post the United States steamer General Sherman, which has a good hull, a good engine, but too much and too fine cabin for this work. It will be kept in the Big Horn as long as the water lasts, and will be employed in carrying up to the post the freight dropped on the river bank by the contract boats. The post already has a good supply of all essential stores, and there is no doubt that long before the season closes all invoiced for its use will be on hand and stored. The day before we reached the post we met General Sheridan and party, who had come across the country from Fort Stambaugh. We had a long conference and agree that this new post is well located, and that it can be supplied with reasonable economy in the future. The new post will be garrisoned by six companies of the Eleventh Infantry and four companies of the Second Cavalry, under command of Lieutenant Colonel Buell, of the Eleventh Infantry, an officer of great energy, and by profession an engineer. He served under me during the war as colonel of an engineer regiment, and afterwards as a brigade commander. He has been on the ground less than a month, but has a steam sawmill at work and a large mass of cottonwood logs being rapidly sawed up into lumber for the new barracks. He has about 200 civil mechanics at work and six buildings in progress, besides temporary shelters for his stores as received, and he entertains no fear but that he will finish his post substantially before winter.

"The location of this post is in the very heart of the Sioux country. With this one and the one at the mouth of the Tongue river, occupied by strong, enterprising garrisons, these Sioux can never regain this country, and they will be forced to remain at their agencies or take refuge in the British possessions. At present there are no Indians here or hereabouts. I have neither seen nor heard of any. General Sheridan saw none nor any trace of any, so that the principal end aimed at by the construction of these posts is already reached, and it is only to make this end permanent that we should persist in their completion. The one at Tongue river can be supplied by steamboats. This one, at the mouth of the Little Big Horn, cannot depend on this river, the current being too strong to be navigated by ordinary boats with a fair cargo. General Terry and his quartermaster, General Card, are at this moment reconnoitering to select some point near the mouth of the Big Horn whereat to establish a supply depot, at which all freight destined for this post can be landed and hauled up here.

"We have on board a company of infantry to guard this depot, and we are nearly agreed that the best place will be a point on the Yellowstone proper, three miles above the mouth of the Big Horn, where the hauling will be about thirty miles by ox trains. These can be hired here, and will do the work more surely and better than the steamboats, for they have been sometimes two weeks in working up the Big Horn and have left their loads strung along its banks at points hard to reach by wagons. I am convinced that this is the wisest course, and thus we can maintain a strong military post in the very heart of the hostile Sioux country, with only a haul of twenty miles, which is insignificant as compared with most of our posts south of this. The country west of this is a good country and will rapidly fill up with emigrants, who will, within the next few years, build up a community as strong and as capable of self-defense as Colorado.

"I have Company L of the Second Cavalry, Captain Norwood, which belongs at Fort Ellis, M.T., now camped on the west bank of the Yellowstone, opposite the mouth of the Big Horn, to escort me up to Ellis. As soon as we have decided on the merits of the point mentioned as a supply depot for this post, I will land and start for Ellis, leaving Gen. Terry with this boat to return to Bismarck for a new load. I will instruct General Terry to report in full all these matters to the adjutant general, so that this letter is only preliminary.

"Here we have no news from Idaho or Oregon, or the world generally, but I suppose in Montana there will be need of the four companies of the Second Cavalry, temporarily taken to Tongue river, and I instructed General Sheridan to so order when he reached Tongue river. This will leave General Miles the whole of the Seventh Cavalry available if the Indian Bureau wishes to escort Sitting Bull from British America to an agency.

"The weather has been intensely hot—as hot as Texas—but last night we had a thunder-squall, since which the air has become perfect. General good health prevails here, and I am impressed with the value of this country. * * * Truly yours,

"W.T. SHERMAN, GENERAL."

Letter III.

"Fort Ellis, M.T., August 3, 1877.

"Dear Sir: I wrote you last from the steamboat Rosebud, coming down the Big Horn in company with General Terry and others on the 25th of July. We had concluded that the current of the Big Horn was too swift to be managed economically, and that the garrison at Post No. 2, at the mouth of the Big Horn, could best be supplied by establishing a depot on the Yellowstone, just above the mouth of the Big Horn, where stores could be hauled thirty miles to the new post. A company of the Eleventh Infantry was left there to establish and guard the depot when the steamer Rosebud dropped down to the point just below the mouth of the Big Horn, where Company L, Second Cavalry, Captain Norwood, was camped with an outfit. This consisted of six Indian horses, two light spring wagons, and one light baggage wagon. The Rosebud landed us at 2 p.m., when she started down the river, leaving us to begin our real journey. In a few minutes the escort saddled up, and we started on horseback up the Yellowstone.

"The valley is strongly marked, about three miles wide, flat, with good grass, the banks of the river and the streams well wooded with cottonwood trees. In this valley, the Yellowstone, a broad, strong stream, meanders back and forth, forming on both sides strong, perpendicular bluffs of rock and clay, forcing the road constantly out of the flat valley over the points, and causing wide deflections in the road to head the ravines or 'coolies,' which flow to the river. There is a strongly-marked wagon trail, but no bridge or cuts, a purely natural road, with steep ascents and descents, and frequent gullies, about as much as wagons could pass. We sometimes shifted into our light wagons, to save the fatigue of travel.

"Thus we journeyed for four days, when we sent a courier from Fort Ellis with a copy of General Townsend's dispatch to me, saying that the President desired my immediate return, unless I had information that the serious riots then in full career had ceased.

"Light wagons can out-travel horses and baggage wagons. Up to that date we averaged twenty-five miles a day. I therefore turned the courier back with a fresh horse, and orders to reach Fort Ellis in two days with answer, to be sent from Bozeman by telegraph, and, with my immediate party, I followed, taking one more day, being time for answers. On reaching Fort Ellis the day before yesterday (August 1), was delighted to hear that the riots had ceased, and that you and the President had consented that I should go on as originally intended.

"The escort company came in yesterday, so that we are now all here at Fort Ellis. When we arrived there was but one company of the Seventh Infantry here, Captain Benham, thirty men. The arrival of the escort gives an addition of sixty men.

"There is no seeming danger here or hereabouts, but the Nez Perces are reported to have entered Montana, from Idaho, and are now in the valley of the Bitter Root, about 300 miles west of this; they are reported en route to the buffalo range, east and north of this point. It seems that for many years these same Nez Perces, along with some Flatheads from the western part of Montana, have been accustomed to come to the sources of the Musselshell and Yellowstone to gather meat for the winter, traversing the whole of Montana, doing little or no damage. But the buffaloes of the great northern herd, like that of the southern, are being rapidly slaughtered for their skins, so that now they are becoming scarce. We only saw four buffaloes, two of which were killed, in our course, whereas ten years ago we would have encountered a million.

"The time has come when these restless Indians must cease to look to buffaloes as a means of maintenance, and they should not be allowed to traverse the scattered and explored settlements of Montana, where hunger will sooner or later compel them to kill tame cattle and steal horses, thus leading to murder and war.

"Besides these the Nez Perces should be made to answer for the murders they committed in Idaho, and also to be punished as a tribe for going to war without just cause or provocation.

"Hitherto all danger to Montana has come from the north and the Sioux to the east, and the few troops stationed in the territory were posted, as it were, at the eastern doors or passes through the mountains, over Ellis, Baker, Benton and Shaw, but last year a new post was selected at or near Missoula, the door of the western frontier. Two small companies, not over sixty men, of the Seventh Infantry, under Captain Rawn, were sent to Missoula to build a post there, but he had hardly arrived when the Nez Perces war began. When it was reported that General Howard had defeated the hostiles and that they were retreating to Montana by what is known as the Lo-Lo trail, some of the citizens of the neighborhood joined the soldiers for the purpose of stopping the Indians until the troops from Idaho could come up with them. But it seems the Indians passed around Captain Rawn's fortified point and then entered the Bitter Root valley, but in such force (300 armed warriors) as to claim to be able, if opposed, to force their way through.

"The country is so large and the passes so scattered that concert of action is most difficult, if not impossible.

"Gen. Gibbon, colonel of the Seventh Infantry, has command of this district, and General Terry is the department commander. Gibbon is stationed at Fort Shaw, on Sun river, 200 miles north of this. As soon as he perceived Captain Rawn's critical position, he collected about 100 men, and has gone rapidly toward Missoula to take command and control them. The governor of the territory, General Potts, has also gone in the same direction—Deer Lodge—and has organized some volunteer companies, and these may be able to get ahead of the Indians somewhere on the Big Hole or Wisdom river, and hold them in check or turn them back toward Idaho, where General Howard must have a pretty respectable force, able to destroy them, unless, as I suspect, they will scatter, when pursuit becomes impossible. I do not propose to interfere, but leave Howard or Gibbon to fight out this fight.

"Too many heads are worse than one.

"I have sent word to Governor Potts that if the citizens in their own interest will join the regular troops and act with and under them, that the commanding officer will loan them arms and ammunition when possible, and may certify to beef or food taken en route, but that congress alone can raise troops for any purpose. I have telegraphed to General McDowell that I expect that his troops now in Idaho will follow up those Indians to the death, go where they may, regardless of boundaries. He answered that such are still, and were General Howard's orders from the beginning. So I expect soon to hear of the arrival at or near Missoula of the troops from that quarter. The nearest point from which troops may come to Montana from the east is by the route I came. When I parted with General Terry at the Big Horn it was understood he would detach for General Miles' command at Tongue river the companies of the Second Cavalry which belong here. It will be two weeks before they reach here, but if they arrive in time, and the troops and volunteers now in the Bitter Root country do not succeed in stopping this band of Nez Perces, these three companies and the one I brought will get on their trail, and change their proposed buffalo hunt into a fight. If, however, they escape, I see no alternative but to drive them across the British border to join Sitting Bull.

"Tomorrow I will start for the park, taking only five soldiers with me, so that my presence here will not materially reduce the fighting force, for I have sent word to General Gibbon that my escort company is subject to his orders. I do not suppose we run much risk, for we are all armed, and the hostile Indians rarely resort to the park, a poor region for game, and to their superstitious mind associated with hell by reason of the geysers and the hot springs. We expect to be gone from here about fifteen days, during which we can receive or send no letters. On our return here, say August 18th, I will go rapidly to Helena, when I will learn all about the movements of the troops, and I will be governed somewhat by them. But I still intend in August to visit Forts Shaw and Benton, and to reach Missoula in the first week of September.

"It is all important that a route or trail be opened between Missoula and Walla Walla, but I can better judge of this after I have passed over the road.

"We found ranches established all along down the Yellowstone, and the mail contractors have already put on a line of two-horse spring wagons, so that soon the route we passed over will fill up with passes. The land is susceptible of cultivation on a small scale, but admirably adapted to cattle raising.

"Fort Ellis is a small post, built of pine logs, all the mountains around being covered with pines.

"We are all perfectly well, and enjoy the isolation and freshness of camp life. Truly yours,

"W.T. SHERMAN, GENERAL."

Letter IV.

"Fort Ellis, M.T., August 19, 1877.

"The Territory of Montana, though very large, and surrounded on all sides by Indians liable to become hostile on the slightest provocation, has for ten years been a district forming a part of the Department of Dakota, and has usually been garrisoned by a regiment of infantry and a battalion of cavalry— four companies. The danger usually lay to the east, toward the Sioux, and therefore the posts were Fort Benton, at the head of navigation of the Missouri; Fort Shaw, on Sun river; Camp Baker, at the head of the Musselshell, and Fort Ellis, at the head of the Gallatin.

"The infantry regiment should be 1,000 men, but the policy of reduction has gradually reduced it to 300, and early this spring the four companies of the Second Cavalry, by order of the department commander, were dispatched to Tongue river to assist General Miles in his active campaign against the

Sioux, and when I passed up the Yellowstone in July three of these companies had been sent by General Miles to the east of Tongue river, and one company (L, Captain Norwood) was held to escort me to this, their proper post.

"On reaching Fort Ellis I found that General Gibbon, colonel of the Seventh Infantry, commanding this district, had, at the request of General Howard, hurriedly called for every man that could be spared, and marched to Missoula to head off the Nez Perces Indians that had been defeated by him (Howard) in Idaho. Gibbon was absolutely without cavalry, and his small infantry companies marched with extraordinary speed, making twenty-six miles a day. * * * General Gibbon got on the trail, followed it with great earnestness, and over-hauled the Indians at a place known as Big Hole. He got into their camp and fought them bravely and well a whole day, inflicting heavy loss and sustaining a corresponding loss himself. Of this you have full reports.

"If General Gibbon could have had 100 more men, there would now be few hostile Nez Perces left. But his force was inadequate, and he did all that a man possibly could do.

"The next day Howard got ahead of his command, and he now has taken up the pursuit, and I hope to hear that he has finished up what General Gibbon so well began.

"I believe these Indians are afraid to return to Idaho, and think they will try to escape to the great plains to the east of the Rocky mountains, by way of the head of Wind river, in which case they will fall to the charge of General Crook or General Miles, either of whom is capable of running them down.

"The moment I reached Ellis I caused General Gibbon to be informed that I had reached the territory, and that I did not wish to interfere with his legitimate command, but on the contrary I gave him the company of cavalry which had escort-ed me up from the Big Horn, and that company is now with

General Howard's command in pursuit of the Nez Perces.

"Our little army is overworked, and I do not believe the officers and soldiers of any army on earth, in peace or war, work as hard or take as many risks of life as this little army of ours. In what we call peace I am proud of them, and I hope you are also, or soon will be.

"Meantime I suppose you want to hear something of the National Park."

Having been in the National Park for fifteen days, and giving a graphic description of its spouting geysers and their performances, its majestic mountains, lakes and canyons, the extremely beautiful formation of which neither pen, words nor painting can equal, and that "Wonderland" must be seen to be appreciated and felt, the general in closing his sketch, says:

"This is Sunday, a real day of rest, and I have endeavored to give this wide and rapid sketch in hopes to account for the fifteen days' absence from duty at this period of military activity, but I have faith that there are plenty of good officers on duty at their posts to do all that is demanded of the army. I now propose to go to work to study closer the present condition and future prospects of Montana as bearing on the great military problems, all of which will be duly reported.

"With great respect, etc.,

"*WILLIAM T. SHERMAN, GENERAL.*"

The Nez Perces War.

It was in Idaho, in the summer of 1877, that Chief Joseph, of the Nez Perces tribe, declared war by butchering his defenseless white neighbors. It may be that the death of Custer and the fame of Sitting Bull awoke the evil spirit in him by birth. The only excuse he tried to give was that the government wanted to move some of his people off a certain tract of land. All of this could have been settled satisfactorily if he had waited but a few weeks, and to this end he agreed. But before the time was up he commenced his murderous deeds. The following is from the Spokesman-Review, Spokane, Wash., in reference to Chief Joseph:

"By nature he was proud, defiant and warlike. His summer home was in the Wallowa valley of eastern Oregon, but when not engaged there at hunting and fishing he roamed at will from the California line to the Canadian boundary, and from the Blue mountains to the summits of the Rocky mountains.

"The invasion of this broad realm by miners and settlers forced upon the government its policy of framing a new treaty with the Indians for the purpose of confining them to two or three reservations. At a conference held at Lapwai in 1873, between the various Indian chiefs and representatives of the government, Joseph refused to go upon either the Nez Perces reservation in Idaho or the Umatilla reservation in Oregon. This being reported to the secretary of the interior, an order was issued that Joseph's band should be permitted to remain in the Wallowa valley during the summer and autumn, and later the President set aside the Wallowa and Imnaha valleys for Joseph and his non-treaty Indians.

"Thus matters drifted until 1875, when, under pressure from the settlers, the President rescinded his order, and another commission was appointed to negotiate with Joseph and his band. Joseph haughtily replied that he had not come to talk about land; the maker of the earth was his mother, sacred to his affections, and too precious to be sold. He did not wish to learn farming, but to live upon such fruits as the earth produced for him without effort. (From these principles Joseph has never departed. To this day (1898) he and his little band on the Colville reservation refuse to take up the arts of peace. They hunt and fish, and dwell in tepees.)

"The government replied that unless in a reasonable time Joseph consented to be removed he should be forcibly taken with his people and given lands on the reservation. He answered this by taking to the warpath. Joseph, Whitebird and Looking Glass gathered their forces on Cottonwood creek, sixty-five miles from Lewiston, ostensibly to comply with the government's command, but really in preparation for the fierce war that followed.

"Their first victims were four white men, killed on White Bird creek. On June 14, 1877, while playing cards, they were surprised by a band of hostiles."

Joseph's fighting force was about five hundred. General O. O. Howard took the field with seven hundred men and officers. Several skirmishes were fought, in which Joseph was badly beaten, although about fifty of Howard's men were killed. Finally, with his men, followed by many women and children, he crossed into Montana with Howard in pursuit. General Gibbon, then located at Fort Shaw, Montana, was notified of Joseph's movements, and at once, with about 150 men, crossed the main range of the Rockies, by going over the "Cadott Pass," making the march in two days. His force was infantry and a few were mounted. About thirty citizens joined him from the Bitter Root valley.

Gibbon attacked Joseph on August 9th in the Big Hole valley in Beaverhead county, and had a hard fought and bloody engagement, lasting several hours. When the battle was nearly ended, stray bullets kept coming and killed several of Gibbon's men before any one could tell where they came from. Finally one of the soldiers discovered that a redskin had climbed and fortified himself in a fork of a large tree and about thirty feet from the ground. A fatal shot was sent and "he fell like a dead squirrel," as one of the men said. The Indians retreated leaving eighty-nine dead. Gibbon lost twenty-nine killed and forty wounded. Bostwick, the interpreter, who was at Gibbon's office, and of whom I have made mention in my letter, "The Indians Stealing My Horses," was one of the killed.

Gibbon was burying the dead when Howard came up. Joseph knew that Howard must be near, and perhaps this saved Gibbon from meeting the same fate as Custer, for the Indians outnumbered him more than three to one.

A magnificent monument has been erected on this sacred ground in memory of those who crossed the main range of the Rockies, and, but a few days later, went down "through the valley of the shadow of death" for the sake of generations to come.

After the battle Joseph crossed into Idaho, killing many settlers on the way, for now all the Indians were in a rage. It appears that he hardly knew where to go; finally he took to the mountains and into the National Park. Here he met some tourists, and two of them, Charles Kenk and Richard Detrick, were killed by his warriors, while at the same time an Indian named Charley was doing all in his power to pacify the other Indians; at this juncture Joseph interfered and forbade his men to harm any more of them. But they were all taken as prisoners for several days. The women who were in the party were treated with the greatest respect, for which Joseph received great praise through the Eastern press as well as that of the West. Howard was still on their path, and Joseph knew it, and knew that his only hope was to get to Canada. From the National Park he went due north as near as the lay of the country would permit, killing several settlers and destroying property as he went. This time he came in contact with Colonel Sturgis, but made his escape.

In the latter part of September news came to Fort Benton that the Nez Perces were heading to cross the Missouri river and on to Canada. Knowing that there were but few people at the several trading posts further down the river, Major Elges, who was in command at Fort Benton, sent what men he could spare down the river in a Mackinaw boat, while he and Colonel J. J. Donnelly, with thirty-five mounted citizens, with rifles and belts full of cartridges, crossed the country. Many of them were picked marksmen, "old prairie men," who would just as soon go into a fight as eat a Christmas dinner. On their way they learned that Joseph was heading for Cow island. On their arrival there they found that the Indians had crossed the river and had a fight with a small party of men that were guarding some goods that had been taken off a steamboat and piled on the levee. Joseph took some of the goods and burned the balance. But this brave little party, who were intrenched, fought like demons, and, although one was killed and three of them wounded, they stood off the enemy and held their fort. Judge Foley, now of the city of Belt, was one of them. About the same time Joseph was having a fight with O. G. Cooper, Frank Farmer and other freighters, who were in camp on Cow creek, a few miles further north, when he had already robbed and was burning their wagons. Without hesitation, the Benton party took a hand in the fight, in which E. B. Richardson (Bradley) was killed. Colonel Donnelly, who had been an officer in the Civil War, borrowed a small boat from Captain Mc-Garry, of the steamer "Benton," and was in camp several miles down and on the south side of the river. Runners were sent by Major Elges on the north side to direct Miles the way the Indians had gone. The balance of the party were watching the course of the Indians, which was to the Bear Paw mountains. Miles immediately crossed to the north side on the steamer that brought his command up the river. Afterwards Miles met Donnelly, thanked him for the dispatch and thanked the citizens for what they had done.

The Montana volunteers who served against the Nez Perces in 1877 numbered 442, who were from different localities and were recognized by the war department as belonging to the Montana militia of that year, and their names are on the rosters of the court of claims, who drew pay for their services. In the list I find "Donnelly's Company, No. 5," consisting of the following names:

John J. Donnelly, William Foster, Sol A. Jantis, Charles B. Buckman, Louis Cobell, Joseph Morrison, J. W. Hanna, W. B. Smith, Samuel Neall, J. C. Lilly, Ed L. Smith, John Samples, C. E. Deanville, Ed Tingle, James Dare, G. A. Croff, C. S. Davis, J. H. Evans, Hiram Baker, Crow Davis, Trev Hale, Murray Nicholson, Powder Bull, William Preston, P. H. Estes, Wolf's Head, George Farmer, Jos. Gauty, Isaac N. Clark, Eph Woolsey, J. W. Tattan, Richard Maloney, Thomas O'Hanlon, John Egan, W. S. Evans, George C. Smythe, John Kavannaugh, E. B. Richardson, George Hammond, Martin Moran, William Rowe, William Murphy, Jeff Talbert and Nicholas Walsh.

I make mention of this little company of citizens because they were my neighbors and because they were the last volunteers that fought in the final battle in the last Indian war in Montana. Colonel Donnelly was then and is now an attorney at law at Fort Benton, and Judge J. W. Tattan, J. H. Evans, William Rowe, J. C. Lilly, Louis Cobell, John Kavanaugh and others are citizens of Fort Benton and vicinity at the present time.

After crossing the river, Miles went right after the Indians. Now, for the first time, Joseph realized that there was a

"Rough Rider" on his trail, for Miles then was as daring a rider as there was in the country. After being in the saddle for four days he captured Joseph in the Bear Paw mountains, and but a few miles from Canada. The day before the surrender General Howard came up with an escort to twelve men, remaining with Miles over night, and was present next morning at the surrender of Joseph and his entire force of 400. And when the conquered chief with his men came into camp he first offered his arms to General Howard, who declined to receive them, at the same time waving him to General Miles. This was considered at the time a generous act on Howard's part, for then he was the ranking officer. Now Howard had come to the end of his long march of nearly two thousand miles, crossing up and down the Rocky mountains in pursuit of the Indian Chief Joseph and his desperate band. It was a feat or achievement of personal heroism, hardihood, persistence and pluck. The extracts below are from a private letter written by Colonel Corbin, of the "Sitting Bull Commission," to a friend in the East. He says:

"Of course we are feeling glad at the happy close of the Nez Perces business—it has been the most remarkable of all our Indian wars; and in a stern chase no troops could have caught them as long as they did not want to be caught. They left their former homes with at least three good horses to each warrior and a reserve of at least a thousand head for families and pack animals. So they were on a fresh horse every third day. While after a few days' march Howard's horses were worn down, and it required every effort to get them through the most damnable passes you can imagine, in the highest range of the Rocky mountains. Howard's troops have endured hardships seldom, if ever, known to the American soldier. They have been in the sun and rain so long that any of them would make a first-rate model for a veteran. Howard, himself, is looking like a frontier teamster after a long streak of bad luck.

"When the Nez Perces surrendered to General Miles, they were yet well provided with provisions. They brought to bear all the cunning of their race and had the most improved arms; in fact it would seem that they had taken advantage of all our experience in war. Their camps were like ours when going to Atlanta, marked by rifle pits thrown up every night, and the site of their last stand is wonderful in its hastily constructed fortifications.

"Lieutenant Jerome of our escort was a prisoner two days, and was well, even kindly, cared for, the women digging a trench for his protection from the fire of General Miles' troops. The men wounded in the first charge of Miles fell into the Indians' hands. They were disarmed and assured of their safety. The admiration felt for Joseph's pluck and general conduct is very warm among both officers and men. They fought until nearly three-fourths of their warriors were either killed or wounded in open battle, and when worn out by Howard, Gibbon, Sturgis, Norwood and Miles, they hoisted the white flag and came down from their mountain fastness and each surrendered his rifle to General Miles in person."

There is no doubt but that Chiefs Joseph and Looking Glass have proven themselves to be the greatest leaders, displayed the best generalship and carried out their plans with more skill than any of the American Indians that ever waged war against our government.

No one can give a better account of the last battle with Chief Joseph and his band of Nez Perces than General Nelson A. Miles, himself. The general says:

"On leaving the Missouri river for the march north, the command was organized to move with the pack trains, leaving the wagons with a strong escort to follow as best they could. Every precaution was taken to conceal the command as far as possible, and the march was made with all the celerity and secrecy practicable. Strict orders were given against firing a shot or in any way disturbing the vast numbers of buffalo, deer and elk which we encountered. In this way we moved from early dawn to dark for four days on the grassy plain and foothills which bordered the eastern slope of the little Rockies, and on the 29th tidings regarding the trail to the left reached us. Captain Maus, commanding the scouts, had used his sleepless vigilance to good purpose and had gained the information desired without disclosing his presence or that of the command.

"Here occurred an excellent illustration of the loyalty of the true soldier. Captain Maus and his small band, while engaged in their scouting duties, suddenly came upon a huge bear sometimes called the 'grizzly,' but in that region more properly the 'silver tip,' who, evidently conscious of its strength and power, rose upon its hind feet in an attitude of defiance. Captain Maus, with the instincts of a thorough sportsman, quickly brought his rifle to his shoulder and ran his eye along the sight. Just then he remembered the rigid orders against firing and as quickly brought it down to his side, the spirit of the soldier overcoming the strong temptation of the hunter. His small detachment then passed on in search of larger game.

"That night I received dispatches from General Howard stating that he had turned his cavalry back to Idaho and was going to move his infantry down the Missouri river, leaving the battalion of Colonel Sturgis, six troops of the Seventh cavalry, on the Missouri river. This made it clear that whatever encounters we might have with the Nez Perces we were entirely beyond support.

"At daylight on the morning of the 30th the command had its light breakfast and was in the saddle pushing on again in search of the enemy, everyone realizing the probability that a conflict would soon occur.

"Our Cheyenne and Sioux Indian scouts had now assumed a more serious attitude. They were well in front of the command, and began to show more earnestness and activity than they had heretofore. Suddenly one of these advance scouts, a young warrior, was seen bounding at full speed back over the prairie. He said something in Sioux or Cheyenne to the other Indians as he passed them, and it was evident that he brought information of the discovery of the Nez Perces camp. Then an almost instantaneous transformation scene was enacted by these savages. Hats, coats, leggings, shirts, blankets, saddles and bridles were quickly thrown into one great heap in a ravine, or 'cache,' as the Indians call it.

"A lariat was placed over the neck of each war pony, and a double knot around his under jaw. The warrior painted for the fray was bedecked with the usual gorgeous long and high head-dress of eagle feathers, and wore a buckskin covering about the loins, which was his only clothing except a pair of buckskin moccasins. Springing upon their war ponies, with rifle in hand, they looked like game champions prepared for the fray, or the ideal picturesque warrior arrayed for the fight. They appeared to be perfectly wild with delight, as unlike what they had seemed twenty minutes before as two scenes of a drama.

"A similar spirit was manifested among the entire body of troops. 'The Nez Perces over the divide' was the word that was passed quickly in low tones from mouth to mouth along the entire column. The command immediately took a trot, with an occasional canter, where the ground would admit of it, over the rolling prairie and the grass-covered valleys. Rounding the northeast base of the Bear Paw mountains, the distance that was supposed to be a few miles proved to be eight, and the disposition of the troops was made while they were at a trot or rapid walk, and the pace quickened to a gallop and charge as they neared the camp.

"Orders were sent by Lieutenant Baird, of my staff, to

Captain Tyler's command (the Second cavalry) to sweep around to the left and then down the valley and cut off, if possible, the herd of horses from the camp, in order, to use the familiar phrase, to 'set the Indians afoot,' the Seventh cavalry was thrown in the line of battle while moving at a gallop, the commanding officer, Captain Hale, riding in advance. He presented the ideal picture of the cavalier, splendidly mounted on a spirited gray horse, and he wore a jaunty hat with a light gray cavalry short coat, while his whole uniform and equipment were in perfect order. Inspiring his followers to courage by his own example and splendid heroism, with a smile upon his handsome face he dashed forward to the cruel death awaiting him. The battalion of the Fifth infantry, under Captain Snyder, was deployed in the same manner a little in the rear of the Seventh cavalry at first, and finally extending the line to the left, charging directly upon the camp, while the battalion of the Second cavalry was sweeping the valley of the vast herd of 800 horses, mules and ponies there grazing. This gallop forward preceding the charge was one of the most brilliant and inspiring sights I ever witnessed on any field. It was the crowning glory of our twelve days' forced marching.

"The Nez Perces were quietly slumbering in their tents evidently without a thought of danger, as they had sent out scouts the day before to see if there were any troops in the vicinity, and the scouts had reported 'none discovered,' but that they had seen vast herds of buffaloes, deer, elk and antelope quietly grazing on the prairie undisturbed, and no enemy in sight. When the charge was made the spirited horses of the Seventh cavalry carried that battalion a little more rapidly over the plains than the Indian ponies of the mounted infantry, and it was expected to first strike the enemy with the Seventh cavalry. The tramp of at least 600 horses over the prairie shook the ground, and, although a complete surprise to the Indians in the main, it must have given them a few minutes' notice, for as the troops charged against the village, the Indians opened a hot fire upon them. This momentarily checked the advance of the Seventh cavalry, which fell back, but only for a short distance, and was quickly rallied again and charged forward at a gallop, driving that portion of the camp of the Indians before them.

"At the same time the battalion of the Fifth Mounted infantry, under Captain Snyder, charged forward up the very edge of the valley in which the Indian camp was located, threw themselves upon the ground, holding the lariats of their ponies in their left hands, and opened a deadly fire with their long-range rifles upon the enemy with telling effect. The tactics were somewhat in the Indian fashion, but most effective, as they presented a small target when kneeling or lying upon the ground, and their ponies were so accustomed to the din and noise of an Indian camp, the buffalo chase, and the Indian habits generally, that they stood quietly behind their riders, many of them putting their heads down to nibble the green grass upon which they were standing. During the desperate fight the horses and ponies were, of course, exposed. The infantrymen had become so attached to their strong and handsome ponies that when one was shot it was a real bereavement to his owner; and in more than one case it was noticed that tears filled the eyes of the soldier as his pony fell dead.

"Sergeant McHugh had galloped forward with his Hotchkiss breech-loading gun, keeping in line with the mounted infantry, and went into action throwing shells into the camp with decided effect. The infantry swept around to the left to inclose that portion of the camp and force the Indians into a deep ravine. The battalion of the Second cavalry had stampeded nearly every animal in the valley and portions of that command were used immediately in circling the camp in order to inclose it entirely.

"As I passed completely around the Indians over the ground occupied by the mounted infantry and Second cavalry, to the line occupied by the Seventh cavalry, I was shocked to see the lifeless body of that accomplished officer and thorough gentleman, Hale, lying upon the crest of a little knoll with his white charger dead beside him. A little further on was the body of the young and spirited Biddle. Captains Moyland and Godfrey were badly wounded, and in fact a great part of the line encircling the camp was dotted with dead and wounded soldiers and horses.

"The loss of the Nez Perces was even more severe. The fight had been sudden, rapid and most desperate on both sides.

"From what was at first a wide circle, the troops gradually closed their lines, forcing the Indians into a narrow ravine, and charging them on all sides until the grip of iron had been completed. In this way the losses on both sides had been serious, considering the number engaged. Captain Carter, in one charge, had 35 per cent of his men placed hors de combat, but I felt positive we had secured the beleaguered Indians in their camp beyond the possibility of escape. I did not, therefore, order a general assault, as I knew it must result in the loss of many valuable lives and possibly might end in a massacre. I, therefore, directed the men to hold their ground, and then from a high point watched the fight going on further down the valley.

"As the cavalry charged the camp a few of the warriors, including White Bird, ran out, secured their horses, and fled to the hills. As the battalion of the Second cavalry swept down the valley the Indian herd became somewhat separated. Captain Tyler captured some 300 of the ponies; Lieutenant Gerome another large band, and Lieutenant McClernand, who had swept on still further, finally secured upwards of 300 more three or four miles down the valley. While driving them back, the small number of Indians who had escaped, undertook to rescue the animals and made several counter attacks, which were all successfully repelled by the judicious and brave action of McClernand and his men. The ponies were all finally gathered up in a secluded valley in rear of the command and proved to be 800 in number.

"That afternoon our train came up under the escort of Captain Brotherton, and this escort, together with the Napoleon gun, was used in strengthening the line then encircling the Indian camp, making the escape of the Indians doubly difficult. As a result of the desperate encounter, I found that the two officers before mentioned and twenty soldiers had been killed. My assistant, Adjutant General George W. Baird, while carrying orders and inspiring the command with his own bravery, was severely wounded, his right arm being broken and part of one ear shot away. Beside Captains Moylan and Godfrey, Lieutenant Romeyn was also injured while leading a charge, together with thirty-eight soldiers.

"The Indians occupied a crescent-shaped ravine, and it was apparent that their position could only be forced by a charge or a siege. The first could not be accomplished without too great sacrifice, while the latter, in my judgment, would be almost sure to result satisfactorily. My one concern then was whether the Sioux Indians, whom I knew to be encamped under Sitting Bull north of the Canadian boundary line, some fifty miles distant, and to whom the few Indians who had been able to escape from the village had fled, might not come to the assistance of the Nez Perces. During the last eight months numbers of disaffected Indians, who had been driven out of the valley of the Yellowstone and its tributaries had sought refuge on Canadian soil and joined the large camp of Sitting Bull, this greatly increasing his force. I afterwards learned, however, that when the Nez Perces' messengers reached the camp of Sitting Bull, instead of coming to the assistance of the besieged, the whole camp, numbering between 1,000 and 2,000 Indians, who evidently had not forgotten their experience during the autumn and winter, immediately moved forty miles further back into the interior of the Canadian territory. But as I did not know this fact until several weeks later, I was bound to make provision for this large body of Indians should they advance to the assistance of the Nez Perces.

"I, therefore, desired that the military authorities should have some intimation of my position, and to that end sent word to General Terry, commanding the department, who was then at Fort Benton, nearly 100 miles to the west, apprising him of our movements and success. I also sent orders to General Sturgis to move up and join us without delay. He was then eighty miles to the south and separated from us by the Missouri river. I likewise informed General Howard of our position.

"As we were besieging this camp of Indians and holding their large herds of stock in the valley, with our large number of wounded to be cared for, I did not relish the idea of being besieged in our turn by the hostile Sioux, and, therefore, took every precaution possible to meet such an emergency. We had no interpreters who could talk Nez Perces well enough to be of any use; some of the scouts could speak Chinook and they called out to the Indians to surrender. Joseph came up under the flag of truce, and from him we learned that the principal chief, Looking Glass, and four other chiefs had been killed, besides a large number of others killed and wounded. Joseph was informed that they must surrender by bringing up their arms and laying them on the ground. They pretended to do so and brought up a few, which amounted to nothing, but hesitated greatly about surrendering the balance.

"While this was going on I directed Lieutenant Gerome to ascertain what they were doing in the village, supposing that he would go to the edge of the bluff and look down into the camp. But misunderstanding my instructions, he went down into the ravine, whereupon he was seized and held until he was exchanged for Chief Joseph.

"It continued to snow during the day, but the siege was pressed continuously and a sharp lookout kept for any force that might come to the assistance of the Nez Perces. On the morning of the third day the ground was well covered with snow, and the scouts reported a large body of black objects on the distant hills, moving in our direction. This occasioned much excitement among the troops, and every eye was turned to the north, whence it was feared that Sitting Bull's hostile Sioux and possible the Assinaboines and Gros Ventres (both of whom were known to be to the north of us) might be moving to the assistance of the Nez Perces.

"It had been reported that the moving column was a large body of Indians. Every officer's field-glass was turned in that direction, and as the long, dark column moved through the midst of light snow, slowly developing its strength as it made its way towards us over the distant hills and rolling prairie, I watched it with very great anxiety. Considering our condition, the large herd of captured stock we were holding, and the hostile camp we were besieging, and the number of our wounded, such a formidable reinforcement would, of course, be a very serious matter and the thoughts ran quickly through my mind as to the best dispositions to make in order to hold what we had gained and repel any effort, no matter how strong, to rescue the besieged or overcome our small but very efficient force. We could use our artillery and quite a large portion of our troops against any additional enemy and still keep the fruits of victory already gained. The mysterious and apparently formidable force drew nearer, when some of the scouts on the extreme outposts shouted 'buffaloes!' and it was a most gratifying cry. The relief occasioned by this announcement was like that afforded to the marines by the appearance of a beacon light or like sunlight bursting through the dark and angry clouds of a storm.

"The snow and cold caused great suffering to our wounded, although they were made as comfortable as possible, and while the siege continued detachments were sent some five miles distant up into the Bear Paw mountains to get poles with which to make travois and stretchers, knowing that the wounded must soon be transported to the nearest hospital.

"On the evening of the 4th of October Howard came up with an escort of twelve men, remaining in our camp over night, and was present next morning at the surrender of Chief Joseph and the entire Indian camp. As Chief Joseph was about to hand his rifle to me, he raised his eyes to the sun, which then stood about 10 o'clock, and said: 'From where the sun now stands, I fight no more against the white man.' From that time to this he has kept his word. Those who surrendered with Chief Joseph and those taken outside the camp numbered 400. There were killed twenty-six in all, and forty-six wounded. The work of securing the arms of the Indians, burying the dead, and preparing the wounded for their long journey occupied the entire day; but on the following morning we commenced our slow and difficult march back to the Missouri river."

Immediately after the surrender of Chief Joseph a runner was sent to Fort Benton with a message to be forwarded to the war department, and General Terry, on his return from Northwest Territory, who was at Fort Benton at the time, received the following dispatch:

"Chicago, October 11, 1877.
"To General A. H. Terry, Fort Benton, M.T.:

"The honorable secretary of war expresses to me his congratulations to General Miles and yourself, upon the important success achieved by the capture of Joseph's band of Nez Perces

GEN. NELSON A. MILES.
Courtesy Montana Historical Society, Helena

on October 5th. The general of the army also desires me to offer his congratulations to General Miles and his command, and to assure them that the capture of Joseph's band is exceedingly important especially on account of the influence on other Indians in Oregon who have been watching the result of Joseph's movements with intense interest. To these well-merited commendations I again offer my own to General Miles and the officers and men who have brought about this exceedingly desirable result.

"(Signed.)

P. H. SHERIDAN,
"LIEUTENANT GENERAL."

This was the last Indian battle fought in Montana; and the "straw" which broke the Indians' back was when Miles captured Chief Joseph. This brave soldier, who is now the commanding general of the United States army, is still on the trail of the enemy, for it was but yesterday, July 25, 1898, that, after a skirmish with the Spanish troops, General Miles successfully landed the American expedition on the island of Porto Rico. Those who surrendered with Chief Joseph numbered 413 by actual count; about 100 escaped to Canada, Chief White Bird among the number. The killed numbered twenty-six and forty-six wounded. Among the killed were Chief Looking Glass and Joseph's brother. Miles had forty-three wounded and twenty-two killed, who are now peacefully sleeping safe from battles, pain or sorrow, in a little dell overlooked by cliffs and ancient mountain pines.

Although those mothers' sons never had a monument to mark their beds of clay, nevertheless the high peaks of the Bear Paws, touching the sky, can be seen from hundreds of miles on all sides and are pointed out by the passer-by, saying: "There's where lie twenty-two American patriots."

CHIEF JOSEPH.
Courtesy Montana Historical Society, Helena

Most of the Indians were taken to the Indian Territory, but Joseph was taken to Washington, D.C., to give an account of his wicked ways.

Howard followed Joseph for two months and a distance of nearly two thousand miles. It cost the regular army one hundred and seventy-nine lives, and the Northwest half that many of its citizens.

When writing the above article I wrote to General Miles asking him for permission to quote his letter, or if he would kindly write me another one on the same subject. In reply, he sent me the following.

"Headquarters of the Army,
"Washington, Jan. 26, 1899.
"Mr. Robert Vaughn, Great Falls, Montana:
"Dear Sir: I have your letter of the 9th instant. So far as I know, you are at liberty to copy the letter referred to in your letter, but I do not at present recall it and would like to know what it is, if convenient for you to give me the information.
Very truly yours,
"NELSON A. MILES,
"MAJOR GENERAL COMMANDING."

After finishing the Nez Perces campaign letter, I sent to General Miles a copy of it, and in reply received the following communication from Lieutenant Colonel Maus:
"Headquarters of the Army,
"Washington, March 4, 1899.
"Mr. Robert Vaughn, Great Falls, Montana:
"My Dear Sir: Some time ago you kindly sent to General Miles an excellent article on the Nez Perces campaign, in which you quote from General Miles' book. The article is certainly very good. The general has been too much occupied to

write anything further at this time, but it is believed his book stated very clearly the main facts regarding this campaign. He says that he does not see any reason why you should not quote from his book, if you so wish.

"I am sure your are right about the service that was done by the Montana people. A number of scouts from Montana were under my charge, as I had command of both the white and Cheyenne Indian scouts in the location of the Indians after they crossed the river. By the aid of these scouts word was sent to General Miles regarding Chief Joseph's band, as well as the direction in which they were going, etc., and in time to be of assistance to him in locating their camp, where we joined him about the commencement of the fight.

"The men of those days were a brave and hardy race, inured to all kinds of hardships, excellent shots, and made a class of fighters of which we have no equal for the kind of warfare in which they were engaged. As civilization advances this type is fast disappearing.

"I should think it would be very interesting for you to write the history of those times, in which your state is especially interested.

"With kindest regards and the thanks of the general for your kind wishes, believe me,

"Very truly yours,

"Marion P. Maus,
"Lieutenant Colonel, Inspector General."

At the time, Joseph was looked upon as a great general, and, no doubt, if it had not been for the Benton parties and other citizens aiding Miles to locate the Indians, Joseph would have carried out his plan and escaped into Canada.

Robert Vaughn.
Great Falls, Montana, July 26, 1899.

An English Tribute to the American Scout.

The Western pioneer will appreciate the following tribute to the American scout by that gallant English soldier, General Baden-Powell, the hero of Mafeking, at one time, the chief scout and "rough rider" in the British army:

General Baden-Powell

Scouting as a fine art had its origin in America, when the pioneer settled first upon the shores of the new country which stretched away, away, to the westward, how far they knew not.

They were surrounded by hostile savages, who came and went like shadows, who found their way as straight as the flight of a carrier pigeon through countless miles of trackless forest; who appeared and disappeared as quickly and completely as the elfs of the fabled fairy-lands. But the instinct of self-preservation sharpened their wits; no man sleeps soundly when danger threatens.

They learned first the secrets by which the Indian made his way from place to place, and tracked his foe for vengeance or his game for sustenance.

They quickly discovered how by training and vigilance the eye became quick, the ear alert, and the touch sensitive.

A crushed blade of grass or a weed, a broken twig, a bent bough, all these things were to the Indian as they are to Sherlock Holmes, sufficient to construct a theory as to the character and numbers of those he pursued.

From him the white man quickly learned his lore, but he could add to it something which instantly made him the superior of the red man, and that was, a higher order of intelligence and reason, and that conquered the aborigine and drove him farther and still farther from the lands of his fathers.

As time passed, some striking figures emerged from the people, as all history demonstrates men have done in all ages.

Daniel Boone crossed the Alleghanies, behind which the Indians made their first stand, thinking the white man would not cross that great breastwork thrown up by nature, and discovered Kentucky.

Then, following Boone, came Crockett, Bridger, Kit Carson and Cody, as the men who were the acknowledged leaders and chiefs of these wise men of the mountains, woods and prairies, during successive epochs.

Since these men and their kind made scouting a fine art, the great soldiers of Europe have acknowledged that they are matchless for the purposes of fighting in an enemy's country.

Returning of Sitting Bull from Canada.

It was but a few months after Sitting Bull had established his camp in the Northwest Territory in the British possessions that the Canadian government requested the government of the United States to send a commission to have a council with Sitting Bull and induce him to return to the United States. Pursuant to this request, a commission was sent to Fort Walsh, N.W.T., and met Oct. 17, 1877, with General Terry at the head. Colonel Macleod, who was in command of the Canadian mounted police with four officers and forty policemen, were present. The council was held in the quarters of the commanding officers of the police force, commencing at 2 o'-clock p.m., and lasted one hour and a half. Sitting Bull desired to have the meeting take place in the open air, but it was thought judicious by the policemen in charge of the ceremony to have the council held in a convenient room, where the act of every participant could be held under strict surveillance and control. All were seated, and General Terry proceeded to state his mission. The following account of this remarkable meeting was published in the Benton Record, October 21, 1877, and was communicated by Captain J. J. Healy (now of Alaska), who was present at the council. Captain Healy describes Sitting Bull as follows:

"He is a short, thick-set man, about forty-five years of age, and weighs, probably, 175 pounds. He is undoubtedly a full-blooded Sioux Indian, and not a remarkably intelligent looking one at that. He is minus one toe, having at some time or other had his feet frozen. He does not speak and apparently does not understand a word of the English language, and his conversations with the whites are always conducted through an interpreter."

General Terry's Speech to the Sioux.

"We are sent here as commissioners of the United States, at the request of the Canadian government, to meet you (interrupted by Sitting Bull, who objected to a table in front of the speaker. The table was removed). The president has instructed us to say to you that he desires to make a lasting peace with you and your people, and that all the people of the United States may live in harmony. He wishes it for your sake as well as that of the whites, and if you will return to your country and leave your hostile life, a full pardon will be given you for any wrong you may have done in the past. You, or any man among you, shall be forgiven and permitted to enjoy all the liberties of any other Indians at the different agencies. We will not tell you what the president means by saying he will give you a full pardon. Of all the bands of Indians, yours among them, who were at war about a year ago, yours is the only one that has not come into the agency. Of those bands that have come in, not one has been punished, and every man, woman and child has been furnished food and clothing. It is true these Indians have been required to give up their arms and ammunition, which were all sold and the money applied for their benefit. We have already sent 650 cows to one of the agencies, for the use of the Indians. This has been done to get you to leave your wild life and to help you to support yourselves. The president will not consent to have you return unless you give your consent to give up your arms and horses, but he invites you to come to your and his country, give up your arms when you cross the line, thence go to any agency he may assign you to, and there give up your horses (except such as you need for use in civil life), which will be sold and the money applied to buy cows, which will support you after the game has left the country. You will also receive clothes the same as other Indians. We have come many hundred miles to bring this message. Too much blood has already been shed. It is time war should cease. You cannot return to your country and your friends unless you accept these conditions; otherwise you will be treated as enemies of the United States. Think well of these things, and when you have made up your mind we are ready to hear your reply."

The Indians were asked if they wanted to retire and hold a council among themselves, but they said their minds were already made up and they were ready to reply.

Sitting Bull's Speech to the United States Commission.

"For sixty-four years you have kept us and treated us bad. What have we done? Your people are the whole cause of the trouble; we could go no place but to this country. Here is where I learned to shoot, and that is why I came here. What did you come for? I did not give you the country, but you followed me and I had to leave. You took my country from me. I was born and raised with the Red River half-breeds, and wanted to come back. (Sitting Bull here shook hands with Colonel Macleod and said he would live with him.) You may think I am a fool, but you are a bigger fool than I am. This house is a medicine house. You come and tell us lies in it. We don't like it. Don't say two words more, but go back where you came from. I shake hands with these people (shakes hands with Colonel Macleod); so say no more. You gave that part of the country and then took it back. I want you to go home and take it easy as you go.

The Ree's Speech.

"Look at me. Seven years in the country. For the last sixty-four years you have treated us bad. I don't like you. You tell lies. I will keep peace with these people as long as I live. I

SITTING BULL.
Courtesy Denver Public Library Western History Department

shake hands with them. You come over and tell us lies. Go home, and take it easy as you go."

Speech by a Yankton Sioux
Who Was in the Minnesota Massacre.

"I don't wear the same clothes as you do. You come to tell us lies. You have treated us bad for sixty-four years and have been fighting us all the time. There were seven different tribes of us. You promised to take care of us then we were over there, but you did not do it. We like these people and intend to live with them. I don't intend to kill any one." (Shook hands with Generals Terry and Lawrence.)

Speech by a Squaw.

"You would not give me time to raise children, so I came over here to raise children and live in peace."

(To allow a squaw to speak in council is one of the worst insults that an Indian can offer.)

Crow's Speech.

After kissing all the English officers, he said: "What do you mean by coming over here and talking this way to us? We were driven out of your country and came to this one. I am afraid of God and don't want to do anything bad. These people give us plenty to eat. You can go back, and go easy. I come to this country, and my grandmother knows it, and is glad I came to live in peace and raise children."

After the Crow had spoken, Sitting Bull sat down and said they were done. General Terry then stated that the commissioners had nothing further to say. The Indians then left, after shaking hands with the English officers.

The commission left the following day, and a few days

later arrived at Fort Benton. No disappointment was expressed by the citizens of Montana that the commission did not succeed. The average citizen was glad rather than sorry that the old savage, imbued with the blood of Custer and his companions, decided to remain on British soil. To live in peace on their reservation—receiving no punishment for what they had done—board and clothes free—to help to lead them from savage life, were some of the inducements proffered for the return of these hostiles. All offers were not only scornfully rejected, but the commission was treated to studied and offensively displayed insults.

After remaining in Canada nearly three years, and finding that the Canadian government had no use for him and that his people were starving, the old fugitive now sings a different tune and is anxious to return.

On February 4, 1880, he sent a commission to the agent at Pine Ridge Agency, indicating that he and his followers wanted to make arrangements with the United States government so that they could come back and live in peace, and, as a token of friendship, he sent a pipe hatchet; in case terms could not be had, it was to be returned. But, to his disappointment, the government did not wish to make any terms with him then. His followers kept coming, however, in small parties, and in a destitute and starving condition, to Fort Peck Agency, in northern Montana, turning over their guns and what ponies they had left; the other ponies they had eaten to keep from starving. By May 1st, 1,116 of the refugees had returned.

Again Sitting Bull made an application to the government, through the war department, for permission to return, and all the property he wanted was his horse and gun. After both the Canadian and United States governments had several communications in regard to the matter, and after Sitting Bull had been in Canada five years, he was permitted to return to the

United States. He stood his trial and was taken to Standing Rock agency and kept there as a kind of prisoner of war. Now, he was not looked upon as a warrior, even by his own people. But it was not long before he began to gain influence, and many of them looked upon him as a kind of high priest and dreamer. It appears that he was determined to be a leader, if not in one thing he would be in another. The next letter will show him up in his new profession, or whatever you may call it, for he was one of the prime movers in the Indian Messiah craze and the floor manager of the ghost dance, which was finally the cause of his death.

ROBERT VAUGHN.

JULY 15, 1898.

The Indian Messiah and the Ghost Dance.

To give a true history of this phenomenal influence that had taken possession of the Indians at that time, I will here give the Indian commissioner's report, which gives a very correct account of this remarkable occurrence, also of the establishing at various agencies of an Indian police system which has been in force since 1877 and now is a perfect success. It will be seen hereafter that this police force made the arrest of Sitting Bull at the time of his death:

"The one best thing that marked the vigorous policy and the giving place to sense for sentiment, was the appointment of Indians to take care of Indians. Some of them had long since served in the regular army, indifferently well, but it was not until 1877 that the experiment of appointing Indian policemen to guard Indians and watch ill-disposed whites was seriously considered. From the report of the United States commissioner of Indian affairs in 1880 it appears to have been a success from the very first. The practicability of employing an Indian police to maintain order upon an Indian reservation is no longer a matter of question. In less than three years the system has been put in operation at forty agencies, and the total force now numbers one hundred and sixty-two officers and six hundred and fifty-three privates. Special reports as to the character and efficiency of the service rendered by the police have recently been called for from its agents by this bureau, and those reports bear uniform testimony to the value and reliability of the police service, and to the fact that its maintenance, which was at first undertaken as an experiment, is now looked upon as a necessity.

"The discipline of the force is excellent, failure to obey an order being followed by immediate dismissal. It is made up of the best young men of the tribes, many of them being mem-

bers of the native soldier organization. There are also enlisted
two chiefs—White Bird and Little Big Man, the latter being a
northern Indian, and having taken a prominent part with Sitting Bull in the Big Horn campaign of 1876, afterwards surrendering at the agency with Crazy Horse.

"A member of the force is on duty all night at the guard
house, making the rounds of the government buildings at intervals of fifteen or thirty minutes, which precluded the possibility
of government supplies being surreptitiously made away with."

Says the Sioux agent, 1880: "The Indian police force at this
agency consists of fifty members, all Indians: one captain, two
lieutenants, ten sergeants and corporals, and the balance privates. The force is in charge of one of the white employes,
who also acts as deputy United States marshal. There is also
attached to the force one special detective and one special interpreter. The members are all armed with the Springfield and
Sharp's army carbine.

"In the autumn of 1890 we find the once famous disturber
of the peace in Montana, Sitting Bull, established at Standing
Rock agency on the Dakota side of the Missouri. He was now
nearly sixty years of age, and had been fully half that time a
formidable leader of wild red men. He lived in two little cabins in comfort and indolence, but was no longer rich in property or influence. As observed in his return from the British
possessions he was still a true aborigine and superstitious as a
child. Still he was dauntless in spirit, reckless of results, and
fearless as a lion in the face of danger. It is something to know
that this remarkable figure in the history of Montana fell not
by the hands of those whom he had always counted as his enemies, but at the hands of his own people. For, gainsay it who
will, as time goes forward he will grow taller, grander in the
estimation of men, especially in the minds of imaginative red
men, and it is very well for all, especially the Indians, to know

that his following was not great in the end, and that he was slain by his own people.

"During the summer and fall of 1890 reports reaching this office from various sources showed that a growing excitement existed among the Indian tribes over the announcement of the advent of a so-called Indian Messiah or Christ, or Great Medicine Man of the North. The delusion finally became so widespread and well defined as to be generally known as the 'Messiah Craze.'

"In June, 1890, through the war department, came the account of a 'Cheyenne Medicine Man, Porcupine,' who claimed to have left his reservation in November, 1889, and to have traveled by command and under divine guidance in search of the Messiah to the Shoshone agency, Salt Lake City, and the Fort Hall agency, and thence—with others who joined him at Fort Hall—to Walker River reservation, Nevada. There 'the Christ,' who was scarred on wrist and face, told them of his crucifixion, taught them a certain dance, counseled love and kindness for each other, and foretold that the Indian dead were to be resurrected, the youth of the good people to be renewed, the earth enlarged, etc.

"From the Tongue River agency in Montana came a report, made by the special agent in charge, dated August 20, 1890, that Porcupine, an Indian of that agency, had declared himself to be the new Messiah, and had found a large following ready to believe in his doctrine. Those who doubted were fearful lest their unbelief should call down upon them the curse of the 'Mighty Porcupine.' The order went forth that, in order to please the Great Spirit, a six days' and nights' dance must be held every new moon, with the understanding that at the expiration of a certain period the Great Spirit would restore the buffalo, elk, and other game, resurrect all dead Indians, endow his believers with perpetual youth, and perform many other wonders well calculated to inflame Indian superstition. Dances, afterwards known as 'ghost dances,' were enthusiastically attended. About the same time the Cheyenne and Arrapaho agent in Oklahoma reported that during the autumn of 1889 and the ensuing winter rumors had reached that agency from the Shoshones of Wyoming that an Indian Messiah was located in the mountains about two hundred miles north.

"In August, 1890, Agent Gallagher stated that many at the Pine Ridge agency were crediting the report made to them in the spring that a great medicine man had appeared in Wyoming, whose mission was to resurrect and rehabilitate all the departed heroes of the tribe, restore to the Indians herds of buffaloes, which were to make them entirely independent of aid from the whites, and bring such confusion upon their enemies (the whites) that they would flee the country, leaving the Indians in possession of the entire Northwest for all time to come. Indians fainted during the performances which attended the recital of the wondrous thing soon to come to pass, and one man died from the excitement.

"The effect of such meetings or dances was so demoralizing that on August 22, 1890, when about two thousand Indians were gathered on White Clay creek, about eighteen miles from the agency, to hold what they called a religious dance connected with the appearance of this supernatural being, the agent instructed his Indian police to disperse them. This they were unable to do. Accompanied by about twenty police, the agent himself visited the place, and, on hearing of his approach, most of the Indians dispersed. Several men, however, with Winchester rifles in their hands and a good storing of cartridges belted around their waists, stood stripped for fight, prepared to die in defense of the new faith. They were finally quieted, but the dances continued, and October 12, 1890, Agent Royer, who had just taken charge of the agency, reported that more than half the Indians had already joined the danc-

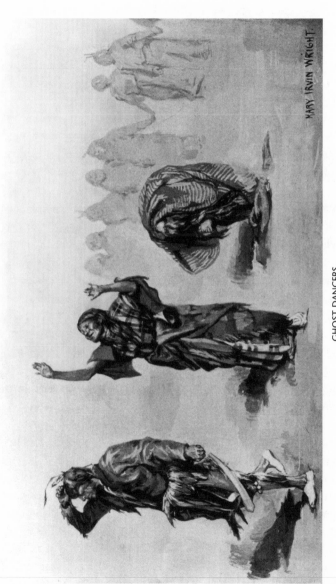

GHOST DANCERS.
Photo from the 14th Annual Report of the Bureau of Ethnology, 1892-93

ing, and when requested to stop, would strip themselves ready
for fight; that the police had lost control, and if his endeavors
to induce the chiefs to suppress the craze should be unavail-
ing, he hoped for a hearty co-operation in invoking military
aid to maintain order.

"About the same time the Cheyenne river agent reported
that Big Foot's band were much excited about the coming of a
'Messiah,'" and, armed with Winchester rifles and of very
threatening temper, were beyond police control. A similar
condition of affairs existed among the Rosebud Sioux.

"Agent McLaughlin also reported from Standing Rock October 17th, as follows: 'I feel it my duty to report the present
craze and nature of the excitement existing among the Sitting
Bull faction of the Indians over the expected Indian millenni-
um, the annihilation of the white men and supremacy of the
Indian, which is looked for in the near future and promised by
the Indian medicine men as no later than next spring, when
the new grass begins to appear, and is known among the Sioux
as the 'return of the ghosts.' They are promised by some
members of the Sioux tribe, who have lately developed into
medicine men, that the Great Spirit has promised them that
their punishment by the dominant race has been sufficient,
and that their numbers having now become so decimated will
be reinforced by all Indians who are dead; that the dead are all
returning to reinhabit this earth, which belongs to the Indians;
that they are driving back with them, as they return, immense
herds of buffaloes, and elegant wild horses to have for the
catching; that the Great Spirit promises them that the white
men will be unable to make gunpowder in the future, and all
attempts at such will be a failure, and that the gunpowder
now on hand will be useless as against Indians, as it will not
throw a bullet with sufficient force to pass through the skin of
an Indian; that the Great Spirit had deserted the Indians for a

long period, but is now with them and against the whites, and will cover the earth over with thirty feet of additional soil, well sodded and timbered, under which the whites will all be smothered; and any whites who may escape these great phenomena will become small fishes in the rivers of the country; but to bring about this happy result the Indians must do their part and become deliverers and thoroughly organize.

"Sitting Bull is high priest and leading apostle of this latest Indian absurdity; in a word, he is the chief mischief maker at this agency, and if he were not here, this craze, so general among the Sioux, would never have gotten a foothold at this agency.

"On Thursday, the 9th inst., upon an invitation from Sitting Bull, an Indian named Kicking Bear, belonging to the Cheyenne River agency, the chief medicine man of the ghost dance among the Sioux, arrived at Sitting Bull's camp on Grand river, forty miles south of this agency, to inaugurate a ghost dance and initiate the members. Upon learning of his arrival there I sent a detachment of thirteen Indian policemen, including the captain and second lieutenant, to arrest and escort him from the reservation, but they returned without executing the order, both officers being in a dazed condition and fearing the powers of Kicking Bear's medicine. Several members of the force tried to induce the officers to permit them to make the arrest, but the latter would not allow it, but simply told Sitting Bull that it was the agent's orders that Kicking Bear and his six companions should leave the reservation and return to their agency. Sitting Bull was very insolent to the officers, and made some threats against some members of the force, but said that the visitors would leave the following day. Upon return of the detachment to the agency on Tuesday, the 14th, I immediately sent the lieutenant and one man back to see whether the party had left or not, and to notify Sitting Bull that his insolence and bad behavior would not be tolerated longer, and that the ghost dance must not be continued. The lieutenant returned yesterday and reported that the party had not started back to Cheyenne before his arrival there on the 15th, but left immediately upon his ordering them to do so, and that Sitting Bull told him that he was determined to continue the ghost dance, as the Great Spirit had sent a direct message by Kicking Bear that to live they must do so, but that he would not have any more dancing until after he had come to the agency and talked the matter over with me; but the news comes in this morning that they are dancing again, and it is participated in by a great many Indians who become silly and intoxicated over the excitement. The dance is demoralizing, indecent and disgusting. Desiring to exhaust all reasonable means before resorting to extremes, I have sent a message to Sitting Bull by his nephew, One Bull, that I want to see him at the agency, and I feel quite confident that I shall succeed in allaying the present excitement and put a stop to this absurd 'craze.'

"Agent Royer, of the Pine Ridge agency, was especially advised October 18th, that Major General Miles, commander of the military division in which the agency was situated, also chairman of the commission recently appointed to negotiate with the Northern Cheyennes, would shortly visit the agency, and that he would have opportunity to explain the situation to him and ask his advice as to the wisdom of calling for troops. October 24, 1890, this office recommended that the war department be requested to cause Sitting Bull, Circling Hawk, Black Bird and Kicking Bear to be confined in some military prison and to instruct the proper military authorities to be on the alert to discover any suspicious movements of the Indians of the Sioux agencies.

"Early in November reports received from the agents at Pine Ridge, Rosebud and Cheyenne River showed that the Indians of those agencies, especially Pine Ridge, were arming themselves and taking a defiant attitude toward the government and its representatives, committing depredations and likely to go to other excesses; and November 13th this office recommended that the matter be submitted to the war department, with request that such prompt action be taken to avert an outbreak as the emergency might be found by them to demand. On that day the president of the United States addressed the following communication to the secretary of the interior:

" 'Replying to your several communications in regard to the condition of the Indians at the Sioux and Cheyenne agencies, I beg to say that some days ago I directed the war department to send an officer of high rank to investigate the situation and to report upon it from a military standpoint. General Ruger, I understand, has been assigned to that duty and is now probably at or on his way to these agencies. I have directed the secretary of war to assume a military responsibility for any threatened outbreak, and to take such steps as may be necessary to that end. In the meantime, I suggest that you advise your agents to separate the well-disposed from the ill-disposed Indians, and while maintaining their control and discipline, so far as may be possible, to avoid forcing any issue that will result in an outbreak, until suitable military preparations can be made.'

"November 15th Agent Royer sent to this office the following telegram from Pine Ridge: 'Indians are dancing in the snow and are wild and crazy. I have fully informed you that employes and government property at this agency have no protection and are at the mercy of these dancers. Why delay by further investigation? We need protection, and we need it now. The leaders should be arrested and confined in some military post until the matter is quieted, and this should be done at once.'

"A military force under General John R. Brooke, consisting of five companies of infantry, three troops of cavalry, and one hotchkiss and one gatling gun, arrived at Pine Ridge November 20, 1890. Two troops of cavalry and six companies of infantry were stationed at Rosebud. Troops were ordered to all agencies that were on the Sioux reservation. When the troops reached the Rosebud agency, about one thousand and eight hundred Indians—men, women and children—stampeded toward Pine Ridge and the bad lands, destroying all of their property before leaving and that of others en route.

"Sitting Bull's camp, where the dancing had been going on, was on Grand river, forty miles from the agency. The number of Indian policemen in that vicinity was increased and Sitting Bull was kept under close surveillance. December 12 the commanding officer at Fort Yates was instructed by General Ruger, commanding the Department of Dakota, to make it his special duty to secure the person of Sitting Bull, and to call on Agent McLaughlin for such co-operation and assistance as would best promote the object in view. December 14th the police notified the agent that Sitting Bull was preparing to leave the reservation. Accordingly, after consultation with the post commander, it was decided that the arrest should be made the following morning by the police under the command of Lieutenant Bullhead, with United States troops within in supporting distance.

"At daybreak, December 15th, thirty-nine Indian police and four volunteers went to Sitting Bull's cabin and arrested him. He agreed to accompany them to the agency, but while preparing to get ready he caused considerable delay, and during this time his followers began to congregate to the number of one hundred and fifty, so that when he was brought out of the house they had the police entirely surrounded. Then Sitting Bull refused to go and called on his friends, the ghost dancers, to rescue him. At his juncture one of them shot Lieutenant Bullhead. The Lieutenant then shot Sitting Bull, who also received another shot and was killed outright. Another shot struck Sergeant

Shavehead and then the firing became general. In about two hours the police had secured possession of Sitting Bull's house and driven their assailants into the woods. Shortly after, when one hundred United States troops under command of Captain Fechet, reached the spot, the police drew up in line and saluted. Their bravery and discipline received highest praise from Captain Fechet. The ghost dancers fled from their hiding places to the Cheyenne River reservation, leaving their families and dead behind them. Their women who had taken part in the fight had been disarmed by the police and placed under guard and were turned over to the troops when they arrived. The losses were six policemen killed (including Bullhead and Shavehead, who soon died at the agency hospital) and one wounded. The attacking party lost eight killed and three wounded." Report of the Indian Commission for 1891.

Sergeant Joe Thompson, who was with the United States troops at the time, is present employed at the Boston and Montana smelter at this place, and is drum major of the Black Eagle band. Mr. Thompson had been in many battles during the campaign of 1876–77, of which I have not given an account. In one of those battles "twenty-seven saddles were emptied," as he said, by one volley from the Indians; and Mr. Thompson is now carrying with him a scar which he received by a bullet from the enemy during one of these engagements.

A wonderful change has taken place since then. Now the Northern Pacific railway runs through the center of the Sioux country, and also the Burlington railroad passes in sight of the Custer battlefield, and settlers from the Eastern and Middle states have come and turned the old battle grounds into productive farms and pasture lands. The Indian villages have disappeared and thriving towns and incorporated cities have taken their places. The Indians have been compelled by the government to stay on their reservations where there are agencies.

According to the statistics in 1891 there were 32,286 of the Sioux nation alone, who are gathered at eleven agencies, where there are schools, mechanical and agricultural institutions, established to teach the young Indians the arts and customs of the white man. And they are fast becoming civilized. They are engaged in raising cattle, sheep and horses, and growing grain and vegetables.

Charles A. Smith, county commissioner of Choteau county, Montana, stated a few days ago that Indians at Fort Belknap have supplied about 350,000 pounds of beef to the agency this year at $3.87 per hundred, from which they derived a revenue of about $13,000.

Major Luke C. Hays, agent of the Fort Belknap Indian reservation, said:

"My Indians will, and do work." That was demonstrated to my satisfaction some time ago. I have about 1,300 Assinaboine and Gros Ventres Indians on my reservation and they are good Indians, although very much alive.

"This promises to be an unusually busy year on the Belknap reservation. Last summer the government started to build a canal, tapping the Milk river at Belknap, where a dam is to be built. Only one mile of this canal was completed, but work on the remainder will be commenced as early as practicable this spring. Indians have been hauling rock all winter for the dam. The canal, when completed, will be ten or fifteen miles long and will irrigate about 5,000 acres of the Milk river valley lands south of the river. These lands will grow excellent crops of grain and hay.

"A new enterprise that will be commenced this summer (1899) is a big reservoir on Warm Springs creek in the Little Rockies. This reservoir will cover 160 acres of land and will have an average depth of eighteen feet. It is designed to furnish a supply of water for irrigating purposes in the southern part of the reservation.

"These two irrigating systems will cost in the neighborhood of $70,000, but that money is available. It is not government money in the sense that the government would not expend it unless appropriated for that use, for it belongs to the Indians themselves, having been appropriated for their benefit and in lieu of lands turned over to them by the government.

"Seeing the success of these Indians, others are endeavoring to go into the stock-raising business—on a small scale, to be sure—but in time the stock interests of these two tribes will be considerable. I have no doubt that in a few years the Indians will become almost self-supporting."

The same can be said of other tribes that are in the northern part of the state of which I have personal knowledge. There is one non-reservation boarding school for Indians in Montana. It is located off the reservation at the old Fort Shaw military post in the Sun River valley and in the center of a well-to-do settlement, and but twenty-four miles from the city of Great Falls. This school was opened December 27, 1892; its enrollment in 1898 was 305, average attendance 283. The pupils are recruited from reservation schools, the policy being to place therein pupils who, by reason of sound physical health and natural aptitude, are capable of receiving further advantages, with facilities for special instructions in agriculture, stock breeding, the mechanical and domestic arts, for normal and commercial training, and for taking up other subjects as occasion requires. Modern facilities for instruction have been introduced. The industrial and literary progress this school has made is wonderful. The report of the commissioner of Indian affairs will bear out my assertion. Manual training and industrial education has gone hand in hand with the intellectual development of the untrained young Indian mind, and has given good results. The exhibit by the Fort Shaw Indian school at the Cascade county fair held at Great Falls last October in the way of carving on woods, shoemaking, plain and fancy needle work, embroidery, drawing and penmanship was excellent, and would do credit to young pupils of the same age of any race. There were about thirty of the young Indian boys and girls accompanying the exhibit, with Dr. Winslow, the superintendent, in charge. Among the number there was a brass band of sixteen pieces; they marched through the city dressed in uniform and playing national airs with as much grace and skill as if they belonged to some military post.

According to statistics there are 234 schools in all for Indians under exclusive control of the government. The average attendance during the year 1897 was 18,676 pupils.

The other day a young Cree Indian by the name of Young Boy, with whom I was acquainted, and who could speak fair English, came to my office, sat by a table and began writing in a small account book that he had. Seeing it was a peculiar looking manuscript, I asked him what he was writing. He told me that he was writing down what he had been buying that day, and he read it to me, first in Cree and afterwards translated into English, and handed it to me. The following is a photograph from the original writing in the Cree language:

A CREE MANUSCRIPT.

A CREE INDIAN.

The translation into English is as follows: "To day I paid three dollars and twenty-five cents for a blanket and three dollars for a bridle, in all six dollars and twenty-five cents.

YOUNG BOY."

Again he wrote the Cree alphabet, and, after speaking the letters, he handed me the manuscript of which the following is a photograph:

A CREE ALPHABET.

The Cree Indians are from the Northwest Territory in Canada. Part of the tribe are in Montana at the present time selling polished buffalo horns and other trinkets to the citizens.

Recently they held their sun dance near the town of Havre, in the northern part of this state. To those who have never witnessed this ancient performance, the following may be of interest: For four days preceding the dance the tribe gathered about the chief's tepee, and at sundown of each day they sang the Indian songs which told of the past glories of the tribe and listened to the words of the chief concerning their welfare and exhorting them to eschew the use of whisky (firewater), extolling the beauties of the ancient sun dance and discussing other topics.

All their songs were accompanied by the beating of tom-toms, the blowing of whistles and performing on various

LITTLE BEAR, CREE CHIEF.
Courtesy Montana Historical Society, Helena

other musical instruments. The preliminary singing and speechmaking continued all night on the fourth day. The dance began the next night and continued for three days, during which time no Indian ate or drank anything. The dancing was done in a huge circular tent, or pavilion, on the crest of a hill. The dancers performed in stalls that were arranged around the pavilion, with the bands of musicians seated on their haunches in the center. The ceremonies closed with a grand feast. Chiefs Little Bear and Little Bird conducted the ceremony. After all was over the Indians dispersed to their several camps.

The younger Indians of this tribe are considerably advanced in civilization. The intelligence which Young Boy displayed to me is an evidence that the Indians are fast becoming civilized in the British possessions as well as in the United States. For several years peace and good order have prevailed among all the northern tribes. It will not be long before the Indians will be self-supporting. The effect of the march of civilization on the most warlike tribes even indicates that Indian wars are a thing of the past. And to the West, the nation's pleasure ground, with its extensive plains, carpeted with luxuriant grasses, with valleys unsurpassed in fertility, many of them overlooked and sheltered by pine-covered mountains in which lies hidden a wealth of nations, can come millions more of our people and live in peace.

ROBERT VAUGHN.

FEB. 21, 1899.

An Indian Legend.

While on my recent visit to the home of Edward A. Lewis a pleasant evening was passed listening to the family telling old Indian stories which were told to them by Black Bear (Sikey-kio), an old Indian woman who lived with them for many years. One of those stories is here given. It is a legend passed from father to son in the tribes of the Blackfeet from time immemorial. The early residents of Northern Montana will remember this old Indian woman. Though time had left its imprints in countless wrinkles, and had bent her once lithe figure with a burden of one hundred and sixteen winters, it could not dim the brightness of her black eyes nor dull the vigor of her remarkable intelligence.

When the century was young, while she was in camp with her people at the mouth of the Sun river, where now the city of Great Falls is located, she saw several members of the Lewis and Clarke expedition, who were the first white men she ever saw.

As time passed Black Bear (as she was called in memory of her father, a Piegan chief), left the Indians and lived more and more with the whites. She was at Malcolm Clarke's house the time he was murdered and was the means of preventing the Indians from killing Mrs. Clarke, and, by doing so, she came near losing her own life.

Finally Black Bear became a nurse in the family of Mr. Lewis, at whose house she died some twenty years ago. Like the 'old woman who lived in a shoe,' she was very fond of children and to them she told many of her Indian stories. One of the children to whom she told these weird tales of Indian folklore was Isabell, the oldest daughter of the Lewis family, now Mrs. John Taber. At my request Mrs. Taber, with the aid of her mother interpreted and reduced to writing the Indian legend referred to for publication in this book. It is as follows:

"Listen," said Black Bear to the little ones who crowded expectant around her knee. "Listen and I will tell you how the Great Spirit gave horses to the Indians.

"It was long, long ago and the Piegans were camped on a large flat. The two daughters of the chief one evening were looking at the stars. One star was so bright that it attracted the attention of the younger daughter. As she looked a strange feeling came over her and she murmured half to herself:

"'Were that star a young man I would marry him.'

"And she looked long at the star, marveling at its brightness. The next day the chief gave orders to hitch the dogs to the travois and move camp. On the trail the daughter, who had charge of one of the travois, had fallen behind on account of a broken travoi. The rest of her people had passed out of sight, and, as she was about to start again, she looked up and, behold, before her stood a young man, beautiful in form and features. As she knelt frightened before him he said:

" 'Do not be alarmed, maiden. I am he thou wished to marry. Close your eyes and I will take you to the happy hunting grounds far away.'

"She did as she was told, and when she opened her eyes she was in her husband's lodge, far above the stars. It was a happy life she led in that distant land. Her husband's father was the great chief of many lodges and every one was kind to her and her people looked after her every want and desire. Her life was one of idleness and happiness until one day came a longing she could not conquer. In the wide fields of this great land grew many delicious roots, but of one of these it was forbidden to eat.

"'Of all the other roots thou mayest dig and eat, but of this root thou must neither dig nor eat.'

"And as she thought of it the desire grew and one day, being alone in the fields, she took her sharpened stick and, finding the great root on the little mound, the temptation became greater and greater. Then, after many hesitations, she began to dig. (Just as the secret longing conquered Eve and Pandora.) And as she dug, the little mound yielded and rolled away, leaving a great hole. Kneeling down she looked and lo! She could see her father and her sister and her people coming and going in their camp far below. And as she looked she became sad and her heart ached with homesickness and she wept.

"Thus they found her—her husband and his father. And they were sad at heart, for they knew that she must leave them. In the morning they made a long rope of buffalo hides and gently lowered her through a hole in the sky to her old home. All her people were happy and made great rejoicing at the return of the long lost daughter of their chief. Soon after she gave birth to a son, and when the boy was five years old a great plague broke out and his mother died and also many of her people. The child was left to the care of his uncle, who now had become chief of the tribe. But they were very poor, for there was no one now to make moccasins or to dress buffalo hides for them, and hunger stalked through the camp and the lodges were without food and there were no dogs for the travois.

"The father of the little boy and the Great Chief and his wife, far up in the sky, saw the suffering and it made their hearts sad, and they took thought to see what they could do. Finally the Great Chief and his wife came to the earth and, finding the boy alone, told him their mission and wept with him.

" 'Now, then, my son,' said the Great Chief, seating himself on the grass, 'bring me some mud.'

"And the boy did as he was told and the Great Chief fashioned it in his hands, and as he did so he made strong medicine and muttered strange words as the wet clay took form under his fingers. Then the Great Chief put the thing on the grass, and as the boy looked at it he saw it grow and grow until it was large and moved with life at a word from the Great Chief.

"Then he looked at his work and was pleased and called a great council of the trees of the forest and the birds of the air and of all the beasts that roamed the plains. They all came as he called, for he ruled over them. And as they gathered around he said to them:

" 'I have made a horse for my son; an animal for him to ride and one that will carry his burdens. Now give me of your wisdom to make this horse perfect.'

"And the pine tree said: 'Oh, Great Chief, thy work is good. But the horse has no tail. From my plenty I will give it.'

"And the pine tree did as it said and the Great Chief murmured, 'It is good.'

"Then the fir tree said: 'Oh, Great Chief, thy work is good. But the horse has no mane. From my plenty I will give it.'

"And it was so and the Great Chief murmured, 'It is good.'

"Then the turtle said: 'Oh, Great Chief, thy work is good, but the horse has no hoofs. Out of my plenty I will give it.'

"And it was so and the Great Chief murmured: 'It is good.'

"Then the elk said: 'Oh, Great Chief, thy work is good, but the horse is too small; I am too large. Of my plenty I will give.'

"And it was so, and the Great Chief murmured: 'It is good.'

"Then the cottonwood said: 'Oh, Great Chief, thy work is good, but the horse has no saddle. Out of my plenty I will give it."

"And it was so, and the Great Chief murmured: 'It is good.'

"Then the buffalo said: Oh, Great Chief, thy work is good, but the saddle is bare. Out of my plenty I give to cover it.'

"And it was so, and the Great Chief murmured: 'It is good.'

"Then the buffalo said again: 'There is no hair rope with which to lead the horse. Out of my abundance will I give again.'

"And it was so, and the Great Chief murmured: 'It is good.'

"Then the wolf said: 'Oh, Great Chief, thy work is good, but there is no soft cover for the saddle. Out of my plenty I will give.'

"And it was so, and the Great Chief murmured: 'It is so. The horse is now complete. Take it, my son,' and the great council was ended.

"Then the grandmother turned to the boy and gave him a sack of pemmican, saying:

"'My son, treasure this carefully. It is a magic sack of pemmican and will never be empty, though you eat from it all the time.'

"And with this they left him wondering. Then he mounted his mare and rode to his people who marveled at the strange animal. The mare soon had a colt, and then another, and in a short time there were horses enough to pack his uncle's lodge-skins and lodge-poles from camp to camp. Then the others became envious and the young man told the chief, his uncle, to take his tribe on the morrow to the great lake and that there he would make strong medicine and perform a miracle. And the chief did as he was told.

"In the morning all the people dug holes near the edge of the lake and waited, hiding in them, and then the young man came riding down from the hills on his mare, with her many colts following behind. Calling his uncle he said to him:

" 'I am going to leave you. You will never see me again. Here is the magic sack of pemmican. Keep it and you will never go hungry. I have made strong medicine and before I go I will make every fish in the lake turn into a horse so that there will be plenty for all your people. Tell them to watch and when the horses come rushing from the lake to catch as many of them as they can. But do you wait and catch none until my old mare comes from the water; then do you catch her and her alone. Do then as I tell you and all will be well.'

" 'With these words the young man mounted on his mare, rode onto the lake and was soon lost to view in the deep waters. Soon the surface of the lake began to bubble and foam and the Indians were frightened and would have run away had not the old chief ordered them back to their posts. And in a little while horses' heads could be seen on the water as the animals came swimming towards the shore. There were hundreds and hundreds of them, and as they dashed up the bank the Indians sprang out and captured many of them and many escaped, and those which got away formed the wild bands which even to-day are found on the wide plains. But the chief caught none of them until the old mare came out of the water, and the last to come out of the lake. She he caught while the people laughed, for the old mare was aged and feeble, but he answered never a word to their jeering, for he had faith in his nephew. At night he picketed the mare near his lodge, and just as the moon was coming up over the distant hills the mare neighed three times and out of the thick brush thousands of colts came running up. Soon the lodge was surrounded and the chief had hundreds and hundreds of horses and his people no longer jeered at him, for he was rich and richer than them all.

"And that was how the Great Spirit gave horses to the Indians."

This is the tale the chief's daughter heard as she crouched at the feet of her grandfather listening, wondering, awed as the slow words came from his lips as he sat in the dim light of a smouldering lodge fire. As Black Bear said, "it was told to my father's father and to his father's father hundreds of winters ago."

Many other legends existed among the Northern tribes of

Indians. They believed in good and bad spirits and that there is some kind of a hereafter. The first missionaries who visited the Flatheads for the first time said that those Indians then believed that after death the good Indians went to a country of perpetual summer and there met their relatives; and that the buffalo, elk, deer and horses were there in great numbers and in its rivers fish were in great abundance. And, on the other hand, that the bad Indians were doomed to a place covered with perpetual snow and there they would be forever shivering with cold. They would see fire a long ways off, but could not get to it; also water was in sight, but, though dying for the want of it, they could not reach it. It may be that those ideas which exist in the minds of the red people of the forest are but human instincts, but to me they seem to be the intellectual ruins of a prehistoric race that was once versed in the architecture of the universe, and believed in the Creator of all things.

ROBERT VAUGHN.
OCT. 14, 1899.

The Round-up.

It will not be long before the "round-up" will be numbered among the things that are of the "then," and the reading of this letter will be of more interest twenty-five years hence than it is now. Many do not know what is meant by "round-up;" I will try and give a brief description of it. The one that tells a story best is the one that commences at the beginning, and for me to tell how the cattle herds that are on the Western plains are conducted I must begin right.

In order to distinguish one animal from another of the cattle running at large on the public domain, the owner must have them branded. In Montana, for instance, there is a state law governing brands. A record of brands, with the names of the owners attached, is kept by the secretary of the Board of Stock Commissioners.

A brand of the same resemblance can be used by other parties, but it must be placed on a different part of the animal and so described in the recorder's book. A brand book is published by the Live Stock Association and every member of the association is furnished with a book. By this method, whenever a stray animal is found, by referring to the brand book the owner can be informed of the whereabouts of his animal. The law of Montana further provides that whenever an animal is sold the person who sells must vent, or counter-brand, such animal upon the same side as the original brand, which vent, or counter-brand, must be a fac-simile of the original brand, except that it may be reduced one-half in size; the venting of the original brand is prima facie evidence of the sale or transfer of the animal. Those herds live summer and winter without care or shelter. But, as a matter of course, during the winter months, some will wander many miles from their home range. The range, in a general way of speaking, extends, in

"THE HERD QUITTER"—PAINTING BY CHARLES M. RUSSELL.
Courtesy Montana Historical Society, Helena, gift of Col. Wallis Huidekoper

St. Ignatius Mission Indian School.
REV. GEO. De La MOTTE, Superior.

Earmark,

Pioneer Cattle Co.
P. O. Address, Deer Lodge, Montana.
CONRAD KOHRS, Manager.
Foreman, J. B. SPURGEON, Shelby.

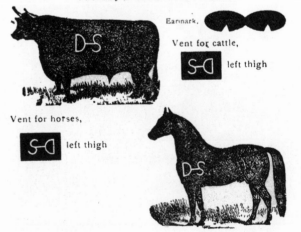

Earmark,

Vent for cattle,

left thigh

Vent for horses,

left thigh

SAMPLES FROM THE BRAND BOOK.

many localities, for one hundred miles or more without a fence or any kind of barrier that will prevent stock from drifting before storms in winter when the streams are frozen over. The home range is a sectional portion that lies between streams that are partly settled by farmers and stockmen. About the latter part of April the spring round-up commences and sweeps the whole country over. This is the time cattle that strayed off during the winter are gathered together and taken back to their home range.

Often, on this round-up sixty to seventy-five horsemen are at work with six to ten horses to the man; the extra horses are herded and driven with the camping outfit which consists of several covered wagons. One would at first think that an army was crossing the country when these "rough riders" turn out in the morning. It is a wonder the many miles they cover in a day; on an average they will ride seventy to eighty

"NO KETCHUM"—PAINTING BY CHARLES M. RUSSELL.
Courtesy Montana Historical Society, Helena, gift of Armand Hammer

"THE ROUNDUP #2"—PAINTING BY CHARLES M. RUSSELL.
Courtesy Montana Historical Society, Helena, Mackay Collection

miles in one day during the round-up. Many of the horses may have been but partly broken the previous winter. To see these excellent horsemen mounting their bronchos, and see the bucking and the capers of those untamed steeds, is a circus in itself. Those young men who are out in the open air exercising as they do are strong and healthy; every inch of them is full of vim and nerve which makes them fearless and daring. The cowboys are not now, generally speaking, of the rough element, but are a highly intelligent class of young men; many of them are from the best families in the country, and, during the school year, are students of some of our foremost colleges and universities. Colonel Roosevelt well knew where to go to get the "rough riders" when he called for cowboys and frontiersmen to fill his regiment.

The spring round-up lasts from three to four weeks; after that the several home range round-ups take place and branding commences. The riders will gather several thousand cattle in one bunch and surrounded by the riders, and this is the round-up proper. The bellowing of the cows and calves is pitiful, for at first they are constantly in commotion and many of them become separated from each other; the noise they make is so awful one can hardly hear his own voice, but it is not long before each cow discovers her calf and then all is well. A fire is built near by and branding irons of all owners of cattle on the range are heated. Then the ropers will ride into the ring, lassoo the young cattle by the hind feet and pull them by the horn of the saddle to where the fire is, and each calf is branded the same brand as the mother. An account of all calves and of each brand, separately, is kept, so that, at the end of the branding season, the owner can tell the number of calves branded. After getting through in one place the camp is moved to another part of the range, and so on, until the work is finished. It is hard work, but fascinating, and many seek to go on the round-up. In the same way the beef cattle are gathered in the fall and shipped east. The round-up, like the buffalo, will soon be a thing of the past and the Western plains will be dotted with homes occupied by actual settlers.

ROBERT VAUGHN.

JULY 7, 1898.

Traveling "Then" And Traveling "Now."

Some one said that to many persons, especially those in the East, the country west of Chicago is still a hazy geographical proposition, and that the Twin Cities, St. Paul and Minneapolis—those posts at the gateway of an empire—seem to be on the confines of civilization, and to those less informed, the words Minnesota, Washington, Oregon and Montana, which represent new and powerful states, may mean some new patent medicine or the names of noted race horses. In fact it does seem but yesterday that west of the Mississippi was but a dimly-known region when all traveling was done by stage and on horseback; even the first locomotive that entered the state of Minnesota is now in the possession of the Great Northern Railway Company. But "now" there are within the limits of the states of Minnesota, North Dakota, South Dakota, Montana, Idaho, Oregon and Washington over 17,000 miles of railway.

As I now write the name "Great Northern" I cannot but think of the powerful agency this transcontinental road has been to bring about the "then and now" in the Rocky mountain regions, and, for that matter, from the Great Lakes to Puget Sound, its eastern terminus being Duluth, on Lake Superior, and St. Paul and Minneapolis, on the Mississippi river, and extending westward to Everett, on the Pacific coast, a distance of 1,782 miles. It crosses the main range of Rocky mountains without a tunnel at an elevation of 5,202 feet above sea level, with a grade on the easterly slope of 1 per cent and on the westerly slope of 8 per cent. A few miles west of the main divide and but three miles from the Great Northern track, lies the famous Lake McDonald, almost concealed by remarkably high and steep mountains and thick forests. It is difficult to one that loves nature's beauty and the wild sublimity of the mountains as I do, to pass such a vast region as this without making a passing note of it. Lake McDonald is a picture of marvelous beauty, a superb stretch of water eighteen miles long. Professor John H. Edwards, in the New York Observer, describes this beautiful lake and the regions surrounding it, as follows. He says:

"In the very heart of the Rockies in the Northern part of Montana, surrounded by mountain peaks in bewildering varieties of form, lies beautiful Lake McDonald. Not quite so large as Yellowstone Lake, it surpasses that loftiest of American mountain lakes of approximate size in grandeur of scenery. Nineteen peaks shoot skyward along its emerald shores or within easy eyeshot. Snow and glacier ice rest upon some of their summits and shoulders throughout the year. The editor of Forest and Stream says of it: 'There is every scenic beauty here of an Alpine lake, with a far greater choice of game and fish.' If Dr. Van Dyke, of New York, would cast his taking fly in these near-by waters, and then cast his irresistible literary book amid the endless beauties of nature in this favored region, his double catch would furnish forth a two-fold feast of choicest quality.

"It would be a hopeless task for any less gifted pen to attempt a description of the noble scenery hid away in this mountain wilderness. The profound blue of the stainless sky, the manifold green of the dense forests that environ the lake and march up the steep flank of the mountain to the vertical height of half a mile above its perfect mirror, that reflects every fine needle and also photographs on its steely plate another half mile of rock and snow towering above the forest line, and then are the rich sunset hues thrown upon peak and glacier—all these seen twice in reality and by reflection. The rare coloring lavished on heights and depths is worth a long journey to see.

"Fish and game abound for experts with rod and gun who

will follow them to their haunts. The cold water of streams that are born of melting snow and ice of the upper ranges produce trout of solid sweetness and finest grain. Twelve miles of bridle path take on to Avalanche basin, a deep recess shut in between a horseshoe sweep of granite cliffs that rise 2,500 feet above the torquoise lakelet in its center, while all around the mountains lift their proud heads to the height of two miles, more or less, above sea level. Half a score of white streamlets leap over the edge of the curving precipice and drop a clear 1,000 feet upon the shelving detritus below, over which they slide and jump in broken lines of foam down into the deep, green waters of the lake. One is reminded of Jean Paul's imagery of a mirror upheld by snowy ribbons, when he was writing of a German lakelet among the hills.

"These lakes and rivulets are all fed by the melting glacier above. This neighborhood furnishes the best opportunity to study living and dying glaciers to be found within our national boundaries, Alaska excepted. John Muir, the king of western naturalists, whose name is born by the finest of Alaska glaciers, has written in ardent appreciation of the region we are describing. Thirty-three hundred feet above Lake McDonald, 6,500 above sea level, is Glacier camp, seven miles from Hotel Glacier, at the head of the lake. From this fine camping place an hour's climb leads to Sperry glacier, named after the indefatigable explorer and popular lecturer, Professor Lyman B. Sperry, of Oberlin. He has spent eight summer vacations here and knows the places round about better, probably, than any other person. The serrated edge of this interesting ice formation measures in width over two miles, and from its upper edge to the end of the longest finger is a stretch of five miles of blue ice. At one time this ice sheet extended a mile further down and plunged over the abrupt precipice that walls the Avalanche basin. Its deserted track furnishes to-day an open page whereon the process of glacial erosion and deposit may be studied even more plainly and instructively than in the days of its greatest extent. Nearly every glacial phenomenon described in the books, it is said, may be found illustrated in this unique body of ice."

The Lewis and Clarke expedition crossed the Rocky mountains ninety-four years ago, and only a few miles further south from where the Great Northern now crosses. Those glaciers, and beautiful Lake McDonald, were not known then, and, for that matter, for over sixty years afterwards. For all that, those phenomena of nature may have been there for thousands of years. One thing is certain, they are there now.

It may not be out of place to give a brief history of the "then and now" of the Great Northern railway, for it is and has been one of the great factors in developing the mines, valleys and plains of the Northwest.

In 1857 a grant of land was made by congress to aid the Territory of Minnesota in the construction of a line of railway to extend from Stillwater via St. Paul and St. Anthony, to what is now Breckenridge, on the Red river, and a branch via St. Paul to St. Vincent, near the international boundary line. At that time the Territory of Minnesota included all of the two Dakotas to the Missouri river. The legislature of the territory accepted the grant which amounted to six sections of land per mile. In the following year Minnesota was admitted as a state and a constitutional amendment was adopted allowing the state to issue bonds to carry along the work. Contracts were let and considerable grading was done at different times, but the financial crash which preceded, and the war, delayed the progress and it was not until 1862 that any track was laid, and that was only ten miles; it was from St. Paul to St. Anthony, and was all trackage of the first division of what is "now" the Great Northern railway; also the first railway ever built in the state of Minnesota. All the material and rolling stock was brought by steamboat on the Mississippi. Minnesota was at the time but a sparsely settled and remote section of the Union.

I shall not attempt to detail the gradual upbuilding of this great transcontinental railway to its present system—its growth from a "then" ten-mile railroad to its "now" grand proportions of 4,786 miles. Its existence as a strong commercial force in the Northwest dates from 1879, when it passed into the control of the St. Paul, Minneapolis & Manitoba Railway Company, organized by J. J. Hill.

In 1880 the trackage of this company was a little in excess of 600 miles, with gross earnings under $2,000,000, while according to its last annual report, its gross earnings amounted to $25,017,903.66. The building of new track, from the time Mr. Hill acquired control in 1876, to 1894, averaged about a mile every working day for the entire period, and the average in gross earnings amounts to an increase of over $1,000,000 a year. Since 1894 extensions have been confined to branch lines and improvements to the betterment of the entire system. Aside from the original grant to the company within the state of Minnesota, the Great Northern system has extended itself into eight states and to British Columbia.

Thirty-five years ago the only method of traveling to and from the Pacific coast was on horseback or in a wagon, with many obstacles on the way—crossing streams, climbing high mountains and cutting the way through thick forests. Now railway cars, drawn by the iron horse, which climbs mountains and leaps over rivers and ravines with an untiring speed, go all the way to the Pacific ocean; and during all the journey the traveler enjoys the comforts, almost, of his own fireside. The solitude that was then

"In pathless woods where rolls the Oregon,
And hears no sound save its own dashing,"

is now broken by the sound of the woodchopper's ax, the reaper, the steam whistle, and the rattle of thousands of wheels. The railway is there now and has made a path of its own in which towns and cities of many thousands of inhabitants have sprung up, where a few years ago was a wilderness. And the valleys and plains of the arid region that were once covered with the brown native grasses, are now interspersed with fields of grain and meadows that are green, and evidence of the white man's civilization.

Before the railway it was a journey of as many months as it is now days to reach the Pacific coast. The following bit of history of the northwest corner of our country, and of that historical horseback ride of Marcus Whitman in 1842 from Oregon to Washington, D.C., and which was worth three stars to our flag, is from the Omaha World-Herald of August 4, 1899, and is as follows:

"The ride of Marcus Whitman was over snow-capped mountains and along dark ravines, traveled only by savage men. It was a plunge through icy rivers and across trackless prairies, a ride of four thousand miles across a continent in the dead of winter to save a mighty territory to the Union.

"Compared with this, what was the feat of Paul Revere, who rode eighteen miles on a calm night in April to arouse a handful of sleeping patriots and thereby save the powder at Concord.

"Whitman's ride saved three stars to the American flag. It was made in 1842.

"In 1792, during the first administration of Washington, Captain Robert Gray, who had already carried the American flag around the globe, discovered the mouth of the Columbia river. He sailed several miles up the great stream and landed and took possession in the name of the United States.

"In 1805, under Jefferson's administration, this vast territory was explored by Lewis and Clarke, whose reports were popular reading for our grandfathers, but the extent and value of this distant possession were very slightly understood, and no attempt at colonization was made save the establishment of the fur-trading station of Astoria in 1811.

"Strangely enough, England, too, claimed this same territory by virtue of rights ceded to it by Russia and also by the Vancouver surveys of 1792. The Hudson's Bay Company established a number of trading posts and filled the country with adventurous fur traders. So here was a vast territory, as large as New England and the state of Illinois combined, which seemed to be without any positive ownership. But for Marcus Whitman, it would have been lost to the Union.

"It was in 1836 that Dr. Whitman and a man by the name of Spaulding, with their young wives, the first white women that ever crossed the Rocky mountains, entered the valley of the Columbia and founded a mission of the American board. They had been sent out to christianize the Indians, but Whitman was also to build a state.

"He was at this time thirty-five years old. In his journey to and fro for the mission he soon saw the vast possibilities of the country, and he saw, too, that the English were already appraised of this and were rapidly pouring into the territory. Under the terms of the treaties of 1818 and 1828, it was the tacit belief that whichever nationality settled and organized the territory, that nation would hold it. If England and the English fur traders had been successful in their plans the three great states of Washington, Oregon and Idaho would now constitute a part of British Columbia. But it was not destined to be.

"In the fall of 1842 it looked as if there would be a great inpouring of English into the territory, and Dr. Whitman took the alarm. There was no time to lose. The authorities at Washington must be warned. Hastily bidding his wife adieu, Dr. Whitman started on his hazardous journey. The perils, hardships and delays he encountered on the way we can but faintly conceive. His feet were frozen, he nearly starved, and once he came very near losing his life. He kept pushing on, and at the end of five terrible months he reached Washington.

"He arrived there tired and worn; a bearded, strangely picturesque figure, clad entirely in buckskin and fur, a typical man of the prairies. He asked audience of President Tyler and Secretary of State Webster and it was accorded him. All clad as he was, with his frozen limbs, just in from his 4,000-mile ride, Whitman appeared before the two great men to plead for Oregon.

"His statement was a revelation to the administration. Previous to Whitman's visit, it was the general idea in congress that Oregon was a barren, worthless country, fit only for wild beasts and wild men. He opened the eyes of the government to the limitless wealth and splendid resources of that western territory. He told them of its great rivers and fertile valleys, its mountains covered with forests, and its mines filled with precious treasures. He showed them that it was a country worth keeping and that it must not fall into the hands of the British. He spoke as a man inspired and his words were heeded.

"What followed—the organization of companies of emigrants, the rapid settlement of the territory and the treaty made with Great Britain in 1846, by which the forty-ninth parallel was made the boundary line west of the Rocky mountains, are matters of history.

"The foresight and the heroism of one man and his gallant ride had saved three great stars to the Union."

Compare those perils and horseback rides of Whitman "then" to what Vice President Stevenson says of his ride from the Pacific coast to Washington, D.C., "now."

He said: "The passenger service on the Great Northern railway is equal to the best in the land, not to speak of the buffet car, which, in itself, is one of the greatest conveniences to

GREAT NORTHERN RAILROAD (MONTANA CENTRAL RY.)
Courtesy Montana Historical Society, Helena

tourist in making long journeys I ever enjoyed. So elaborate and complete are the accommodations that a man hardly realizes that he is traveling. It is a comfortable thing to find a library of books and tables spread with magazines, daily papers and writing materials, easy chairs and bath rooms, a barber shop and smoking room. It really seems as though a man had left his home and gone to his club, to step aboard this car."

Think of the perils, hardships and delays the traveler encountered "then" and the comforts and accommodations he is having "now." "Then" for protection against hostile Indians he had to equip himself with gun and ammunition, "now" for comfort and pleasure he equips himself with Havana cigars, daily newspapers and magazines. And he sings:

> Riding o'er the mountains in a buffet car,
> Writing loving letters, not a shake or jar;
> Leaping over rivers, flying down the vale;
> "O bless me, ain't it pleasant riding on a rail."

I know of no other section in the United States where there have been greater changes made since "then" and "now" in the way of traveling and otherwise, and in the same length of time, than in Northern Montana. A few years ago this part of the Union was but a region in the wilderness. Then the only mode of traveling or transporting goods was with vehicles drawn by horses or mules, and, not infrequently, by the slow and tedious ox or on the backs of animals. Now there are in Northern Montana over seven hundred miles of railroads in operation. The Great Falls and Canada extends from the north and south, a distance of over one hundred and fifty miles. The Great Northern system has its Montana Central, with its Sand Coulee and Neihart branches, besides the two lines that lead to both sides of the falls of the Missouri; and the Great Northern itself extends for over three hundred and fifty miles through the center of this northern Eden.

Some one may ask why I should name this remarkable section Eden. Well, I will answer by asking a few questions myself. Why was it that tens of thousands of buffaloes used to roam here from time immemorial until they were killed off by white people? And why was it that from fifteen to twenty thousand Indians lived here "then," and without doing a lick of work or receiving a single ration from the government? And why is it that there are "now" over two hundred thousand cattle roaming on the same land and feeding on the same kind of grasses as the buffalo did then and without care or shelter, except that provided by nature?

ROBERT VAUGHN.

GREAT FALLS, MONT., NOV. 2, 1899.

Yellowstone National Park.

It would be hardly proper for me to lay down my pen and make no mention of the Yellowstone National Park, which is in the heart of the "Rockies." Besides, in my letter headed "Stampede to the Yellowstone," I stated that "Wonderland was not known then." That indicated that there was such a region in existence somewhere. Therefore it is necessary, at this time, to give a brief sketch of this wonderful place. The time of its first exploration was in 1869–70. It lays mostly in the northwest corner of Wyoming, extending a few miles into Montana on its north and Idaho on its west. It extends from a few miles east of 110 degrees to a few miles west of 111 degrees west longitude from Greenwich. Here the United States government, by an act which passed both houses of congress unanimously, and was approved March 1, 1872, has withdrawn from sale and occupation and set apart as a National Park or perpetual pleasure ground, for the use and enjoyment of the people, a region fifty-four by sixty-two miles and covering an area of 3,312 square miles or 2,119,680 acres. Its average elevation above the sea is from 7,000 to 7,500 feet, while its highest peak rises to the height of 11,155 feet.

A tourist wrote that in this remarkable region nature has assembled such a surprising number of the most sublime and picturesque objects, and amidst the grandest scenery of mountains, lakes, river, cataracts, canyons, and cascades exhibits such a variety of unique and marvelous phenomena of spouting geysers, of boiling and pulsating hot springs and pools of steam jets, solfataras, femerells and salses, rumbling and thundering and pouring out sulphurous hot water, or puffing out clouds of steam and throwing out great masses of mud that its early explorers gave it the name of "Wonderland."

The first public conveyance to enter the Yellowstone National Park was a stage coach, owned by J. W. Marshall, which made its first trip, leaving Virginia City, Montana, at daylight, Oct. 1, 1880, following the beautiful Madison valley for over thirty miles, crossing the Rockies and thence going by Henry Lake, which is a sheet of water two miles wide and five miles long. One of the passengers described the lake as being then "full of salmon trout." Ten miles farther, and in a northwesterly direction, was Cliff Lake, another remarkable sheet of water having a total length of three miles and a breadth of half a mile, in whose azure depths 1,400 feet of line failed to reach bottom. It took sixteen hours to make the trip, a distance of ninety-five miles, from Virginia City to the National Park House, Lower Geyser basin, then the only hotel in the park. This pioneer hotel was a two-story, hewed log structure, the property of Mr. Marshall.

And now the Monida & Yellowstone Stage Company, in connection with the Oregon Short Line railroad and the transcontinental lines, conducts a line of concord coaches from Monida to all points in the Yellowstone National Park. Monida is a station on the Oregon Short Line railroad, and the starting point for the stage ride, and is less than one day coaching distance from the Yellowstone Park. It is on the crest of the Rocky mountains, 7,000 feet above the tide. The lower Geyser basin in the park is about the same elevation.

The name "Monida" is a composite of the first syllables of "Montana" and "Idaho."

The Rev. T. De Witt Talmage writes: "A stage ride from this place to the park 'is a day of scenery as captivating and sublime as the Yellowstone Park itself.'

"The road threads the foothills of the Rocky mountains, skirting beautiful Centennial valley, the Red Rock Lakes, and after passing through Alaska basin, crosses the divide to Henry Lake in Idaho, whence it recrosses the range into Montana via

MAMMOTH HOT SPRINGS HOTEL, YELLOWSTONE NATIONAL PARK.
Courtesy Montana Historical Society, Helena

Targhe Pass near the western entrance to the park. Red Rock Lakes are one of the sources of the Missouri river, and in Henry Lake originates one of the branches of the Snake. From Henry Lake are distinctly visible the famous Teton peaks. Near the western entrance to the park, prettily situated on the south fork of the Madison river, is Grayling Inn (Dwelles), the night station for tourists going in and out of the park. After passing Grayling Inn the road enters the reservation, winding through Christmas Tree Park to Riverside Military Station, following the beautiful Madison river and canyon to the Fountain Hotel in Lower Geyser basin."

I will not attempt to write a description of this wonderful region myself, but will give the picturesque sketch of it written by my friend, Olin D. Wheeler, for the Northern Pacific railway's Wonderland series of books. After reading the account of this trip given by Mr. Wheeler, the reader will find that there is a great contrast in the way of getting into the National Park now in comparison to what it was in 1880, and that vast change has taken place since General Sherman made his trip through the "Sioux Country" in 1877.

Speaking of the train he was about to take passage on, and which was standing in the station awaiting the hour of departure, Mr. Wheeler says: "At its head is a huge, ten-wheeled Baldwin locomotive. On each side of this machine there are three driving wheels sixty-two inches in diameter. As it stands, its length from peak to pilot, or in common parlance, cowcatcher to end of tender, is about fifty-five feet. From the rails to top of smokestack it stands fourteen feet five inches. With its tender loaded with coal and water it weighs nearly ninety-four tons. Behind this noble combination of iron, brass and steel extends a long train. First comes the mail car, in which Uncle Sam's messengers run a traveling postoffice. Then follows the express car, carefully guarded by ever vigilant expressmen. The third car is the principality of the baggage man. Then follow the various classes of passenger coaches—the free colonists' sleeping car, where man or woman may find a fair bed at night and a comfortable seat by day. The smoking car, and the first-class coaches with their high-backed, easy, reclining seats, are succeeded by the Pullman tourist car. Behind the tourist car is the dining car, which is a feature of this train. Behind the dining car are the first-class Pullman sleeping cars—from two to four of them. These are of the most approved type, with heavy trucks and wheels of large diameter, insuring smoothness of motion. This entire train is vestibuled and the car wheels are of paper and steel tired.

"But the bell of that monster engine is ringing, the conductor is signaling to start. Jump aboard and we will continue our dissertation as we glide swiftly along."

The Northern Pacific through trains from St. Paul to Portland, Oregon, a distance of 2,050 miles, are of the same description, only on a larger scale. The average time these trains make is twenty-seven miles an hour, schedule speed, including all regular stops.

After describing his journey through Dakota and up the great valley of the Yellowstone for 341 miles in Eastern Montana until arriving at Livingstone, where the National Park branch of the Northern Pacific began and on which the tourist train continued to the country of wonders, fifty-one miles away, Mr. Wheeler was still in his observation seat taking notes of the grand scenery that the swiftly moving train brought to view. Again he said:

"The entrance to the heart of Wonderland is through an enormous gateway. The gateway, or opening, was made by a river, through a mountain wall, and it is known as The Gate of the Mountains.

"Through this gateway pours the river, fresh from the

eternal snows far back in the mountains; from the great lake, a vast reservoir into which the melting snow banks drizzle in a million streamlets; from the wondrous canyon between whose divinely sculptured and colored walls it throws itself in an ecstasy of fury. Beside the stream lies a railway, which, following it in its sinuosities, leads the pilgrim to the very border of Wonderland. As the river flows out of the mountain gate into the broad, unpent valley, it seems to sing, in the words of Colonel Norris, whose name is indissolubly connected with Wonderland, of the region it is leaving far behind.

> 'I sing in songs of gliding lays
> Of forests scenes in border days;
> Of mountain peaks begirt with snow,
> And flowery parks, pine girt below;
> Of goblins grim and canyons grand,
> And geysers spouting o'er the strand
> Of Mystic Lake, of Wonderland.'

"After having passed through the gate of the mountains one is in Paradise valley, for such is the name of the beautiful valley which stretches up to the portals of Wonderland. The farther one invades these precincts, the more one comes to feel that the valley is rightly named. The great mountains, the very temples of the gods, loom high above. Mighty canyons, rocked ribbed, ragged, gloomy, forest-garbed, deep and fascinating, have been gouged from their very vitals. From out these latter the mountain streams rush, singing songs of deliverance as they dance down the long, sweeping slopes to the mightier river. In their courses the streams have been harnessed by man, and their fructifying influences are seen in the broad fields of waving grain and alfalfa that checker the slopes.

"Mountains, fields, streams, trees, slopes, form truly

enough such a picture that the thought of paradise is borne in upon me.

"The scene changes! The mountains crowd together, the valley contracts, the rocky sides of the former rise high above, the river is throttled by craggy canyons and rushes madly along far below us—we are in a wild eyrie where the echoes of the iron horse's brazen throat reverberate among the crags and cliffs. Sweeping through this scene of wildness we reach the threshold of the Wonderland of Wonderlands, nature's greatest wonderland—

Yellowstone National Park.

"The scene here hinted at is that beheld by the tourist as he rides from Livingstone, on the main line of the Northern Pacific, up the valley of the Yellowstone to Cinnabar, the terminus of the National Park branch line at the northern edge or boundary of the great park.

"The valley is indeed one to arouse enthusiasm. At two places it becomes constricted, forming small but ragged canyons that but pave the way for the grander visions which, in the days to follow, are to break upon the eye.

"Well up the valley Emigrant Peak, a noble, snow-capped mountain of august mien, stands sentinel, thrusting his crown above brawny shoulders to a height of 10,629 feet.

"Just before reaching Cinnabar, Cinnabar Mountain, famous for its Devil's Slide, is rounded. Soon there comes into view the giant peak of the region, Electric Peak, which, with its 11,155 feet of altitude, may well be termed the guardian peak of the park. Facing it, but of lower altitude, stands Sepulcher Mountain, a rough, imposing mountain, the origin of its name involved in obscurity.

"On the opposite side of the valley rise the sister peaks of the Emigrant and its companion, the Absaraka, the range

GIANT GEYSER, YELLOWSTONE NATIONAL PARK.
Courtesy Montana Historical Society, Helena

swinging to the eastward and forming the eastern boundary and mountain wall of the park. High up on the flanks of the range in and about the town of Crevasse, men are toiling with more or less of success for the gold that everybody covets.

"But our train has stopped at the platform at Cinnabar. We step from the cars, ready with our hand bags for the next move on the program.

First Day's Ride.

"Soon there come prancing round the corner six splendid horses, drawing behind them a huge Wonderland stage coach. Another appears, and, if necessary, still others come swinging up to the platform to transport the waiting throng on to Wonderland. How the people scramble aboard! Some climb up the sides of the coaches to the broad, open seats on the roof, where they will obtain, as they ride along, unobstructed views of the landscape. Other, less agile or venturesome, clamber into the interior of the coaches, satisfied with less elevation, less sun, and nearly as much advantage in sightseeing. The bags and valises are strapped on the trunk racks behind the vehicles or thrown into the boots, the conductor calls out, "All set," the driver tightens the reins, speaks to his horses, and the stage is off and away over the hills bound for Mammoth Hot Springs, seven miles distant.

"After a short ride, a collection of low and in some cases mud-roofed houses is seen. Through the heart of the little frontier town, Gardiner, the coaches carry us, when, swinging at right angle, we are soon skirting the Gardiner river, a typical mountain stream with which one falls in love at first sight. For several miles, first on one side then on the other of this torrential, beautiful river, the coach is slowly dragged up an ascending grade. The stream is beset with boulders against which, over which, under which, yea, through which, as one will easily see, the tremendous current dashes in a chorus of

CASTLE GEYSER, YELLOWSTONE NATIONAL PARK.
Courtesy Montana Historical Society, Helena

sound, and a mass of spray. It is a royal trout stream and the heart of the angler leaps within him even as does the trout itself leap within the boiling waters.

"This stream of turmoils and fascination gathers its streamlet threads from widely extended sources. Much of it comes from the northern slopes of some of the mountains about the Grand Canyon, Observation Peak, Storm Peak, etc. Another branch swings around Bunsen Peak, forming an elongated horseshoe, and insinuates its watery tentacles among the slopes of Electric Peak—the south side—Quadrant Mountain, and Antler Peak. A sub-system of this branch stream—the Middle Gardiner, so-called—extends southward from the toe of the horseshoe, past Obsidian Cliff and Beaver Lake to the region about Roaring Mountain, nearly to Norris Geyser Basin.

"The scenery along the Gardiner is striking. The dun-colored clay and conglomerate walls rise in massive buttressed slopes surmounted by palisades, to a height of a few hundred feet on one side and 1,000 and 1,200 feet on the other. The eastern walls are by far the finer. Spires and pinnacles have been eroded from the soft earthen slope and form conspicuous objects. The most striking and noted is Eagle Nest Crag, a solitary, rounded column upon the inaccessible apex of which is perched an eagle's nest. Yearly the parent birds raise broods of young eagles whose protruding heads can frequently be seen and whose plaintive cries are plainly heard.

"Soon after crossing the stream for the last time a sharp ascent is begun. This continues until the hotel plateau is reached at Fort Yellowstone. As the coaches mount the grade the outlet of a river is seen on the western bank of the Gardiner. The rocky ground there is more or less broken and quantities of steam arise. This river flows from the hot springs of the terrace at Mammoth Hot Springs, underground through the hill over which the road winds.

"In olden days this was a favorite camping place. The hot water made bathing agreeable, culinary and laundry work easy, and if one was inclined he could easily catch his trout in the Gardiner and then, swinging his line, plunge the victim into Boiling river and cook his fish, all at one operation—so they say.

"Passing Fort Yellowstone when the plateau is reached, the coaches are whirled swiftly across a geyserie or travertine plaza, upon which the fort or cantonment—and it is one of the best posts in the country—fronts to the hotel, a mammoth structure which commands a fine view to the south.

"At last we are fairly within the great Yellowstone Park—the heart of Wonderland.

"From the time our train started from Livingstone until it again sets us down there, six days will have passed. When we leave the coach at the hotel the first half of the first day has passed into history. The afternoon will be spent in clambering over the parti-colored terraces of Mammoth Hot Springs.

"After the tourist has registered, retired to his or her room, performed the usual ablutions, and shaken off the dust of travel from one's garments, the luncheon is eaten. It is then customary to make all arrangements with the transportation company, as a new order of exercises will be inaugurated upon the morrow.

"When next, we start, the coach, horses and driver, to which we are assigned, became ours for the entire round of the park. It is advisable, therefore, if particular acquaintances or friends desire to ride in company, to explain this to the powers that be, that such an arrangement may be effected. By the time this matter is attended to, the voice of the guide is heard announcing that all is ready for the event of the day—the visit to the formation, as it is termed.

"To the right, from the hotel front, rises Terrace Mountain. At the extremity of the plaza and at the base of the mountain as viewed from here, and a part of the mountain, rise the wonderful terraces. Even at this distance they present a remarkable appearance. As we approach them the singularity of their origin and appearance becomes more and more pronounced; but as we climb the slopes and view the pools of rainbow colored waters, and examine the terrace fronts with their infinite patterns of etchings and bead work, we stand in open-eyed amazement at what seems a miracle of creation.

"Whether we stand in front of the terrace walls and examine the exquisite chased work, built up by minute secretions from the hot waters as they trickle slowly down; whether we stand on the heights above and gaze upon acres of water divided and subdivided into many shaped basins, and so brilliantly colored as to seem impossibly colored; or whether, as we climb higher, and are transfixed almost, at the beautiful, delicate, fragile and algaic forms seen—it is all the same, we now begin to understand what the word Wonderland means, and are prepared for whatever we may stumble upon, and ready to admit that the half has not been told and cannot be—seeing only, if not believing, is certainly understanding.

"The water found in these pools varies in temperature, but it is all hot. Some of the pools are very small, others almost lakelets.

"Such brilliancy of coloring was never excelled, and the variety of color, sometimes even in the same pool, is simply astounding. What one sees here is found upon successive terraces on the mountain side, and is reached by easy gradation by using foot paths or trails. After a time we are somewhat bewildered as to where we are, whether in the infernal regions; with the ancient deities; in a zoological garden; among Egyptian queens and mummies; where angels tread, orange trees bloom, or where railways are being built, or cupids shoot arrows.

"The Upper Geyser Basin is the goal of the tourist, so far as the geysers are concerned. There are here about a dozen geysers that expel the contents of their reservoirs to heights ranging from one hundred to two hundred and fifty feet. There are as many more that play to elevations less than one hundred feet. This family of geysers is like a large family of children; a strong family resemblance runs through all of them, but individually no two are much alike.

"The Castle has a very large, castellated, siliceous cone; the Grand has none whatever, nor is there any resemblance in their eruptions. The Oblong and the Giantess each expel their contents from deep, pit-like reservoirs, but there the resemblance between them ends. The Bee Hive and Old Faithful each have cones, as entirely unlike as are their splendid columns of water and vapor. Some throw the water as straight in the air as a tree stands; others hurl it out at various angles, or even in arches. Some send it forth in a solid, steady, majestic column; others in an irregular, churn-like fashion.

"But there are other things than the geysers here. Emerald Pool, Sunset Lake, and Black Sand Pool are, with one possible exception, the most delicate, beautifully colored bowls of water to be found in the park. The word color acquires a new significance as one stands at the verge of these truly heavenly pools, shut in among mountains.

"The particular attraction at the Fountain Hotel has been the Fountain Geyser near the hotel. This geyser has a basin some thirty feet in diameter, connected with another of about the same size just north of it. Much of the time these basins are full of water, thus, apparently, forming a large double crater.

"In 1899 a new geyser, called the New Fountain, broke out in the north basin, resulting in a decided curtailment of the old Fountain Geyser's eruptions. The new geyser is not yet old enough so that its periodicity and peculiarities are fully known.

Its eruptions, however, are more stupendous and much beyond those of any other geyser which the writer has seen. Excelsior Geyser at Midway Basin, the greatest geyser—when it plays—in the world, is closely approached by this new giant, in both the magnitude and the grandeur of the display.

"The geyser is rather spurty in character, and when in full operation plays from three orifices. In its general action it is not unlike the Fountain or the Great Fountain. It will boil furiously and throw the water quite regularly to a height of ten to fifteen feet. Then, becoming semi-quiescent for a few moments, it will again break loose, a solid body of water of immense bulk, to a height of fifteen to thirty feet. Then changing again it will send upward an enormous volume of water to a height of 100, 150, or even, in exceptional spurts, 200 feet.

"After a period of momentary quiescence, the geyser will often break out with a violent explosion, when the scalding flood, transformed into millions of white, beautiful beads of crystal and spray, is sent in all directions, to all heights, at all angles, from the three apertures. The water is all torn to pieces and is thrown out and comes down in a perfect avalanche. The geyser then is a very leviathan at play. It throws out pieces of geyser formation, bits of trees, and geyser eggs, as they are called, small, white, rounded stones.

When the eruption ends it comes abruptly, at once, not as the Great Fountain's, with a series of dying, tremendous throbs as if its great heart were broken. The eruption ceases, the great body of water drops rapidly down into the central cistern and runs into it from the geyser knoll in pretty little cascades, until the surplus is thus carried away and the water level outside of the basin is lowered. Then it is all over.

"Regarding the Canyon let me again quote from Dr. Hill:

"And now I want to say a word in regard to the Grand Canyon. You stand on Inspiration Point and look down 100, 300,

1,000 feet, and there, away below, is a green ribbon, worked in and out as if to hold together the lower edges of the canyon's walls. It is the Yellowstone river. You look off toward the south and see, in a sort of recess, a little column of white. It is the Great Falls of the Yellowstone, 308 feet high. You examine the slanting walls of this tremendous canyon and you see such a display of color as the eye of man never looked upon. Someone has said that it looks like a blown-up paint shop. Just there to the right some huge pots of white and yellow and red paint have been tipped over, and it has flowed right down in parallel streaks to the water's edge. Farther along is a gigantic tower carved out of a solid crimson rock. Here to the left all along are turrets and castles and cathedrals, there a Parthenon, over there St. Mark's glittering in gold, there Taj Mahal, as white as spotless alabaster. Colors green and brown and saffron and orange and pink and vermillion and russet cover every rock until the scene is bewildering. What shall one say as he looks upon such a scene? Nature teaches us about God. Then the Grand Canyon has been cut and painted by the divine hand as if to give some idea of John's vision of heaven. Walls of jasper, streets of gold, gates of pearl, foundation stones of emerald and sapphire, and topaz and amethyst. Yes, they are all there. Who can look upon such a scene and say there is no God and no heaven?

"If the enthusiast wishes to get a sight of the canyon much different from any other, and in the opinion of many the finest obtainable, he should go beyond Inspiration Point. The Lower Mount Washburn trail leaves the road near Inspiration Point. There is an enormous boulder right at the intersection, of which more anon. Follow this trail for a mile perhaps, and a projection will be noticed leading well out into the canyon. From this crag the walls are emblazoned with every color or combination of colors that are probably to be found anywhere in the canyon. It is perhaps less brilliant than the magnificent array found at Grand View. In each case it is a canyon view pure and simple. The Lower Falls, so conspicuous a factor of the landscape from both Lookout and Inspiration Points, do not appear in either of these.

"I have mentioned a boulder at the junction of the main road and the Washburn trail. This boulder is worthy of inspection by tourists. It is of granite, eighteen feet high and twenty-four feet long by twenty-feet in breadth, dark in color. It was transported from its native heath by a glacier and deposited where it now lies when the glacier receded. Mr. Arnold Hague of the United States Geological Survey states that the nearest point from whence it could have been torn is at least thirty or forty miles distant.

"To thoroughly appreciate, yes, I will say to fall in love with the canyon, one must needs see it under different conditions. See it when the sun is flooding it with noon-day radiance; when the winds sweep the masses of vapor through it, deluging its walls with moisture; when the sun is vanished from earth and evening's shadows slowly creep from crag to crag and base to summit. To look upon the canyon when in the full glare of the sun, one would never realize what a softness and mellowness comes over it when the clouds hide the golden orb.

"I had seen the walls under varying lights and shades, but upon one occasion I saw it in a new dress. It had snowed somewhat during the night. When I reached the road at the canyon brink, everything seemed transformed. The trees were cottonwood over the snow, the road was a white avenue, rocks were whitened. But the canyon itself—what a change had come over it! The sun, of course, was invisible. The heavy masses of foliage that on either side crown the precipice with a ribbon of green were powdered with snow. The crevices and moderate angles of the walls wore a soft mantle of purest white. The other parts of the canyon were gently sprinkled with the fleecy material. The leaden clouds hung in parallel ridges above the gorge. Nature was in exquisite attire, and how softened! I wouldn't have missed it for a good deal."

After returning to the Mammoth Hotel with his soul filled with the wonders of nature, Mr. Wheeler said:

"As we leave behind these scenes, now almost sacred, we muse and then regret—regret that we had not arranged to spend at least another week here, and see more of what we have seen, and search out much that we have not seen.

"There are so many side trips that can be made, so much to study, such comfort and health in this elevated region, that now, when it is too late, we see where we made a mistake in not planning for a two-weeks' trip. Well, there is this silver lining to our cloud: We can take the trip over again and spend a month if necessary.

"And that is just what we determine to do some other year. So we reach Mammoth Hot Springs in a happier frame of mind, eat our last dinner in the park, mount the outgoing coach, and end our sixth and last day of our park tour by stepping into the Pullman car at Cinnabar and being whirled homeward at forty miles an hour."

"In 1885 Mr. Charles T. Whitmell of Cardiff, Wales, in a paper read before the Cardiff Naturalist Society regarding the Yellowstone National Park, said: 'Were there but a living glacier and an active volcano the cup of wonders would be full.' The volcano is yet to be found, but the glacier is here, was there when Mr. Whitmell made his address, but the existence of perpetual ice was not known then."

"About eleven miles southeast of the Hoodoo Basin, between Stinkingwater Peak (11,600 feet high) and Sunlight Peak (11,977 feet above sea level), the United States Geological

Survey found a large glacier, or, indeed, a series of them. They gave to it the name of Sunlight Glacier. It is more than a mile across. The surface is crevassed with walls of clear green ice, and it has a typical terminal moraine. It is deep within the mountains, and in the summer of 1895 Col. W. S. Brackett of Peoria, Ill., and others saw it from a distance. Residents of Montana have also seen it. While it lies just outside the limits of the park proper, it is, notwithstanding, part and parcel of the wonders of the Park region. It is difficult of approach, owing to the rough character of the country.

"There are glaciers in the Bear Tooth Range, south of Red Lodge, east of the Park, and several on the Three Tetons, just south of it."

Verily, the variety of wonders in "Wonderland" are many, and still they come. Many people have heard of Death Gulch, in a portion of Yellowstone National Park, where beasts soon die. This summer (1899) a party of Montana Scientists visited Death Gulch. "Truth is stranger than fiction, and Dame Nature herself has surprises that are past all perfect explanation." The following is from the Helena Independent Sept. 16, 1899:

"Many persons have heard of the wonderful gulch in the northeastern part of the Yellowstone National Park named Death Gulch, but while accepting many other stories of Wonderland, have only passed this particular story by as a fabrication. The story is that all things living that enter this gulch never come out again. That was the story as it was once told, but a year or two ago a member of the United States Geological Survey wrote a scientific article about the canyon in which it was explained that only under certain conditions was animal life taken in the mysterious gulch. Even after that article appeared many who heard of the gulch and its strange secret called it all a fairy tale.

"A semi-scientific expedition of well known Montanians

has just returned from a visit to Death Gulch and the Granite range. The party was composed of Rev. James Reid, President of the Agricultural College, Bozeman; Dr. Frank Traphagen, who has the chair of natural sciences at the college and who is a chemist of wide reputation; Peter Koch, cashier of the Bozeman National Bank and treasurer of the college, and his son, and Ed. C. Alderson of Bozeman, one of the best known mountaineers and guides in the state. Rev. Mr. Reid, who came over from Bozeman last week, said that the party had visited Death Gulch and that Dr. Traphagen, the scientist of the party, had made some interesting investigations. The trip was begun more than a month ago, and although the weather was not at all times propitious, it was on the whole an enjoyable outing.

"Death Gulch, said President Reid, is in the National Park, on Cache creek, about three miles from the point where it empties into the east fork of Yellowstone river, and twenty miles from Cooke City. Its sides are steep and high, but wild animals have no difficulty in creeping down to the bottom where there is a little stream. In the gulch, and within the space of a quarter of a mile, we saw the carcasses and bones of eight bears, one or two coyotes and an elk. All had met death in a strange, but, in the light of science, not mysterious way. They had been asphyxiated, nothing more nor less. Rising out of the bottom of the gulch is a gas resembling, and which practically is, sulphuretted hydrogen. The smell of the gas was strong upon us and could not be mistaken. This gas is poisonous, and I can readily see how, on a still, sultry day or night, the gulch might become filled with the gas and be a menace to every breathing thing that entered there. The day we visited the gulch there was a strong breeze blowing up the canyon, but, in spite of that, the odor of the gas was strong.

"The theory has been that the gas, being heavier than the

air, settles in the bottom of the gulch, and that animals might die of it where a man who was taller than they would feel no bad effects. That theory may be all right, but I noticed that our dogs, who accompanied us, didn't seem to feel any bad effects from the gas; however, as I said, the wind was blowing up the canyon, and I believe that on a sultry, still day the gulch would not even be a safe place for a man.

"The bodies of the animals that met death in the gulch have been well preserved, the gas seeming to have the effect of embalming them to a certain extent. Two of the bears that we saw must have weighed in life in the neighborhood of four hundred pounds each. I suppose some of the bears have been attracted into the gulch by the smell of elk or other animals that have died there, entered in and been overcome themselves.

"Dr. Traphagen took several samples of the gas, intending to make some experiments with them upon arriving at his laboratory. How did he obtain them? That was a simple thing. He filled several bottles with water then emptied them at the bottom of the gulch. The air, impregnated with the gas, rushed into the bottles as the vacuums were formed. The bottles were then securely corked and preserved. Of course the gas obtained in that form was diluted, but it will be sufficiently strong, I believe, to answer Dr. Traphagen's purpose.

"The Bozeman party visited the famous Grasshopper mountain, near Cooke City, the first published description of which appeared in the Independent less than a year ago. On this mountain, buried in solid ice and snow, are two strata of grasshoppers.

"There are many persons, perhaps, said President Reid, who may doubt the story of this wonderful mountain, but, after all, it is not such a strange phenomenon. The grasshoppers are certainly there, and while it is not an easy task to reach this mountain, which is in the heart of the Granite range, any one of a scientific or curious mind can convince himself by going there. The presence of the grasshoppers in the glacier may be explained by the probable fact that two great flights of the insects attempted to pass the mountain at different times, and, becoming exhausted or stiffened by the cold, lit upon its side and were buried in the snow storm.

"The expedition saw many glaciers and little lakes high up in the mountains of the Granite range, which was explored for the first time in 1898 by Dr. Kimball of New York and party under the guidance of Ed Alderson. Many of the lakes visited, said President Reid, are still frozen and most of them are surrounded by vast snow fields. Kersey lake, the largest one of these explored by the party, empties into the Broadwater, a stream larger than Clark's Fork. The lake is about half a mile long, and was the only one visited where there was good fishing.

"The party had intended to make the ascent of Granite Peak, believed to be the highest mountain in the state, but owing to storms it was unable to reach the top. The mountain is about 13,000 feet high, and with Dewey Peak, 11,400 feet, and Snow Bank, 11,750 feet high, were named by Dr. Kimball and party. The East and West Rosebuds rise in the glaciers of the Granite range. The Granite range has been visited by but few white men. There is no big game among its glacier-locked peaks, and even the prospector has not penetrated its fastnesses."

On account of its vastness, the depth of its canyons, its perpendicular cliffs, and its high and rugged mountains, there is no doubt but that there are many wonders in the Yellowstone National Park region yet to be found.

It is not strange that foreign travelers have named it "The Wonderland of the World." Professor Hayden, the chief of a division of the United States Geological Survey, said: "Such a vision is worth a lifetime, and only one of such marvelous beauty will ever greet human eyes." I often think of the time myself and companions, in 1864, were within a few miles of this marvelous place prospecting for gold, and those geysers were there then puffing spitting out brimstone; and the indications show that they have been carrying on this wonderful performances for ages—wild animals and birds of the forest being the only audience to witness the play—not a civilized soul knew of such a place then, and, for that matter, for several years after.

All the natural scenery in the park is carefully guarded and is now as it was when first discovered. But millions of dollars have been expended in a mechanical way to improve the park. The drive that begins at the railway depot is 150 miles in length and is stocked with elegant stage coaches and cabs made especially for the mountain roads. Hundreds of horses are constantly at work during the summer season conveying the thousands of people from all over the world to and fro from one hot spring and geyser to another. There are hotel accommodations for a thousand people. The Mammoth Hot Springs Hotel, which is located at Mammoth Hot Springs, is a very large one. At other points hotels and lunch stations are maintained through the park season. These hotels are heated by steam, lighted by electricity, and supplied with bath rooms and in one case—the Fountain Hotel—with water from one of the hot springs. There is also telegraph communication from this place in the heart of the Rockies with all the civilized world.

And it would not surprise me to hear that Old Faithful and Mount Ætna were whispering to each other through the means of the wireless telephone one of these days. Thus are the wonders of nature and of science—all in one.

The management of the park is under the exclusive supervision of the government. The military has general control of everything. A garrison of two or three troops of cavalry is stationed here, who are distributed in small patrols all through the park during the summer to protect the wild game that is there in abundance, principally elk, deer, buffalo and bears; also to see that no one carries away any of the curiosities in the way of specimens of the various formations, and to see that the forest is not destroyed by fire or otherwise. For the violation of any of the laws that govern the park a severe penalty is imposed. The same military force serves as a police protection to the people as well. While this Wonderland is the property of the general government, it is in fact the pleasure ground of all nations.

ROBERT VAUGHN.

APRIL 2, 1900.

From the Prospector's Hole to the Greatest Mining Camp on Earth.

Go where you may and if the state of Montana is spoken of the name will not be repeated many times before someone will inquire and ask something in reference to her mines; and for me, who claims to be one of her pioneers, to write what I have about Montana and not tell the story of her first gold discoveries and of her great copper mines, would be a breach of trust.

To commence with, I will give the old prospector's theory of how gold came into the streams and gulches of the Rocky mountains. In the first place gold is in quartz, and quartz is in fissures or clefts in the mountains caused by volcanic action, and, evidently those mountains have been at one time under water, for on the higher elevations boulders and gravel can be found. The gulches and channels where gold is found are but some ancient river beds; all goes to show that some powerful water current has been in action at one time in these mountains, whether it was an ocean current or not is a mystery. Quartz is softer than granite, in which formation gold is invariably found, and, having been washed down the mountains and gulches, and coming in contact with harder stones, the quartz is worn off until nothing but the gold is left; and, as the gold is heavier than the gravel, it lodges on the solid bed rock in the beds of those ancient streams. As neither fire nor rust injures gold, every particle remains as perfect as it was when laid there by nature's own hand centuries ago.

In all of the vocations of man, there is nothing that he enters into with more enthusiasm, takes more risks, endures greater self-sacrifices, than gold hunting and prospecting in the Rocky mountains; neither is there anything that has brought him wealth or made him an independent fortune as quickly as gold mining has, therefore, as long as ariseth the mountains

ANACONDA SMELTER - 1903.
Courtesy Montana Historical Society, Helena

above the plains the gold hunter will be there. The first record giving indications of gold discoveries in the northwestern portion of the United States, and in what now embraces the state of Montana, dates back to 1739, when Verendrye, a French explorer, reported to the French government that "these mountains were rich in minerals." But previous to the Lewis and Clarke expedition little was known of this part of the country. Many other stories have been written giving names and the location of where the first gold was found in this state. The truthfulness of those I will not dispute. But there is one that I can vouch for to be reliable, and that is what Granville Stuart has written on this subject. Mr. Stuart is a natural born historian; like a tourist, he kept a journal and set down day by day what was of importance. And Montana is lucky that he and his comrades were her first gold discoverers, at least they were the first to find gold in paying quantities.

Mr. Stuart is a Virginian by birth. In 1852, with his father and brother, he went to California. In 1857 he came to what is now Montana. He has written a book, dedicated Virginia City, Montana, January 1, 1865, in which he says:

"About the year 1852, a French half-breed from Red River of the North named Francois Finlay, but commonly known by the sobriquet of 'Benetsee,' who had been in California, began to prospect on a branch of the Hell Gate, now known as Gold creek. He found small quantities of light-float gold in the surface along the stream, but not in sufficient abundance to pay. This became noised about among the mountaineers; and when Reese Anderson, my brother James and I were delayed by sickness at the head of Malad creek, on Hudspeth's cut-off, as we were on our way from California to the states in the summer of 1857, we saw some men who had passed 'Benetsee's creek,' as it was then called, and they said that they found good prospects there, and as we had an inclination to see a little mountain life, we concluded to go out to that region to winter and look around a little. We accordingly wintered on Big Hole just above the 'Backbone,' in company with Robert Dempsey, Jake Meeks and others; and in the spring of 1858 we went over to Deer Lodge and prospected a little on Benetsee creek, but, not having any 'grub,' or tools to work with, we soon quit in disgust, without having found anything that would pay, or done enough to enable us to form a reliable estimate of the richness of this vicinity, but we found as high as ten cents to the pan on Gold creek and we resolved to get more grub and return. We then went back to the emigrant road, and remained there trading with the emigrants over two years, very frequently talking of the probability of there being good mines in Deer Lodge. In the fall of 1860 we moved out to the mouth of Stinking Water river, intending to winter there, and go over and try our luck prospecting in the spring. But the Indians became insolent and began to kill our cattle, when we moved over, later in the fall, and settled down at the mouth of Gold creek and began to prospect. We succeeded, during the following summer, in finding prospects that we considered very good, upon which we began to make preparations to take it out 'big,' and wrote to our brother Thomas, who was at 'Pike's Peak,' as Colorado was then called, to come out and join us, as we thought this a better country than the 'Peak.' How events have fulfilled this prediction will be seen hereafter. Thomas showed our letters to quite a number of his friends, and they became quite excited over them, and in the spring of 1862 many of them started out to find us, but became lost and went to old Fort Lemhi, on Salmon river, and from there they scattered all over the country, a few of them reaching us about the first of July. We were then mining on Pioneer creek, a small fork of Gold creek, without making more than a living, although some of the adjacent claims paid good wages.

"About this time quite a number of people arrived who had come up the Missouri river intending to go to the mines at Florence and Oro Fino, but not liking the news from that region when they arrived in Deer Lodge, a part of them went no further, but scattered out and began to prospect. The 'Pike's Peakers,' soon after their arrival, struck some good pay on a small branch of Gold creek, now know as Pike's Peak gulch. The diggings of this region did not, as a general thing, pay very well that summer, and they have not been much worked or prospected since from the following cause: Many of the 'Pike's Peakers' became rather lost and bewildered in their attempts to reach Deer Lodge and were scattered all about through the mountains; this though a source of infinite vexation to them at the time, proved of great ultimate benefit to the country, for one small party of them discovered some gulch mines at the head of Big Hole prairie in the spring of 1862, but they seem to have been exhausted, as they have not been worked since that time. I have been told by men who worked there that they worked across a vein of good coal thirty feet wide in the bed of the gulch, and that they put some in the fire and it burned brilliantly.

"Another party happening to camp on Willard's creek in July, 1862, began to prospect and found very rich diggings, where a great many men made fortunes during the summer and winter. This attracted almost every man in the country to the spot, and the mines at Gold creek were deserted for the richer ones at 'Bannock City,' a small town that had sprung up at the head of the canon of Willard's creek. About the time the Bannock mines began to decline a little and people began to think of branching out again, a party of six who had started to the Yellowstone country on a prospecting tour, and had been driven back by the Crow Indians, who robbed them of nearly everything they had, camped, as they were returning, on a small branch of the Stinking Water river, afterwards called Alder creek because of the heavy growth of that wood. They camped on the creek about half a mile above where the City of Virginia now stands, and on washing a few pans of dirt they 'struck it big,' getting as high as four dollars to the pan. They staked off their claims and went to Bannock City to get a supply of provisions, and to tell their friends to return with them and take claims, which they did. The creek proved almost fabulously rich, thousands of men having made fortunes in it."

A letter was written by Lieutenant James H. Bradly concerning the first gold discoveries in Montana. It was dated Fort Shaw, September 21, 1875, and appeared in the Helena Herald. Bradly, at one time, was stationed at Fort Benton, afterwards at Fort Shaw, and was killed in the Gibbon battle with the Nez Perces at Big Hole in 1877. He was an interesting writer and very fond of reading histories. I have heard some of the old timers of Northern Montana speak of this man Silverthorne and his gold, to whom Lieutenant Bradly refers to. It appears that there is some doubt where this gold came from. In this letter Bradly says:

"I read with interest the extract from the Northwest (published at Deer Lodge), contained in your weekly issue of the 16th instant, relative to the 'First Gold Mining in Montana.' Anything Mr. Granville Stuart has to say about the early history of Montana is sure to be interesting and valuable, and it is probably rare, indeed, that his views should require subsequent modification. But in reference to the first gold mining done in Montana, I am in possession of some facts apparently not known to Mr. Stuart, and which may be equally unknown to the great majority of your readers.

"It is probably generally known that the American Fur Company, founded by Mr. Astor and subsequently controlled by Pierre Choteau, Jr., & Co., had a trading post at or near the site of the present town of Fort Benton. Major Alexander Culbertson was for a number of years in charge of that post, and was at the time of which I have to speak—namely, the year 1856. In the month of October a stranger appeared at the fort, coming by the trail from the southwest, now the Benton and Helena stage road; he was evidently an old mountaineer, and his object was to purchase supplies. Producing a sack, he displayed a quantity of yellow dust which he claimed was gold, and for which he demanded $1,000, offering to take it all in goods. Nothing was known at the fort of the existence of gold in the adjoining country, and Major Culbertson was loth to accept the offered dust, having doubts of its genuineness. Beside, even if gold, he was uncertain of its value in this crude state, and he was, therefore, about to decline it, when an employe of the post, a young man named Ray, came to the aid of the mountaineer, by his assurances as to the genuineness of the gold and the value of the quantity offered, induced Major Culbertson to accept it. Still doubtful, however, he made it a private transaction, charging the goods to his own account. The mountaineer was very reticent as to the locality where he obtained the gold, but in answer to numerous questions, he stated that he had been engaged in prospecting for a considerable period in the mountains to the southwest, that his wanderings were made alone, and that he had found plenty of gold. Receiving for his dust a supply of horses, arms, ammunition, blankets, tobacco, provisions and other supplies, he quietly left the fort on his return to the mountains. Major Culbertson never saw or heard of him afterward, and was ignorant, even of his name. The following year, 1857, he sent the gold dust through the hands of Mr. Choteau to the mint, and in due time received as the yield thereof $1,525, the dust having proved to be remarkably pure gold. Thus, as early as 1857, three years before Gold Tom hewed out his rude sluice boxes on gold creek, Montana gold had found its way to the mint, and contributed a small fortune of the shining pieces to the circulating medium of the country. This much I obtained from the lips of Major Culbertson, just enough to pique curiosity; and the mysterious miner who had been the first to work the rich gulches of Montana, made the earliest contribution to the world of its mineral treasure, and whose subsequent fate and very name were unknown, often returned to my thoughts to vex me in my apparent powerlessness to lift any part of the veil of mystery that shrouded him. But one day I mentioned the circumstances to Mr. Mercure, an old and respected resident of Fort Benton, who came to the territory in the interest of the American Fur Company in 1855. To my great satisfaction, he remembered the old mountaineer, the event of his golden visit to the fort having created quite an enduring impression. When Montana's great mining rush began, Mr. Mercure quitted the service of the fur company and sought the mines. There he met the mountaineer again and immediately recognized him. His name was Silverthorne, and his habits were still of the solitary character that had distinguished him in former days. For several years he remained in the territory, occasionally appearing at the trading posts with gold in abundance; but after supplying his necessities by trade, he would again disappear in his lonely rambles. He could not be induced to divulge the secret of his diggings, but always declared that his mine was not a rich one yielding him only four or five dollars a day. Mr. Mercure believes, however, from the quantity of gold always in the possession of Silverthorne, that he greatly understated the value of his discovery."

After writing the foregoing I sent it to Mr. Stuart for correction and in reply he sent me the following:

Robert Vaughn, Esq., Great Falls, Mont.:
Dear Sir—Your manuscript about the early discoveries of

gold in what is now Montana, and your request that I correct any mistakes therein, received. In the interest of true history, I will gladly do so.

What I wrote in 1865, as quoted by you, is an absolutely correct account of the discovery and first working of gold mines in what is now Montana, except that it does not tell of the mining done on Gold creek by Henry Thomas, known as "Gold Tom," and which I contributed to the first volume of the Historical Society of Montana in 1875, and which is referred to by Lieutenant Bradly.

Upon learning of Bradly's statement about Silverthorne's gold and which was a surprise to a considerable number of old timers, myself included, who were intimately acquainted with him (Silverthorne), I took steps to ascertain where that gold came from and the late W. F. Wheeler and myself found in the journals kept by John Owen at Fort Owen in the Bitter Root valley since the year 1852 the evidence that John Owen brought that gold dust up from the Dalles in Oregon, and sent Silverthorne over to Fort Benton to buy goods with it to trade with the Flathead Indians, and besides all the old timers knew that "Silver," as we used to call him, never owned that amount of gold in his whole life (he's dead now, rest his soul), and never knew of nor worked any secret mines because there never were any in Montana, and we who well knew "Silver" could readily imagine the pleasure it gave him to stuff the American Fur Company's men at Fort Benton (none of whom knew anything about mining) with his yarn about his secret mines, etc., etc.

Very truly yours,

GRANVILLE STUART

Mr. Stuart is one of the self-made men of Montana, and no other man has done more to make Montana what it is than he.

He was elected to the council from Deer Lodge County for the session of 1871–2, and to the house session 1873–4, and to the house from Lewis and Clarke County, session of 1878–9, and extra session of 1879, and from Fergus County to the council, session of 1882–3 and was president of this session. In February, 1894, he was appointed Envoy Extraordinary and Minister Plenipotentiary to Paraguay and Uruguay by President Cleveland, and he served until December, 1897. Mr. Stuart is now in business in Butte, Mont.

Alder gulch, or Alder creek, as Mr. Stuart called it, was discovered in the spring of 1863 and soon became the Mecca of restless prospectors. It was not many months afterwards before Bevan, Last Chance, Nelson, Confederate, Highland, Lincoln, McClellan, and a score of other gulches were swarmed with miners who were taking out gold in great quantities. And thus the history of the mines of Montana began.

Since 1862 her mines and gulches have made rich contributions to the world's treasure. For many years gold was in the lead as the chief production, but after the richest placer mines of the bars and gulches had been worked out, the gold production rapidly declined, and the new era in mining began by giving attention to quartz veins. It was not long before quartz mills and smelters were in operation, and, the consequences were that silver took the lead, but it did not hold the position very long before the base metals took the lead over the two precious metals. And now copper is king over all other metals put together, as can be seen by the following table which I received some time ago from Hon. Eugene Braden, United States assayer, at Helena, to whom I had written for the information. He says:

"The production of gold, silver, copper and lead in the state of Montana from 1862, the year of discovery of gold, until the end of the year 1898 is as follows:

	1862 to 1897 (inclusive)	1898 (estimated)
Gold	$257,533,727	$5,167,958.66
Silver	273,033,393	20,040,407.03
Copper	217,487,224	27,669,000.00
Lead	9,817,112	793,800.00
	$757,871,456	$53,671,165.69"

The regular annual report of Mr. Braden for the year 1899 has just been made public. The value of the minerals mined during the year was $68,457,307.54, an increase of $17,138,240 over the preceding year. The output of the state was as follows:

Copper, fine pounds 245,602,214
Silver, fine ounces 16,850,764
Gold, fine ounces .233,126
Lead, fine pounds 20,344,750

Their value is given as follows:

Copper, at $16.75 per cwt. $40,941,905.74
Silver (coinage value) 21,786,834.52
Gold 4,819,156.95
Lead at $4.75 per cwt. 909,410.33

Total $68,457,307.54

The gain is more than 33 1-3 per cent in the value of the production over 1898. There was an increase of nearly 28,500,000 pounds in the production of copper, and this means a gain of $15,000,000 in this metal alone.

Copper is the paramount feature of the mining industry in Montana. More than 80 per cent of the total values won in the

NEIHART, MONTANA.
Courtesy Montana Historical Society, Helena

state during 1899 came from the mines at Butte in the shape of gold, silver and copper.

Like the story of the "Mustard seed," is the story of the mines of Montana. From the prospector's hole on Gold creek, in 1862, only a few miles away "now" is Butte City, which is today the greatest mining camp on earth, its population being between forty-five and fifty thousand. Though the ore is principally copper, yet as can be seen, it carries much gold and silver and is separated in the refineries at Butte, Anaconda and Great Falls. A writer in the Anaconda Standard, January, 1899, gives an interesting account, in a manner, so that the reader can comprehend the magnitude of this great camp. He says:

"Ten miles of mining shafts have been operating in Butte during the past year. This does not include the old and abandoned shafts on which work has been stopped, but of shafts on which work has been actually done during the year. It includes work done on mines which have been leased or are worked by small owners and not by the companies. The total depth of shafts operated by the regular mining companies amounts to 49,075 feet. Adding to this the depth of mines operated by leasers and operated by small owners, and the total will exceed 52,800 feet, or ten miles of shaft depth.

"More than a mile and a half of shaft depth has been sunk the past year. This is the largest amount of depth ever added to the mining development in the history of Butte. The total depth for the mining companies is 8,512 feet, and the returns from the small mines will increase this total. The development of the past year exceeds anything else in the history of this camp. The total number of men reported employed is 7,548. This includes the big companies only. Individual owners of mines and leasers employ 800 more, which would make the total numbers of miners employed in the camp 8,350.

"Ten miles of shafts—add to that the length of drifts and

stopes that lead in all directions beneath the city of Butte, and the figures would be enormous. These drifts form the streets and by-ways of another city underground. Along these subterranean highways there moves, day and night, a procession of toilers that reproduce beneath the surface the busy scenes that are enacted upon the streets of the surface city and her suburbs. Night and morning the actors in these busy scenes change places. Those from the surface take their turn in the activity under ground and those whose toil has been in the dimly lighted thoroughfares of the city where the sunlight never enters are relieved.

"The visitor in Butte marvels at the bustle and stir that he witnesses upon her streets. Were he to pause and consider that hundreds of feet below him are thousands of men, moving back and forth, repeating down there beneath the very spot upon which he stands the activity that he sees before him, his amazement would be even greater.

"Ten miles of shafts—hundreds of miles of drifts and workings—in these passage ways of the nether city there is life and stir and busy movement that would cause a boom in many a city whose name is in large letters upon any chart; its existence is noted in no atlas. Along the dark streets of this city there daily move 8,300 men in the performance of their duty. Here they labor day after day, creating the wealth that gives Butte her proud rank in the sisterhood of cities.

"Of the two Buttes—the surface city and that under-ground—it is not improbable that the latter possesses more and greater points of interest than the visible town. There are no crimes committed there and vice does not enter. There is no police patrol—none is necessary. The laws that govern this underground city are recognized and obeyed without the ne-cessity of brass buttons and nickel stars. When a man enters this city he lives under new conditions as long as he remains. He is a member of a well organized community, working under its laws and regulations, and for the time he loses his connection with the municipality upon the surface.

"There are no paving contracts let in this city that is out of sight. There are no legislative elections there, and the bungstarter's union has no standing in the remarkable community. The boodler is unknown in the business of Underground Butte and the Salvation Army has no barracks there. All in all, this second Butte is a wonderful place. Many tales might be told of deeds of heroism performed within her limits, of devotion to duty that surpasses many an act that has been emblazoned upon the scroll of fame. The sturdy, honest toilers of this city work on without the inspiration that prompts deeds of valor upon the field of battle. They do their duty because it is their duty. They have made Underground Butte even greater than the greatest mining camp on earth."

For further illustration of the greatness of the mines of Butte I have in my possession the following statement from the Anaconda Company's last year's report. There were brought by rail to the smelters of Anaconda one million four hundred and fifty-nine thousand tons of ore from the Butte mines. This company shipped one hundred and twenty-four million four hundred and eighteen thousand pounds of copper, and paid fourteen thousand dollars express charges, on five million seventy-four thousand and thirty-six ounces of silver and one hundred and thirty-five thousand two hundred and forty-four ounces of gold. One hundred and fifty thousand dollars worth of powder and forty-one thousand seven hundred and sixty-one dollars and forty-nine cents worth of candles, were used in their Butte mines. The pay roll of this company alone amounted to five million three hundred ninety-two thousand three hundred and twenty-three dollars and twenty-three cents. As the above amounts are so large, I put them in words instead of figures, so that the reader will understand that there has been no mistake made, as often occurs in copying figures.

The Boston and Montana, The Butte Reduction Works, The Butte and Boston, The Montana Ore Purchasing Company and other companies that are operating in Butte, I am not familiar with. Acording to Mr. Braden's account for the year 1899, the copper output of the mines of Butte was two hundred and twenty-three million pounds of refined copper.

The monthly pay roll of this "Greatest Mining Camp," including smelters, is over fifteen hundred thousand dollars, or over eighteen million dollars per year.

The wealth of the copper deposits at Butte was first recognized officially by the United States commissioner of mining statistics, Raymond, in his report of 1870. From that date to the present time the development of the copper deposits has been rapid; and, at this writing the state contains not only the richest copper mines of the world, but also the largest and most modern reduction plants. Thus, in brief, are the footprints of the prospector and the "from the cradle to the throne" of the mines of Montana.

After this faint effort to give an illustration of the "Then and Now," I can but think of the "Now and Then" thirty-six years hence, and that someone, perhaps, will have this little book in the year 1936 and take up where I have left off and write the "Now and Then." "I wish I were a boy again;" if I were, I would not give my chances to watch the progress that will be made in the valleys and mountains of the West during the next thirty-six years for the pay roll of the "Greatest Mining Camp on Earth" from the time of its first existence until then.

Now I end this series of letters, hoping that the reader will have as much pleasure in reading them as I had when writing. If so, both of us will be satisfied. Faithfully yours.

ROBERT VAUGHN.
GREAT FALLS, MAY 30, 1900.

Index